A HISTORICAL GUIDE TO
Herman Melville

The Historical Guides to American Authors is an interdisciplinary, historically sensitive series that combines close attention to the United States' most widely read and studied authors with a strong sense of time, place, and history. Placing each writer in the context of the vibrant relationship between literature and society, volumes in this series contain historical essays written on subjects of contemporary social, political, and cultural relevance. Each volume also includes a capsule biography and illustrated chronology detailing important cultural events as they coincided with the author's life and works, while photographs and illustrations dating from the period capture the flavor of the author's time and social milieu. Equally accessible to students of literature and of life, the volumes offer a complete and rounded picture of each author in his or her America.

A Historical Guide to Edgar Allan Poe
Edited by J. Gerald Kennedy

A Historical Guide to Henry David Thoreau
Edited by William E. Cain

A Historical Guide to Mark Twain
Edited by Shelley Fisher Fishkin

A Historical Guide to Edith Wharton
Edited by Carol J. Singley

A Historical Guide to Langston Hughes
Edited by Steven C. Tracy

A Historical Guide to Emily Dickinson
Edited by Vivian R. Pollak

A Historical Guide to Ralph Ellison
Edited by Steven C. Tracy

A Historical Guide to F. Scott Fitzgerald
Edited by Kirk Curnutt

A Historical Guide to Herman Melville
Edited by Giles Gunn

A
Historical Guide
to Herman Melville

EDITED BY
GILES GUNN

OXFORD
UNIVERSITY PRESS

2005

OXFORD
UNIVERSITY PRESS

Oxford University Press, Inc., publishes works that further
Oxford University's objective of excellence
in research, scholarship, and education.

Oxford New York

Auckland   Cape Town   Dar es Salaam   Hong Kong   Karachi
Kuala Lumpur   Madrid   Melbourne   Mexico City   Nairobi
New Delhi   Shanghai   Taipei   Toronto

With offices in

Argentina   Austria   Brazil   Chile   Czech Republic   France   Greece
Guatemala   Hungary   Italy   Japan   Poland   Portugal   Singapore
South Korea   Switzerland   Thailand   Turkey   Ukraine   Vietnam

Copyright © 2005 by Oxford University Press, Inc.

Published by Oxford University Press, Inc.
198 Madison Avenue, New York, New York 10016

www.oup.com

Library of Congress Cataloging-in-Publication Data
A historical guide to Herman Melville / edited by Giles Gunn.
p. cm.—(Historical guides to American authors)
Includes bibliographical references and index.
ISBN-13 978-0-19-514281-5; 978-0-19-514282-2 (pbk.)
ISBN 0-19-514281-0; ISBN 0-19-514282-9 (pbk.)
1. Melville, Herman, 1819–1891—Handbooks, manuals, etc.
2. Novelists, American—19th century—Biography—Handbooks, manuals, etc.
3. Literature and history—United States—History—19th century—
Handbooks, manuals, etc.   I. Gunn, Giles B.   II. Series.
PS2386.H54 2005
813'.3—dc22   2004063564

1 3 5 7 9 8 6 4 2

Printed in the United States of America
on acid-free paper

Acknowledgments

My special thanks to Jacob Berman for helping me review the recent bibliography on Melville, to Mr. Michael Perry, for all of his assistance and thoughtful suggestions in the early stages of the preparation of this volume, and to Ms. Maggie Sloan, for her help in selecting images and arranging for permissions. In addition, I am very grateful to Ms. Jennifer Kowing for her expert editorial assistance and support and to Dr. Toni Mantych for so carefully preparing the index. As always, I owe special thanks to my wife, Deborah Sills, for her shrewd counsel and strong support. But the deepest debt of gratitude goes to all those critics and scholars who have voyaged these seas before and have brought back such troves of insight and understanding.

Contents

A HISTORICAL GUIDE TO
Herman Melville

Introduction

Giles Gunn

Among American writers, Herman Melville remains a kind of colossus; there is no other word for him. Though in sheer number of pages he was outwritten by other American artists of the nineteenth century, such as Mark Twain, Henry James, and the still more prolific E. D. E. N. Southworth, he nonetheless managed to pen some of the century's most massive and, even more, ambitious narratives both in prose and in poetry. *Mardi: And a Voyage Thither* (1849), a romantic quest narrative that turns into an allegorical search for the ideal life; the much better known *Moby-Dick* (1851), his great sea epic named after the whale that is chased around the world by Captain Ahab; and the masterwork of his later years, an 18,000-line poem devoted to exploring the spiritual crisis of modern civilization, *Clarel: A Poem and Pilgrimage in the Holy Land* (1876)—all take their place among the ranks of those mammoth literary productions that the nineteenth century seemed almost obsessed with creating and consuming, as though history had presented it with perhaps the last opportunity to try to say absolutely everything in art. For Melville, there was in this ambition—as there was for such fellow artists as Victor Hugo at the beginning of the century, George Eliot in the middle, and Fyodor Dostoevsky and Leo Tolstoy toward the end—something like a semireligious conviction that art could encompass in its representations very nearly the whole of life itself, or at least that art could tap into and mine some of life's deepest and richest veins of experience. Melville, in other words, belonged to that company of nineteenth-century literary artists of whom it could be said, as Walt Whitman declared so truly of himself, they were large and contained multitudes.

But Melville deserves to be associated with greatness of size and aspiration not merely because of the length of some of his texts but also because of the enormous scope of the themes and issues with which he grappled. Not for him the depiction of local customs, well-worn traditions, regional practices, and conventional morals and manners. Melville's was a mind that from the beginning of his career not only was preoccupied with "the everlasting itch for things remote," as his narrator, Ishmael, remarks about himself at the beginning of *Moby-Dick*, but also was tormented by questions of transcultural, indeed universal, range. Melville's reflections kept extending outward toward the farthest horizons of thought to engage such huge questions as the coherence of life, the existence of God, the goodness of creation, the problem of evil, the nature of truth, the possibilities of justice, the limits of knowledge, and the meaning of death. And even when he succeeded in, or at any rate settled for, reining in some of the more abstract, ultimately unanswerable inquiries, he remained intensely interested in probing the deep structure of more specific but no less complex and recalcitrant issues of the day, from the nature of industrial capitalism, the depredations of colonialism, the dangers of imperialism, and the evils of slavery to the oppression of women, the diversity of sexuality, and the prospects for democracy.

In addition, we should remember that Melville's career as a writer spanned nearly a half century. Beginning well before the outbreak of the Civil War in 1861, with the publication in 1846 of a narrative based on his own South Sea adventures in the Marquesan islands entitled *Typee: A Peep at Polynesian Life*, and not concluding until his death in 1891, when he left unfinished in manuscript the short novella *Billy Budd, Sailor*, which was published posthumously in 1924, Melville's writing straddles an era of incomparable, almost cataclysmic, historical change in

America. Not only did the United States, during this period, undergo in the Civil War the greatest threat to its existence since the American Revolution, it also transformed itself from a society that was predominantly rural and agrarian into one that was industrial and increasingly urban. Add to this the fact that the same period also witnessed America's attempt to bury its problem with race by permitting the South, after the Civil War, to work out its own brutal accommodation with the former victims of slavery. This was an accommodation that quickly led to the institution of Jim Crow laws, the spreading practice of lynching, the establishment of segregation, and the continuation of a regime of inequality that the United States is still struggling to overcome. Then, too, this period experienced, particularly in the North, what Henry James was to call its "great grope of wealth," which led not only to the financial excesses and indulgences of what Mark Twain aptly described, in the title of one of his books, as "the Gilded Age" but also to the expansionist politics that precipitated the Spanish-American War and established America as a colonial power in the Pacific. The times in which Melville wrote were momentous indeed.

All this and more is reflected in Melville's fiction and poetry. *Typee* and its sequel, *Omoo: A Narrative of Adventures in the South Seas* (1847), detail, among other things, the potentially genocidal effects of the West's attempt to discipline native ways of life by bringing them under the tutelage of "civilization." *Redburn: His First Voyage* (1849), the narrative influenced by Melville's memory of his father's bankruptcy and built around Melville's first journey abroad to Liverpool, England, yields images of economic misery that eventually become emblematic of the injustices produced by the entire social order in ante- and postbellum America. *White-Jacket; or, The World in a Man-of-War* (1850), the novel Melville published immediately after *Redburn* ("two jobs . . . done for money"), reveals, amid the social and political inequities of life aboard a naval warship, a betrayal of the democratic ideal that Melville had found so handsomely honored among the gallant foretop men he met and worked with in the naval service. *Moby-Dick*, completed a year later and built on lessons Melville had learned in the composition of all of his earlier books, returns to some of the larger and more unwieldy speculations that Melville had begun in *Mardi* but brilliantly reframes them in a quest narrative that permitted him to expose many of the myths that were soon to fuel America's imperial ambitions abroad and to question the understructure of the ancient Christian beliefs and ethical values that so often—and so paradoxically—supported and reinforced them. Melville's next book, *Pierre; or, The Ambiguities* (1852), shifted ground abruptly by turning away from the ever more perplexing and infinitely elaborate cosmic world without to investigate the duplicities and contradictions of the self within, discovering within the interior corridors that wind down into the center of human willing and striving forces so dark as to leave all attempts at human fulfillment, much less ethical defiance, seriously crippled.

Pierre was eventually followed by *Israel Potter: His Fifty Years of Exile* (1855), another novel that broadened his oeuvre by showing how common people are viciously exploited by the twin demons of war and deprivation, but its weakened literary intensity signaled that Melville's literary agenda had somewhat shifted in the interim. During the years between the publication of *Pierre* and *Israel Potter*, Melville had turned his attention, at least temporarily, toward a different reading audience by producing a number of brilliant, shorter works for literary magazines. Though these texts were more restricted in length and less indifferent to the conventions of the medium, they were no less original, daring, and masterful than some of his earlier, longer books. The story "Bartleby, the Scrivener," the novella "Benito Cereno," and the tales collected in "The Encantadas" display Melville's continuing capacity to depict the human condition in all of its diverse postures of puzzlement, resistance, indifference, stupidity, heroism, meanness, and suffering. But before concluding this phase of his career, which was eventually followed by another phase achieved almost completely in public obscurity, Melville decided to have one last go at a longer narrative that might sum up his disillusionment with the world, his public, and himself. The result was *The Confidence-Man: His Masquerade* (1857), a book that launches an assault on the very grounds of truth itself. Yet despite the cynicism it expresses about all human motives, *The*

Confidence-Man also reveals an exquisitely shrewd social, political, and moral grasp of the myriad ways that nineteenth-century American idealism could be employed for purposes of deceit, manipulation, and corruption.

Melville's later career, which Robert Milder in this volume so persuasively describes as its distinguished second act, displays no less concentrated an absorption with the chief issues and preoccupations of his times. While Melville's preferred literary medium during this phase of his writing life was verse rather than fiction—the exception being his posthumously published *Billy Budd*—his engagements with his age remained in their way as insistent, complex, and passionate as before. There was, apparently, a first volume of poems, which was produced in 1860, some of whose texts appeared in his later *Timoleon* (1891) and the posthumous *Weeds and Wildings Chiefly: With a Rose or Two* (1924), but the first manuscript that appeared in this later period of Melville's career was *Battle-Pieces and Aspects of the War* (1866), a collection that grapples with a world violently torn asunder and seeks to find in writing itself the power to envision a reunited America. *Clarel*, the poetic masterpiece that in many ways matches his epic masterwork *Moby-Dick*, uses Melville's seven-month journey in 1856 to the Holy Land and Europe to stage among a remarkable group of latter-day pilgrims "the conflict of convictions," as the title of one of Melville's later poems depicts it, that was ripping the spiritual fabric of Victorian experience. Their discussions enable the pilgrims to explore virtually all of the great issues of faith and doubt, hope and despair, charity and venality, which vexed the latter half of the nineteenth century in America and England, turning the poem itself, as both Leon Chai and Robert Milder claim, into one of the greatest, though as yet still unacknowledged, works of Victorian literature. This astonishingly long poem represents how an entire age sought, if you will, to realize itself, to lend itself body and expression, in thought.

Clarel was not followed by another volume for twelve years, until Melville published *John Marr and Other Sailors* (1888), where he could finally declare of his struggle with his times, though not without an element of self-doubt, "Healed of my hurt, I laud the inhuman Sea." *John Marr*, however, was succeeded by another book of self-questioning poems, the last of his works that was published (privately printed in an edition of only twenty-five copies) before Melville died on September 28, 1891, called *Timoleon*. Left unfinished on his desk, along with various miscellaneous poems, was an extraordinary manuscript that was initially inspired by a poem called "Billy in the Darbies." That poem became the basis of the novella *Billy Budd* in which Melville returned to a world at war to revisit those ancient questions that had always engaged his deepest curiosity, questions about innocence, goodness, malevolence, truth, treachery, monomania, and moral compromise. In a world where, as the text's Captain Vere remarks (at the drumhead court he has summoned to try Billy for murdering the master-at-arms, John Claggart), "forms, measured forms are everything," Melville finds himself asking if there is any place left for the *Rights-of-Man*, the name of the ship from which Billy was impressed.

Melville's final question attests to the global reach of his vision. His literature encompasses all five continents, examines cultural practices, prejudices, and preoccupations from all quarters of the globe. An "Anacharsis Clootz deputation from all the isles of the sea" is what Melville christened his motley gathering of "meanest mariners, renegades, and castaways" in *Moby-Dick*, and the phrase suggests the catholicity and internationalism of his characters as well as his canvases. They are drawn, like the "congress" of foreigners for which they are named and which the Prussian nobleman Baron Jean Baptiste de Clootz presented to the first French assembly after the French Revolution, as representatives of the human race, and they mark Melville's texts as in certain respects more worldly than anything produced in American writing either before or since.

But Melville was not always viewed in this manner, as America's most cosmopolitan author. In his own time, his writing was recognized as exotic, demanding, ambitious, curious, and sometimes evocative but was greeted with a mixture of interest, perplexity, dismay, and hostility. To some of his readers, his larger and more intellectually challenging texts were simply bewildering if also audacious; to others, they were confounding, sometimes infuriating, and exhausting. But the bulk of those who paid him any serious attention over the extent of at least the first phase of his career regarded him as an able story teller of strange, sensational, somewhat primitive tales who had apparently lost his way. This was somewhat less true of Melville's English readers than of his American audience—the latter was even less patient with Melville's flights of philosophical and metaphysical speculation—but the general estimate of Melville's reputation during his lifetime followed a downward curve from a sense of early promise and rich potential to a perception of later confusion, incoherence, and eventual inconsequence.

While Melville had achieved a measure of artistic celebrity and even financial security with the publication of *Typee* and *Omoo*, he began to jeopardize them with the appearance of *Mardi*. *Redburn* and *White-Jacket* helped him to recover some of those early readers, but then *Moby-Dick* risked losing many of them forever. With *Pierre*'s attack on the literary establishment, Melville managed to insult even his friends—the southerner William Gilmore Simms declared that Melville was now "clean daft"—and he was thus forced to retreat, not, however, without some success in winning new readers, to writing for literary magazines like *Putnam's* and *Harper's*. But this comparatively successful interlude, when he published fourteen stories of the caliber of "Bartleby, the Scrivener," "I and My Chimney," and "The Paradise of Bachelors and the Tartarus of Maids," to say nothing of "Benito Cereno," did little to enhance the reception of his later novels, *Israel Potter* and *The Confidence-Man*, both of which were published under contractual arrangements that virtually guaranteed their critical disappearance. After the publication of *Battle-Pieces* by Harper and Brothers in 1866, Melville's last three books of poetry, including *Clarel*, were privately printed with the assistance of relatives, and by the time of Melville's death, those who took any public notice of it admitted to having lost track of him long since.

This unhappy saga of increasing public neglect and disfavor was eventually terminated with the publication in 1921 of Raymond Weaver's *Herman Melville*. A biography that had originally been commissioned as an article for the *Nation* but turned into something more as Weaver warmed to his subject, it initiated the first phase of a Melville revival that was to pass, during the rest of the twentieth century, through several additional distinct moments. Within less than a decade, Weaver's biography was complemented by another, written by Lewis Mumford, and then accompanied by a series of shorter critical studies by the English writer D. H. Lawrence and others that permanently altered the coordinates of the literary and cultural assessment of Melville's art.

The second phase of this revival occurred in the 1940s, 1950s, and 1960s, sparked on the one side by critical and historical studies such as F. O. Matthiessen's *American Renaissance* (1941), which placed Melville at the center of a literary flowering in the mid-century that was now seen to have shifted the center of gravity in nineteenth-century American writing, and, on the other, by broader changes in the international political climate. Those changes were associated with the Great Depression that followed so closely on the heels of the Great War and the events that occurred in such quick succession throughout the 1930s, from the rise of fascism in Europe and Asia and the collapse of the peace that was to end all war to, finally, the outbreak of war again, first in Europe and then in the Pacific. Such events, which would eventually school so many in suffering and threaten so many others with tragedy, created a new receptivity to Melville's art. But the Melville who thus came to the fore was neither the writer who, for critics of the 1920s and 1930s, had managed at great personal and artistic expense to refuse to compromise his artistic standards for an increasingly materialistic world nor an author unafraid to risk public censure for the sake of diving as deep as Shakespeare into the conundrums and diabolisms of human experience.

As such, this second phase of the twentieth-century revival of interest in Melville's art was precipitated less by scholars of Melville (though they contributed their fair share) than by historians of American literary and cultural history, who had now become convinced that Melville occupied a special place in the American literary pantheon. To them—F. O. Matthiessen, Perry Miller, C. L. R. James, Henry Nash Smith, R. W. B. Lewis, Harry

Levin, Leslie Fiedler, Leo Marx, Daniel Hoffman, and others—
Melville's art not only provided insights into a world grown
treacherous, ambiguous, unstable, brutal, and unjust but also
offered, through the variety of discourses it seemed prepared to
engage—psychological, mythic, ideological, social, ethical, epistemological, linguistic, metaphysical—a set of strategies for cop-
ing with, even successfully surviving, such a world. Criticism
therefore took a decidedly cultural turn, which it has never relin-
quished, as interpreters and historians sought to demonstrate the
relevance that Melville's writing might possess in a world where
wars could be cold as well as hot and where the recovery of even
the most skeptical of writers could be used to renew the national
consensus as well as call it into question.

The third phase of the revival, if it can be so described, came
in the 1980s and 1990s and had as much to do with new discoveries about Melville himself and with the establishment of a reliable set of texts on which to base the estimate of his reputation
as on the way that Melville's writing could now be seen to be im-
plicated in still different issues of the moment—race, gender,
sexuality, nationalism, and class—having to do with efforts to
broaden the canon of American literature and to rethink the
meaning of its multiculturalism. In a strange way, these two
movements, so different from each other, have proved useful to
one another. Just as the continuously swelling phalanx of scholars whose often brilliant editorial, textual, and biographical work
has changed our understanding of Melville himself and of the
production and reception of his writing, so the burgeoning army
of critics and historians committed to wrestling more directly
with Melville's Angel Art have opened up to us new and largely
unexplored geographies of experience.

Melville presents unusual difficulties for any biographer. While
there is no shortage of material about Melville's family and his
surrounding culture, both material and intellectual, Melville left
behind comparatively little testimony that reflects or comments
directly on his inward experience. Nor is there much in the way
of reliable secondhand observation from family, friends, or fel-

low artists that discusses or speculates on his interior feelings and thoughts. Thus in seeking to integrate the private and the public worlds of their subject, Melville's biographers have often found themselves in the awkward position of having to rely on Melville's narratives and poems to tell the full story of his life, and they have had to read a good deal into those texts in order to get anything biographically significant out of them. Robert Milder's beautifully crafted capsule biography is no exception. Melville's life takes on flesh and blood for us not by virtue of any rehearsal of its outward circumstances but because of the way Milder employs those circumstances, and the world around them, to rethread into more plausible patterns of meaning what in his reading appear to be the major tensions and resistances of Melville's most representative literary creations. The result is a story in which many parts of the life are indirectly inscribed within the writing, the writing in many respects rendered as the fullest and deepest realization of the life.

Leon Chai situates Melville's writing between the two great literary and cultural ideologies that divided between them so much nineteenth-century writing on the Continent, in the British isles, and in the United States. But Romanticism and Victorianism are not, as Chai so deftly elaborates them, abstract world views but rather vital frames of mind that influenced the way artists and intellectuals thought and felt about a variety of essential topics from the nature of subjectivity and the constitution of selfhood to the dynamics of intersubjectivity, the forms of human development, the possibilities of ultimate belief, the transparency of language and symbols, and even the meaning of technology. In a certain sense, as Chai makes clear, Melville was predisposed to be a Romantic and never fully got over it. But even if he could never shed all of Romanticism's philosophical, epistemological, and aesthetic aspirations, his later evolution into a kind of Victorian whose view of experience would always be shadowed by doubt and uncertainty forced him in the end to look beyond it.

Myra Jehlen takes up the question of class in Melville from a different perspective. Looking closely at a passage from the first of the famous "Knights and Squires" chapters of *Moby-Dick*,

which has often been taken to represent his indictment of all social hierarchies, she shows that Melville's recurrently expressed
attitude toward class was somewhat different from his ringing
endorsement of the "kingly commons." Unlike Emerson, Thoreau, or Whitman, Melville could address his criticisms of those
oppressed by conditions of labor or, for that matter, of prejudice,
to a class of persons defined in the aggregate but imagined
in their individuality—Jehlen discusses at great length his censure
of the one in "The Paradise of Bachelors and the Tartarus of
Maids" and his indictment of the other in "Benito Cereno"—but
that individual humanity was still evoked more as a postulate
than as a fact. While in the same chapter Melville appealed to the
spirit of "divine equality" that erases all class distinctions, he in
fact viewed class identity as the very marker that prevents one
from fully embodying the spirit of equality, which constituted for
him the essence of democracy. Thus the representatives of what
he took to be transcendent humanity are, paradoxically, those
like Ishmael, Ahab, and the three harpooners who somehow
transcend class precisely to the degree that they seem self-
created. His great theme therefore became the way this project
in democratic self-fashioning was tragically frustrated, in Jehlen's
nuanced, ingenious, revelatory reading, by the imperfections of
American democracy itself.

Sheila Post relocates Melville's writing in relation to the
changing literary marketplace of his era, which not only influenced the public's response to his work but also loaned it some of
its least suspected but more creative elements. This is an aspect
of Melville's career that has too often been underplayed and
frequently misunderstood. Far from ignoring or despising market forces, Melville clearly understood a good many of them
and was prepared to exploit them, where he could, for the purposes of enabling his art to reach multiple audiences. One of the
more popular genres of the day, which he employed very self-
consciously, was the mixed-form narrative that appealed to a
cross-section of readers, and some of his most effective writing
was composed for middle-class magazines like *Putnam's* and
Harper's. Indeed, Melville took great pains, as Post reveals clearly,
to produce stories for each magazine that reflected their differing

stylistic demands. Not that Melville crafted his tales to conform to periodical formulas, but his writing for the periodical marketplace, like his longer works for the book market, furnished him with a richer array of formal alternatives than has previously been acknowledged to reach a multifaceted, mainly middle-class market. Adapting semipopular literary conventions to his own artistic purposes, he thus fashioned between his cultural moment and his own interests, in Post's marvelously felicitous formulation, a kind of "correspondent coloring."

Timothy Marr focuses his chapter on the remarkable diversity of people Melville brought into his art. Constituting a kind of ethnic cosmopolitanism, this worldly orientation placed Melville in sharpest conflict with his fellow Americans who were bent, then as now, on using differentiations of any kind—ethnic, racial, sexual, religious—to deprecate what is different. Melville's global embrace of human multiplicity and variety is evident in his literary representations of Polynesians, Africans, Asians, Jews, and Native Americans, who epitomize for Ishmael in *Moby-Dick* that it is "a mutual, joint-stock world, in all meridians." There is, however, nothing simple or naive about Melville's commitment to this new ideal of human worldliness. From *Typee* on, Melville was deeply sensitive both to the "local and social prejudices" that preyed on the possibilities of achieving this ideal and also to how various peoples were being drawn together and mixed by virtue of being drafted into the world of an emergent, often predatory, capitalism. He also knew that even under the best of conditions the transnational intermixing of the world's people held the potential for great conflict. But he remained steadfast in his belief that the only way to challenge the hierarchical categories used to subordinate others was by, as Marr authoritatively elaborates in such striking detail, "figuring cultural difference as a disguise that obscured an essential human unity."

Emory Elliott then explores some of the religious and philosophical underpinnings of Melville's thoughts about life's possible forms of unity. The problem is that when Melville turned his mind to the ultimate issues of life, he found myriad questions but few answers. As Nathaniel Hawthorne early recognized and Elliott turns to such good purpose, Melville could neither believe in any conventional sense nor be content with his unbelief. All he could do was continue to seek for clarifications and assurances, which almost always eluded him as he intellectually pressed his age ever more vigorously for an accounting of its mysteries, mystifications, and misanthropies. To investigate this extraordinary spiritual drama, Elliott first describes the complex moral and religious anatomy of Melville's era and then moves on to interpret its unfolding in each of Melville's major texts from *Typee* to *Billy Budd*. Elliott's exceptionally rich and thoughtful exposition, which must of necessity display the interlinkages among Melville's ruminations on religion and on psychology, aesthetics, politics, economics, sexuality, and a good deal more, never yields the sense that Melville's odyssey came to some satisfactory terminus or resolution. It is rather as though in each of his texts, if often in differing terms, Melville attempted to carry his spiritual quest, as Captain Ahab said to Starbuck in the great "Quarterdeck" chapter of *Moby-Dick*, "a little layer lower." But what we ultimately discover, as we descend to each lower layer, is not that Melville finally reached some secure level of religious certainty or peace but merely that his realization intensified that religion could be as much a bane as a blessing, as much a source of harm as solace.

Herman Melville
1819–1891

A Brief Biography

Robert Milder

When Herman Melville died in 1891, he was remembered, if at all, chiefly as a writer of the South Seas whose talent lay in investing his Pacific experience with a mixture of verisimilitude and romance and who squandered a promising literary career due to a streak of morbidness and an unaccountable penchant for metaphysics. Even had there been sufficient interest in the decade or two after his death, a full-scale biography would have seemed superfluous. "Of Melville's four most important books," wrote his young admirer and literary executor Arthur Stedman, reflecting the opinion of the 1890s, "three, 'Typee,' 'Omoo,' and 'White-Jacket,' are directly autobiographical, and 'Moby-Dick' is partially so; while the less important 'Redburn' is between the two classes in this respect," and he concluded that the remaining works were mostly failures of one sort or another.[1] Melville was conceived as a writer whose usable experience ended with his return from the Pacific in 1844 and whose enduring claim, even in the more successful parts of *Moby-Dick*, was to have truthfully rendered his life as a sailor. The books *were* the biography, or as much of the biography as contemporaries cared to know.

Melville's own view was quite the reverse. "Until I was twenty-five, I had no development at all," Melville wrote to Nathaniel

Hawthorne in 1851, dating the origin of his life just where Sted-man would locate the close. "Three weeks have scarcely passed, at any time between then and now," he added, "that I have not un-folded within myself."[2] Melville was alluding to that remarkable drama of inward growth (so he always regarded it) that subsumed the achievement of even his greatest individual works and gave them the status of way stations in a continuing intellectual and spiritual journey. Completing *Mardi* (1849), a quantum leap over *Typee* and *Omoo*, Melville envisioned a comparable advance in his *next* book, and no sooner had he finished *Moby-Dick* than he began thinking of bigger fish than Leviathan, of "Krakens" (*WHM* 14:213). American writers have canons, but few have had careers as long and as various as Melville's: a forty-five-year development of mind, character, and art that spanned the historical divide of the Civil War and encompassed both fiction and poetry.

For the first decade or so, the production was rapid, spurred by the sometimes competing demands of "a full heart" and "the ne-cessity of bestirring himself to procure his yams" (*WHM* 3:592), as Melville wrote of the poet Lombardo in *Mardi*. In almost unin-terrupted succession came *Typee* (1846), *Omoo* (1847), *Mardi* (1849), *Redburn* (1849), and *White-Jacket* (1850); then *Moby-Dick* (1851), followed immediately and as if by some interior urgency by the disastrous *Pierre* (1852); then the philosophical retrenchment (but aesthetic mastery) of the magazine pieces (1853–1856) and the comic/pathetic *Israel Potter* (1855), the vertiginous ironies of *The Confidence-Man* (1857), and finally silence. As late as the 1970s it was common to regard Melville's career as effectively ending with *The Confidence-Man* save for the coda of *Billy Budd, Sailor*, begun in the mid-1880s and published posthumously in 1924. But the eleven-year parabola of Melville's rise and putative fall covers only the first act of his career. There was a distinguished second act inaugurated by his trip to the Mediterranean in 1856–1857, extend-ing through the verse collection *Battle-Pieces and Aspects of the War* (1866), and culminating in the magisterial narrative and philo-sophical poem *Clarel* (1876), a fit companion to *Moby-Dick* and in many respects a more profound work. And there was a fertile, if abbreviated third act beginning with his retirement from the New York Customs House in 1885 and expressing itself in the overlapping projects of his final years: the poetry volumes *John Marr and Other Sailors* (1888), *Timoleon* (1891), and *Weeds and Wildings Chiefly: With a Rose or Two* (post. 1924) and the prose novella *Billy Budd*.

All successful biography is a labor of integrating the outer life and the inner life—what Virginia Woolf called the "granite-like solidity" of factual truth and the "rainbow-like intangibility" of "personality."[3] In Melville's case this is particularly difficult because the richness of the surrounding family archive—enlarged considerably since the first generation of Melville scholars set out to separate fact from fiction in the early 1940s—is unmatched by the kind of testimonies to the interior life (notebooks, letters, recollections of literary friends) so abundant with Emerson, Thoreau, and Hawthorne. A handful of extraordinary letters, mostly to Hawthorne and to New York editor and critic Evert Duyckinck; journals from Melville's travels of 1849–1850, 1856–1857, and (fragmentarily) 1860; reading marginalia; a few scattered portraits left by Hawthorne, Duyckinck, Stedman, and others; some family letters; and granddaughter Eleanor Melville Metcalf's revealing but reticent account of his domestic life and legends—these, along with the writings themselves and the circumambient facts and contexts of nineteenth-century life, are the materials from which the biographer must reconstruct or imagine or invent a "Melville."

Nothing in Melville's youth seemed to promise the extraordinary. Descended on both sides from distinguished Revolutionary War grandfathers, Melville began life in New York City in affluence and apparent security, the third child (and second son) of Allan Melvill, an importer of French goods, and Maria Gansevoort Melvill, daughter of a prominent upstate New York Dutch family. The eldest, Gansevoort, was the favorite—ambitious, scholarly, and visibly a genius in his parents' eyes—while the most that could be said for young Herman ("very backward in speech & somewhat slow in comprehension," his father reported of him as a seven-year-old) was that he was "of a docile & aimiable [*sic*] disposition."[4] Commerce seemed to Allan a likely vocation for the boy, but whatever dreams Herman himself might have had were shattered by Allan's bankruptcy in 1830, the family's hasty and humiliating retreat to Albany, and Allan's death early in 1832, when Herman was twelve. In *Redburn*, Melville would project a colored version of his probable feelings in the affliction of his fatherless hero forced "to think much and bitterly before [his] time" (*WHM* 4:10). "And never again can such blights be made good," Redburn adds, "they strike in too deep, and leave such a scar that the air of Paradise might not erase them" (*WHM* 4:11).

One legacy of Melville's reversal of fortune was his complicated and ambivalent class allegiance: on one side, his identification with the sufferings of the dispossessed; on the other, his sense of belonging by lineage and tastes to the class of possessors. Another consequence may have been what Newton Arvin called the "frightful sense of abandonment, the reproachful sense of desertion" that followed upon Allan Melvill's death,[5] an event which seems to have crystallized forever the child's feeling of inadequacy in the father's eyes and which left Melville with a hunger for male approval he would later inject into his relationship with Hawthorne. The unanswerable question, which one is obliged to ask nonetheless, is to what extent the mature Melville's feeling of God the Father's indifference, abdication, or nonexistence was rooted in the boy's sense of paternal undervaluation and desertion. This is not to imply that intellectual or spiritual conflicts are simply transpositions of early emotional conflicts; it is rather to suggest that, compelling as adult issues may be in their own right, they are often apprehended through or inflected by needs and dispositions established in childhood.

During the years immediately after his father's death, Melville passed in and out of school and in and out of various menial jobs, his already limited prospects for professional employment further impaired by the hard times following the Panic of 1837. The social alienation of his early narrators, who rail against the callousness of nominal Christians, have their root in the frustrations of this period. The lessons on land were reinforced by lessons at sea when, in June 1839, after fruitless attempts at finding work, Melville sailed for Liverpool as a green hand aboard the merchant ship *St. Lawrence*. *Redburn* notwithstanding, the character of this first voyage must be conjectural, though there is no reason to doubt Melville experienced the usual hardships, tyrannies, and degradations of shipboard life as well as the glaring disparities between rich and poor in bustling, polyglot Liverpool. His father had visited Liverpool in style some twenty years earlier; now his son wandered the city as a "boy" from a merchant ship, closer in status to many of the emigrants the *St. Lawrence* would carry to America than to the youth raised amid privilege in New York City. Returning home in October 1839 and obtaining no better employment in the next two years than that of village schoolmaster, Melville signed on to the whaling ship *Acushnet* bound for a four years' voyage to the Pacific. Melville sailed from Fairhaven, Massachusetts, on January 3, 1841; he would not return to America until October 1844.

In some respects, contemporaries like Arthur Stedman were not far wrong in seeing Melville's Pacific experience as the fount of his writing. Polynesia gave Melville his initial subject and milieu, but his life at sea and in the Marquesas and the Society and Sandwich (Hawaiian) islands also imprinted itself on his mind and imagination in ways that would take him years to sift and with an emotive power that would mellow into myth as he aged. After eighteen months on the *Acushnet*, Melville and shipmate Richard Tobias Greene deserted on the Marquesan island of Nukahiva (recently appropriated by the French) and made their way over rugged mountains to the idyllic valley of the Typees, a tribe still virtually untouched by Western civilization. Melville remained with the Typees as a willing or enforced guest for fewer than four weeks before he was taken on by the Australian whaler *Lucy Ann*. There, captivity assumed the less exotic form of drudgery under the yoke of incompetence, a situation that prompted Melville to join a number of the crew in a nonviolent mutiny that landed them for a time in a makeshift jail in Tahiti. Melville's opéra bouffe adventures in Tahiti and nearby Eimeo are the subject of *Omoo*, whose title "signifies a rover" (*WHM* 2:xiv), or devil-may-care drop-out, or picaro. In Tahiti, Melville signed on as a boat steerer aboard the Nantucket whaler *Charles & Henry*, which took him to Lahaina, on Maui, where he witnessed what forcibly struck him as the deleterious effects of American missionary civilization upon native life. Three months in Honolulu rounded out his island experience, which ended in August 1843 with his enlistment as ordinary seaman on the frigate *United States* and with the long cruise home that landed him in Boston fourteen months later.

In the absence of primary evidence, one must infer the legacy of Melville's sailor experience from prominent attitudes and patterns in his writings. The Pacific did not "form" Melville, but it did provide an otherwise provincial American with a revisionary perspective on fundamental matters of race, class, sexuality, social organization, culture, and history. Hawthorne intimated something of this when, reviewing *Typee* for the *Salem Advertiser* in 1846, he praised Melville for "that freedom of view—it would be too harsh to call it laxity of principle—which renders him tolerant of codes of morals that may be little in accordance with our own."[6] Polynesia did for Melville what a night and a day with Queequeg did for Ishmael. Melville's residence in Typee was too brief and bewildering for him to begin to comprehend island culture on its own terms, but he did see enough to perceive that in their relation to nature, to each other, and to their own bodies the Typees were not *pre*civilized but *alternatively* civilized, and in ways that seemed a salutary complement to the driving purposiveness of his own hyperconscious, productive, but severely repressive and repressed countrymen.

Melville never articulated it as such, but what he witnessed and intuitively grasped in the newly colonialized Pacific was the replacement of the pleasure principle (spontaneity, freedom, sensuality, immediate gratification) by the reality principle (discipline, toil, austerity, delayed gratification). He associated this process with the logic of history and regarded it as not only inexorable but, on balance, desirable. Yet he could not avoid feeling that history was tragic and wasteful, as it should not be if it were guided by Providence, and that the sacrifices of communal and instinctual life entailed by the triumph of Western culture unnaturally constrained human impulses well beyond the requirements of social order. In this belief he was less like Freud, who saw psychosocial repression with its accompanying discontents as the condition for the stability and sublimated achievements of civilization, than like revisionists such as Herbert Marcuse, who distinguished "civilization" from a particular historical *form* of civilization and who regarded capitalist social, economic, moral, and sexual organization as excessively denying.[7] Even in his later years Melville was poorly read in social theory and could not have translated his cultural insights into a systematic critique of the West. On the level of imagination, however, Polynesia made him realize that while "we can't go back to the savages: not a stride," as D. H. Lawrence wrote in an essay on *Typee* and *Omoo*, "we can take a great curve in their direction, onward."[8] This remapping of human development is the cultural meaning of Ishmael's "marriage" to Queequeg: an assimilation of Polynesian spontaneity, sensuousness, and fraternalism, symbolized by (and partially located in?) homoeroticism, to sophisticated Western consciousness. Returning to Victorian America, Melville had little chance of realizing his ideal, but it remained with him not simply in the restorative memory of a paradise lost (as in the late poem "To Ned," in *John Marr*), but in the vision of a better, because more conscious, paradise to be regained, whether in some distant historical time or in the atemporal reconciliations of art.

Discharged from the navy in October 1844, Melville was scarcely more employable than when he left for the Pacific, but he did have a wealth of accumulated stories to tell. Whether or not "a chance word" decided him on authorship, as one report has it,[9] the fact is that Melville came to narrative prose not through the main portal of the novel or romance but through the side entries of travelogue and autobiography, genres in which the status of the represented world and the speaking "I" are quite different from that in fiction. Descriptively and ethnologically, *Typee: A Peep at Polynesian Life* (1846) is generally accurate so far as it goes, partly because Melville refreshed or supplemented his experience with readings from previous travelers, upon whose accounts he drew for information and paraphrased anecdote with or without citation. Beyond the portion of Melville's story vouched for by his companion Toby, who came forward with dramatic effect soon after *Typee* was published, it is impossible to know how much of the book's minimal suspense plot, turning on threats of tattooing and cannibalism, is based in fact: probably not much. Contemporary readers relished the book for its exoticism and geniality of style (an arch mixture of titillation and chivalric euphemism), but there were also those, not exclusively in the religious press, who took its "freedom of view" as irreverence or worse. "Not that you can put your finger on a passage positively offensive; but the *tone* is bad," a fidgety Horace Greeley complained in the *New-York Weekly Tribune* (*Log* I:248), anticipating what would become a widespread uneasiness about Melville's orthodoxy.

Typee sold well, but not spectacularly, and was largely a critical success, though some English reviewers doubted its authenticity on the ground that a common sailor could never have written it, and some American reviewers objected strenuously to its criticism of missionaries. Pressures from religious conservatives acted on the Presbyterian conscience and New York balance sheet of publisher John Wiley and forced the issuance of what Melville called a *"Revised* (Expurgated?—Odious word!) Edition" of the book (*WHM* 14:60), to which Melville agreed with the complaisance of a novice overwhelmed to find himself a celebrity overnight. As if in reparation, however, he redoubled his criticism of missionary civilization in *Omoo: A Narrative of Adventures in the South Seas* (1847), which he placed with the more prestigious Harper & Brothers, devout Protestants themselves but evidently of a different mix of piety and pecuniousness than John Wiley. *Omoo* is a slighter book than *Typee* but also a more assured one in its grasp of the tragic destruction of Polynesian culture under the double yoke of colonialist rapacity and missionary repression. John Bryant notes that Melville began *Typee* "with no set political agenda" but gradually developed one as he wrote;[10] in *Omoo* the agenda becomes overt as Melville, conscious of the Polynesians' temperamental unfitness for a life of harsh labor and sensuous denial, protests, elegiacally, against what amounts to practical genocide.

Even as Melville the writer was establishing himself as an amiably seductive but sometimes pointedly critical iconoclast, Melville the New Yorker was delighting in his fame and bidding to take his place in the American world against which he sometimes inveighed. He moved freely among the New York literati, especially Evert Duyckinck's Young America group, middle-of-the-road Democrats whose commitment to progressive politics and a national literature coexisted with a literary cosmopolitanism especially advantageous to the undereducated Melville. A convivial man of broad, if conventional tastes, Duyckinck was Melville's closest literary friend during his New York years (through mid-1850); he was host at numerous suppers during which Melville showed a fellowly epicurean side central to his nature (until adversity drove it underground); and, as owner of one of the best private libraries in America, he was an important source of books for Melville. Although Duyckinck was married, the literary group he presided over was exclusively male—figurative "bachelors" (a freighted word in Melville's fictive vocabulary) who temporarily sequestered themselves from female influence and enjoyed the combined pleasures of good food, good wine, and good talk, an ideal of masculine festivity and sometime escapism that would figure prominently, if ambivalently, in Melville's writing from *Mardi* onward.

By late summer 1847, Melville was married—to Elizabeth Shaw, daughter of Chief Justice Lemuel Shaw of the Massachusetts Supreme Court, a former friend of Allan Melvill and a family benefactor since Allan's death. Lizzie was a friend of Melville's sisters; the connection with the Shaws was a prestigious one; and Shaw himself would treat Melville generously and respectfully throughout their lives. Biographer Hershel Parker imagines Melville falling "passionately in love with Lizzie from their first sessions together" (Parker I:521). If so, it is hard to understand why. Lizzie was a kindly, dutiful woman who would make Melville a devoted wife, but she was conventional and lacked intellectuality, vivacity, beauty, and more than ordinary wit—"domestic in her tastes without proficiency," her granddaughter Eleanor Melville Metcalf characterized her.[11] There is no question that Melville was happy with Lizzie as they set up housekeeping in New York City, together with Melville's brother Allan and Allan's bride, Melville's mother, and his unmarried sisters. The strains in the marriage would develop later as Melville deepened as a writer and as his circle of literary friends contracted with the move from New York to a Pittsfield, Massachusetts farmhouse in August 1850. For all of Lizzie's virtues, "her life with a genius husband brought her much that she was emotionally unequal to" (Metcalf 55), her granddaughter commented, and though she gradually came to believe in Melville's writing, she apparently never went far toward fathoming it. On his side, Melville grew to be impatient with Lizzie's perceived limitations as his career frustrations mounted. "Herman was always challenging Elizabeth, that she did not understand it,"[12] Melville's niece Maria Morewood is reported to have said of later years, her words suggesting a pattern of psychological interaction more than a specific source of grievance.

Melville's immediate problem in the fall of 1847 was how to make an adequate living as a writer, something that no American other than Washington Irving and James Fenimore Cooper, both of whom resided in Europe for important parts of their career, had managed to do. Success lay in giving the public more books like *Typee*, but restlessness and burgeoning literary ambition caused him to abandon his "narrative of *facts*" for a " 'Romance of Polynisian [*sic*] Adventure'" (*WHM* 14:106), as he told his skeptical English publisher, John Murray, then to subordinate the romance itself to a philosophical voyage through the imaginary archipelago of Mardi, Melville's representation of the known (to him) geographical, political, and intellectual world.

The transformation of *Mardi: And a Voyage Thither* (1849) from adventure narrative to philosophical quest was prompted by Melville's readings early in 1848 in Montaigne, Rabelais, Sir Thomas Browne, Coleridge's *Biographia Literaria*, David Hartley's *Observations on Man*, Seneca, Ossian, and others. The book set the pattern for Melville's "free yielding to that rush of interior development which served him for education,"[13] and as such it was both essential to his unfolding—"Had I not written & printed 'Mardi', in all likelihood, I would not be as wise as I am now, or may be" (*WHM* 14:149), he later told Duyckinck—and compromising to his solvency and his reputation as a writer. For most readers and reviewers, *Mardi* would always represent the tendency toward obscurity and metaphysics that Melville had to resist, while for Melville himself it was the initiation into a world of thought that irresistibly beckoned. Melville's career-long struggle with his audience thus began with his third book—not simply with its reception but, as William Charvat shrewdly observed, with the exuberance that led Melville to follow the line of his growth and attempt to make the reader "collaborate in exploratory, speculative thinking which is concerned not with commitment but with possibility," "the one kind of thinking that the general reader [would] not tolerate" and "the nineteenth-century critic" would label "subversive."[14] Artistically, *Mardi* is not a successful book, but it is, as Hawthorne said, "a rich [one], with depths here and there that compel a man to swim for his life" (*Log* I:391). It is also, for the study of Melville, an indispensable book—"the first draft of all his subsequent works," as Richard H. Brodhead remarked with more truth than hyperbole.[15]

The composition of *Mardi* occupied Melville for longer than he could well afford, yet even after his wife, Lizzie, described the book as complete in May 1848, Melville took it up again to add a long section of political allegory in response to the European revolutions of 1848, the founding of the antislavery Free Soil party, the California gold rush, and other contemporary events. Melville's attitude toward most of these phenomena can best be described as cautious. Egalitarian in sentiment, Melville was wary of political revolution; responsive to New World millennialism, he recoiled against American chauvinism and brag; and indignant at social injustice, particularly at slavery, he was inclined to see no solutions beyond what might be wrought by "all-healing Time" (*WHM* 3:535). In one form or another these would be lifelong attitudes, and they make it difficult to characterize Melville politically as a progressive or a conservative. It might be truest to say that he was a skeptical idealist: an idealist in his hopes for humanity and his outrage at all abuses of human rights and human dignity; a skeptic in his estimate of actual human motives and behavior and in his distrust both of entrenched power and of violent attempts to dislodge it. In an 1851 letter to Hawthorne, he boasted of his "ruthless democracy on all sides," by which he meant his impatience with class arrogance and pretense, but he immediately qualified this by adding what remains the most succinct formulation of his political creed: "It seems an inconsistency to assert unconditional democracy in all things, and yet confess a dislike to all mankind—in the mass. But not so" (*WHM* 14:190, 191). Estimates of Melville's politics have suffered severely from the politics of the estimators, with radicals, liberals, and conservatives all trying to enlist him for their cause. Yet on this subject, as on so many others, Melville's complex ambivalence resists the pull of reductionism and ideology; there are only questions, problems, and conundrums in Melville, never answers.

The poor sales of *Mardi* sent Melville back to his sailor experiences to keep afloat his growing family, now including an infant son, Malcolm, born in February 1849 (later children include another son, Stanwix, born in 1851, and two daughters, Elizabeth and Frances, born in 1853 and 1855; only Frances had descendants, none carrying the Melville name). In fewer than five months during the spring and summer of 1849 Melville wrote *Redburn* and *White-Jacket*—"two *jobs*, which I have done for money," he told Judge Shaw, yet within whose limits, he added, "I have not repressed myself much—so far as *they* are concerned; but have spoken pretty much as I feel" (*WHM* 14:138-39).

Redburn: His First Voyage (1849) is based on Melville's 1839 voyage to Liverpool, *White-Jacket; or, The World in a Man-of-War* (1850) on his homeward cruise from the Pacific aboard the warship *United States*, fictively renamed the *Neversink*. Curbing his eagerness to outdo *Mardi*—"no metaphysics, no conic-sections, nothing but cakes & ales" (*WHM* 14:132), he promised English publisher Richard Bentley about *Redburn*—Melville established himself in both books as a fervently democratic writer concerned with the inequities (and iniquities) of wealth and class. *Redburn* draws upon his youthful hardships after his father's bankruptcy and death to depict what F. O. Matthiessen called "the latent economic factor in tragedy [that] remained part of Melville's vision at every subsequent stage of his writing."[16] *White-Jacket* focuses polemically on flogging in the U.S. Navy, but its wider subject, announced by its metaphoric subtitle, is the nature of power relations within a martially oriented class society. Melville is passionate about legislation to abolish flogging (a reform already in progress when *White-Jacket* was published), but he is doubtful of the efficacy of political action to remedy what *Redburn* calls "those chronic evils which can only be ameliorated, it would seem, by ameliorating the moral organization of civilization" (*WHM* 4:139). Conservatives typically appealed to "moral reform" to defuse legislative threats to the established order; in *Redburn* and *White-Jacket* Melville invokes it to *arraign* the established order. His point of view is "Christian democratic," terms that converged for him when Christianity was seen as an ethical system and democracy as its translation to the civil and political realm. Both books express—*Redburn* poignantly, *White-Jacket* satirically—Melville's Swiftian indignation at the practical opposition between the Sermon on the Mount and the ways of the world, later an important theme in *Pierre*. Unable to imagine a real or even a fictional solution to the problem, Melville could only fall back upon a rhetoric of New World millennialism (America as defined by its founding idealism, not its sociohistorical actuality) and upon a running paradox involving Christians as heathens, heathens as Christians, which would culminate in *Moby-Dick* in Ishmael's conversion to Christian fraternity through the agency and example of a "savage."

Although *Redburn* and *White-Jacket* are not overtly metaphysical books, neither are they free from Melville's interrogations of the universe and his emerging sense of tragedy. As chapters on sickness, death, and the "armed neutrality" of Fate (*WHM* 5:320) darken the close of *White-Jacket*, *Redburn*'s plea for a brotherhood of man under the fatherhood of God gives way to the mature Melvillean vision of a brotherhood of man asserted in the absence of God. It was as if in thinking about Christianity Melville came to separate God the sovereign (the metaphysical side of Christianity) from the unitarian Jesus (the ethical side of Christianity), revering Jesus as the fount of a soul-stirring idealism utterly impracticable in our man-of-war world while detaching him from a deity whom experience suggested was indifferent or nonexistent. The heartlessness of laissez-faire society seemed to Melville replicated in, and enabled by, the heartlessness of a nonprovidential universe. Yet far from inviting quietism or despair, Melville's sense of cosmic abandonment implied an active historical self-determination summed up in White-Jacket's words "Ourselves are Fate" (*WHM* 5:321). Without being fully cognizant of the development, much less superintending it, Melville in

White-Jacket was beginning to join the social and metaphysical elements of his vision in an egalitarian democracy predicated not on cosmic optimism, as it was for Emerson, Whitman, and most of their less-philosophical countrymen, but on humanistic naturalism.

While generally well received, *Redburn* and *White-Jacket* did little to help Melville's financial situation, lately complicated by the muddled state of the British copyright (an international copyright law would not be enacted until the 1890s). In the fall and early winter of 1849–1850 Melville had journeyed to England and the Continent, nominally to arrange favorable terms for the publication of *White-Jacket* but also to indulge in an abbreviated version of the Grand Tour he had never taken. Anchored off Dover and about to "press English earth after the lapse of ten years," he was awed and amused by his changed status since his last visit— *"then* a sailor, *now* H. M. author of 'Peedee,' 'Hullabaloo,' and 'Pog-Dog'" (*WHM* 15:12). Without the requisite letters of introduction, Melville was unable to meet the leading authors of his time as the young Emerson had done years earlier, but he could at least purchase books, among them the plays of Marlowe, Jonson, and Beaumont and Fletcher, Boswell's *Life of Johnson*, Rousseau's *Confessions*, Goethe's *Autobiography*, Romantic writings by Lamb, De Quincey, Mme de Staël, and Mary Shelley, and the narrative of a Revolutionary War veteran reduced to paupery in England, which would later provide the basis for *Israel Potter*. Instructive, too, were Melville's conversations aboard ship and afterward with George J. Adler, a scholar of German Romanticism with whom he "talked metaphysics continually" during at least one cold Atlantic night, and through whom he came to know something (or something additional) of "Hegel, [Friedrich?] Schlegel, Kant &c" (*WHM* 15:8). In contextualizing Melville, it is essential to keep his literary and philosophical internationalism in mind. History for him did not begin spatially at the American shoreline and temporally in 1776; history was the American present as situated within the Western tradition from the Elizabethans and Montaigne, with crosslights from the classics and from esoterica known to him through authors like Pierre Bayle.

Returning to America in early February 1850, Melville seems to have set to work almost immediately on the book that would become *Moby-Dick; or, The Whale* (1851). The writing went well. By May 1, he was able to report that he was "half way in the work" (*WHM* 14:162), and later that month he told English publisher Bentley that he would have "a new work" finished "in the latter part of the coming autumn" (*WHM* 14:163), a timetable confirmed by Evert Duyckinck in a letter of August 7 that describes Melville's whaling book as "mostly done."[17] As it turned out, *Moby-Dick* would not be completed until the following summer, a delay which has prompted speculation that somewhere during the later months of 1850, *Moby-Dick* underwent not only a significant enlargement, as Melville consulted additional sourcebooks on whaling, but also a profound reconception: what might have begun as a loose and episodic whaling narrative patterned after *White-Jacket* became a grand symbolic hunt.

The catalysts that seem to have transformed *Moby-Dick* and helped to transform its author were Melville's re-immersion in Shakespeare, his reading of Carlyle's *Sartor Resartus* and *On Heroes, Hero-Worship, and the Heroic in History*, and his discovery of Hawthorne's *Mosses from an Old Manse* and his meeting with Hawthorne himself—events that converged to produce the "shock of recognition" (*WHM* 9:249) recorded in Melville's essay/review "Hawthorne and His Mosses," published in Duyckinck's *Literary World* on August 17 and 24, 1850. Melville met Hawthorne on August 5 at a gathering of literary friends in the Berkshires, where Melville and his family were staying at the Pittsfield home of his cousin Robert, partly for a vacation and partly to explore the possibility of settling in the area, which Melville had loved since youthful visits to his uncle Thomas. The two writers took to each other immediately, with Hawthorne making the thoroughly uncharacteristic gesture of inviting Melville to visit at the small red cottage in nearby Lenox to which he had moved his family after leaving Salem. In September, with a loan from Judge Shaw, Melville bought a farm (renamed "Arrowhead") in Pittsfield about a half dozen miles from Lenox, and for the next fourteen months, until Hawthorne left the Berkshires in November 1851, the two men periodically exchanged letters and visits in what would become one of the most extraordinary friendships in American letters.

Melville had interested Hawthorne from the time of *Typee*, when Hawthorne had recognized in its author a freshness and breadth of experience, including erotic experience, he himself admired and wistfully envied—probably all the more so in 1850 with middle age fully upon him (Hawthorne was forty-six when the two men met, Melville thirty-one) and with the pressures of family life displacing the idyll of his early married years at Concord's Old Manse. For Melville, Hawthorne was a revelation— strikingly handsome with a dark repose hinting of depths and mysteries remarked on by nearly all who left record of him, yet also, it seemed to Melville, so sympathetically attuned to his own (Melville's) inner life as to combine, in one person, the roles of friend, brother, father, soulmate, ideal reader, and perhaps fantasized lover.[18] As a writer, Melville had little to learn from Hawthorne; their talents were vastly different. Hawthorne's chief literary service to Melville, as Howard P. Vincent said of the debt inscribed in "Hawthorne and His Mosses," was to demonstrate "that one American was expressively aware of the evil at the core of life, a perception toward which [Melville] had been groping for seven years of authorship, but which he had not completely realized nor dared to disclose."[19] *Moby-Dick* owes much of its boundless ambition to its fertilization by Hawthorne, to whom the book is dedicated, but this only begins to suggest the investment of emotion and self-esteem Melville poured into the relationship even after time and circumstance had distanced him from Hawthorne, indeed even years after Hawthorne's death in 1864.

The drama of Melville's efflorescence in 1850–1851 tends to obscure the fact that *Moby-Dick* was written in a time of national crisis during which the Compromise of 1850 was enacted and, the following April, escaped slave Thomas Sims was arrested in Boston and ordered to be remitted to slavery in compliance with the Fugitive Slave Law; Judge Lemuel Shaw, Melville's father-in-law, issued the decision. Any private comments Melville may have made about the case or about virtually any other political question of the day have not survived.[20] Hershel Parker handles the issue of Melville's politics gingerly, suggesting that though Melville was "not blind to the great national sin of slavery," he was a loyal husband and son-in-law before he was an abolitionist, and a writer of Shakespearean aspirations before anything else (Parker I:832). Melville abhorred slavery and voiced his outrage whenever he addressed it, yet, try as one might to allegorize his writing or draw workable analogies between text and context, politics in general and antislavery politics in particular are not (except in "Benito Cereno" and some of the poems in *Battle-Pieces*) at its immediate center, as James Duban claims when he calls *Moby-Dick* Ishmael's "abolitionist narrative" that "foreshadow[s] the punishment in store for a bellicose, proslavery, and unrepentant republic."[21]

Melville's engagement with the social and political problems of mid-nineteenth-century America needs to be set within his larger understanding of America itself and its place in Western history. By 1850 Melville had come to see America as embodying not simply a new political system but, potentially, what Whitman would call a "different relative attitude towards God" and "the objective universe"[22]—a new consciousness of which the writer was the avatar and his work a proffered medium of cultural transformation. The success of this enterprise depended on America's sloughing off an old mentality, rooted in traditional theocentrism, that shaped not only the perceived coordinates of experience but the affective way of inhabiting those coordinates. "Take God out of the dictionary, and you would have Him in the street" (*WHM* 14:186), Melville wrote to Hawthorne in April 1851; that is to say, dissolve the inherited categories of thought and you would have reality, truth, a new foundation for being, perhaps even Divinity itself, omnipresently around you.

Whitman performs this act of cultural revolution by writing as if it had already occurred and as if he were the Adam of a post-Christian age; *Moby-Dick* enacts it by staging the death throes of an old civilization and the emergence of a new. In his fanatical willfulness Ahab shares in what Melville perceived as the thrust toward aggrandizement that marked America in its rampant individualism, expansionism, exploitation of nature, and emotional and sexual repression. But the Ahab who incorporates elements of the literary and mythic heroes of the past—Prometheus, Job, Christ, Lear, Milton's Satan, Byron's Manfred and Cain, and Goethe's Faust, among others—is also the culmination of 1,900 years of Western thought with its fruitless engagement with the problem of evil, now raised to crisis pitch on both sides of the Atlantic by midcentury doubt. What linked Western intellectual consciousness to forms of social domination was the drive to "comprehend" the world in the double sense of understanding and enclosing it, trying to bring experience under the control of rational, anthropocentric thought and rationalized (i.e., economically productive) modes of social organization and personal behavior. The role of Ahab is to play out and expel this entrenched mindset by venting its accumulated frustrations, calling God to account for not behaving like God and, in the process, immolating itself. It is not simply unregenerate America that goes down with the *Pequod* but Western consciousness itself, of which the reigning American mentality is a provincial variation and slavery a particularly egregious by-product. In this grand apocalypse, reminiscent of the Norse twilight of the Gods that Melville knew from Carlyle, an exhausted cultural order presses its discourse to the point of extremity where it shatters against the obdurateness of naturalistic fact and leaves the mind naked and illusionless, like Ishmael on the empty ocean clinging to Queequeg's coffin. But the end of *Moby-Dick* is also a beginning. With his "free and easy sort of genial, desperado philosophy" (*WHM* 6:226), the Ishmael who returns to tell the story and reflect broadly on his experience is Melville's prototype of the modern man—egalitarian and liberationist in his relation to others, to conventional beliefs and practices, and to his own body, and combining a Whitmanesque delight in the variety and flux of experience with a thoroughly un-Whitmanesque intellectual curiosity and sense of the appalling. Ishmael is a new phenomenon in literature and culture: a fraternal democrat who is *also* a tragic thinker and who locates the ontological ground for democracy not in the cosmic yea-saying of Whitman or in the shallow progressivism of his countrymen but in humanity's common liability to "the universal thump" (*WHM* 6:6).

Reviews of *Moby-Dick* were mixed on both sides of the Atlantic, though on balance more favorable in England. Melville would have been particularly stung by what Evert Duyckinck in the *Literary World* deprecated as Ishmael's "piratical running down of creeds and opinions"—the seriocomic core of Melville's new American sensibility—which Duyckinck found irreverent, "out of place and uncomfortable."[23] If Duyckinck could not rise to *Moby-Dick*, how many American readers could? Like Whitman, Melville saw his vision of a transvalued America founder on national prudishness, sentimentality, and moral and religious conventionalism, and with it foundered his hope of popular success and critical acclaim. "Not one man in five cycles, who is wise, will expect appreciation from his fellows," he wrote to Hawthorne in November 1851 even as he basked in Hawthorne's "joy-giving and exultation-breeding letter" of praise for *Moby-Dick* (*WHM* 14:212). That same month Hawthorne left the Berkshires, and Melville, embittered by the reception and disappointing sales of his book, was forced to deal simultaneously with the loss of the most enlivening intellectual and spiritual intimacy in his life.

According to one theory, Melville began his next book, *Pierre; or, The Ambiguities* (1852), with an eye toward regaining his audience by appealing to female readers with what he disingenuously touted to Richard Bentley as "a regular romance" "very much more calculated for popularity than anything you have yet published of mine" (*WHM* 14:226).[24] As later proved by the reviews, "regular" was the last word contemporaries would apply to *Pierre*, which not only founded its plot on brother-sister incest (with overtones of emotional mother-son incest) but which from its opening pages committed the still graver literary sins of irreverence, morbidness, linguistic obscurity, and abstruse philosophical speculation, any one of which, as Melville well knew, could be fatal to success. *Pierre* is the Melvillean quest for truth recast ironically in a nightmarish subversion of sentimental romance and deconstructed with an unsparing intellectual and psychological acuity all the more painful because Pierre's family history (literally) and authorial career (figuratively) are modeled visibly upon Melville's. It is as if from some buried compulsion Melville were vivisecting himself in public or submitting as analyst and analysand to an unusually drastic and humiliating form of psychotherapy.

Fascinating in its own right, *Pierre* is the pivot of Melville's career intellectually and professionally and, as E. L. Grant Watson long ago remarked, the book "one must understand . . . before all others" in order to understand Melville.[25] Biographically, there is a kind of overdetermination to the conjectural motives behind *Pierre*: Melville's frustration and anger at the reception of *Moby-Dick* and its implications for his literary future; his possible discovery that Allan Melvill, like Pierre's father, had an illegitimate daughter; and his desolation at Hawthorne's withdrawal, which, linking itself to the trauma of Allan's death years earlier, led him to examine his feelings for Hawthorne, their entanglement with unresolved feelings about Allan, and the relationship of both of these things to his literary career.[26] Most intriguing of all is the premonition of imminent decay that Melville confided to Hawthorne in June 1851, when, not yet thirty-two and at the height of his powers, he likened his development to the organic cycle of a plant, adding, "I feel that I am now come to the inmost leaf of the bulb, and that shortly the flower must fall to the mould" (*WHM* 14:193).

Whatever the occasion for *Pierre*, the book's publication was a disaster from which Melville's career as a novelist never recovered. Previously, hostile reviewers had found Melville lurkingly subversive; now, responding to the host of red flags he waved before them—narrative, stylistic, thematic, attitudinal—nearly all reviewers were hostile, and they pronounced him immoral and possibly insane. The diseased *Pierre* was set against the "healthy" *Typee*, and Melville was advised to "diet himself for a year or two on Addison" and leave morbidity and metaphysics alone.[27]

In effect this is what Melville did, or gave the appearance of doing. Happily for him, financial exigency, nervous exhaustion, and the failure of family efforts to secure him a consular appointment in 1853 coincided with the emergence of two excellent periodicals, *Harper's New Monthly Magazine* (1850) and *Putnam's Monthly Magazine* (1853), each of which welcomed his contributions and was willing to pay him at their best rate of $5 per page. This hardly made for a living income, let alone enough to relieve

Melville of mounting debt, but it did help to sustain him as a working author while he recovered from the psychological ordeal of writing *Pierre* and the critical ordeal of having published it. In 1852-1853 Melville evidently wrote and "was prevented from printing" (*WHM* 14:250) a narrative entitled "The Isle of the Cross" based on the history of a Nantucket woman named Agatha Hatch Robertson (see Parker II:136–61). The tale or sketch had never been Melville's genre, but now, with the novel effectively closed to him, he availed himself of the new publishing opportunities and learned to write engagingly for a popular audience while still, through irony, symbolism, and dramatized point of view, managing to have his social and metaphysical say. Where *Pierre* had flaunted its challenges to piety and convention, the magazine pieces of 1853–1856 so subtly insinuated theirs—which included explorations of slavery and racism ("Benito Cereno"), class and gender exploitation ("Poor Man's Pudding and Rich Man's Crumbs," "The Paradise of Bachelors and the Tartarus of Maids"), and human relations under laissez-faire capitalism ("Bartleby, the Scrivener: A Story of Wall-Street")—that "some of the blackest" of the tales, as William Charvat observed, "were praised as 'quaint,' 'fanciful,' 'lifelike,' 'genial,' and 'thoroughly magazinish.'"[28]

Altogether, Melville published fourteen tales and sketches between 1853 and 1856 (another, "The Two Temples," was rejected by *Putnam's* as offensive to genteel churchgoers), along with *Israel Potter: His Fifty Years of Exile* (1854–1855), a serialized historical novel of intermittent comic/satiric brilliance, which, as Walter E. Bezanson said, "gave scope for all but his highest talents."[29] *Israel Potter* appeared in book form in 1855, and the following year five of the *Putnam's* stories ("Bartleby," "Benito Cereno," "The Lightning-Rod Man," "The Encantadas, or Enchanted Isles," and "The Bell-Tower") were collected with a fancifully semiautobiographical preface and published as *The Piazza Tales*. Reviews of both books were generally favorable, if sometimes cursory, but financial returns were meager; Melville's combined income from the magazine pieces of 1853–1856 was less than $1,400. The greater service of the writings was, first, to confirm him in his literary vocation while constructively disciplining his practice of fiction with lasting effect and, second, to assuage a bitterness that threatened to run over into misanthropy and despair. Simply to objectify and seriocomically render his struggle with creditors ("Cock-a-Doodle-Doo!"), his disappointments about fame and success ("The Happy Failure" and "The Fiddler"), and family concerns about his physical and mental health ("I and My Chimney") was to achieve a salutary distance from them and turn his attention outward to the challenges of a new craft. This is not to say that the writing must be read autobiographically. Ingeniously wrought, nearly all of the best tales work simultaneously on the levels of private reference, social criticism, and metaphysical protest; "Bartleby," for example, is about a writer who abandons his vocation, about the dehumanized nature of life and work in laissez-faire society, about a depth of isolation leading to solipsistic withdrawal and self-immolation, and about the tragic, irremediable forlornness of the human condition.

The tension between Bartleby's bleak pathos and the narrator's constitutional but increasingly chastened optimism suggests the antithesis that governed Melville's writing, as it may have governed his life, between the completion of *Pierre* in the spring of 1852 and his departure for England and the Mediterranean four and a half years later. Bartleby is a depressive; his coworkers Turkey and Nippers are manic-depressives; so, too, is the giddily melancholic narrator of "Cock-a-Doodle-Doo!" a tale which takes as its subject the extreme mood swings (and accompanying philosophy swings) of psychic bipolarity. The opposition between "bright" and "dark" views of life permeates virtually all of the magazine pieces and serves as an organizing principle of *The Confidence-Man*. Psychiatrist Kay Redfield Jamison includes a brief section on Melville in her study of manic-depressive illness and artistic creativity, *Touched with Fire*.[30] Melville *was* unusually mood-ridden, especially in times of literary stress and vocational distress, and during at least one period in their marriage (1867) Lizzie Melville questioned her husband's sanity. But if Melville were manic-depressive, it was more likely in a figurative than a clinical sense, and never in the devastating form that afflicted Virginia Woolf. In the aftermath of *Pierre* and with financial burdens pressing more heavily on him as notes on Arrowhead came due and a third child was born in 1853, a fourth in 1855, Melville may well have oscillated between what *The Confidence-Man* calls a "too-drunken" and a "too-sober" view of life (*WHM* 10:134). In making this issue his subject, however—in recognizing that world views, his own included, were as much a matter of temperament and affective condition as of "truth," and in dramatizing the idea in a series of strikingly inventive tales, most comic or darkly comic, some tragic—Melville externalized and psychically controlled what might otherwise have overwhelmed him.

From the thematic materials and genial but rigorous prose of the magazine period, Melville fashioned the consummate ironies of *The Confidence-Man: His Masquerade* (1857). Suggested by the exploits of an actual confidence man and set on the Mississippi riverboat *Fidèle* on April Fools' Day, *The Confidence-Man* is Melville's most "American" book in characterization and local color; in its involutedness and self-conscious artifice, it is also his most prophetically postmodern, ringing dizzying changes on the notion of "confidence" (or want of it) in man, nature, God, the reliability of knowledge, and the stability of the self. Whatever Melville's private demons, *The Confidence-Man* is the work of a writer who has mastered his art and is displaying it with dexterous confidence, save perhaps confidence that he is addressing a responsive audience. At one point Melville apparently thought to serialize the book in *Putnam's*, but whether the manuscript evolved over time or Melville was simply deceived (or deceiving) about its character, *The Confidence-Man* is deeply antithetical to the magazine writing of the time. Indeed, its generic oddity and self-reflexive language—densely laden with qualifiers, insinuating circumlocutions, allegorical patterns defying simple solution, and diabolical jokes (many involving the Devil himself)—so insistently challenge the reader that Melville seems often to have been writing for the sheer virtuosity of it. He may as well have been. The book was barely noticed in America, where Melville had ceased to be a literary presence; English reviews were longer and often more thoughtful, but baffled. *The Confidence-Man* was published on April Fools' Day 1857 by Dix, Edwards & Co., which, in a capstone joke Melville might grimly have savored, went bankrupt by the end of the month.

On April 1, Melville was en route from Padua to Venice as part of a seven-month journey to Europe and the Near East underwritten by his father-in-law, Judge Shaw, in response to family anxieties about his state of mind. Meeting him in November 1856 in Liverpool, where he was now American consul, Hawthorne found him "looking much as he used to do (a little paler, and perhaps a little sadder)" but genial enough for the men to resume "pretty much [their] former terms of sociability and confidence."[31] Melville stayed with Hawthorne for three days—he would visit again (the final meeting of their lives) just before sailing home in May—and during a memorable walk on the Southport dunes, Hawthorne reported in his journal, "Melville, as he always does, began to reason of Providence and futurity, and of everything that lies beyond human ken" (*English Notebooks* 163). The entry is worth quoting at length because it has come to be taken as a touchstone for Melville's spiritual plight:

> It is strange how he persists—and has persisted ever since I knew him, and probably long before—in wandering to-and fro over these deserts, as dismal and monotonous as the sand hills amid which we were sitting. He can neither believe, nor be comfortable in his unbelief; and he is too honest and courageous not to try to do one or the other. If he were a religious man, he would be one of the most truly religious and reverential; he has a very high and noble nature, and better worth immortality than most of us. (*English Notebooks* 163)

From Liverpool, Melville sailed to the Mediterranean, where he visited some of the legendary Greek islands and Constantinople.[32] The heart of the journey was four weeks in Egypt and Palestine, including stays in Cairo and Jerusalem, excursions to the Pyramids, and a three-day circuit through the Judean desert to the Jordan, the Dead Sea, the Mar Saba monastery high in the mountains, and Bethlehem, a trip that would serve as the geographical basis for the pilgrims' ten-day journey in *Clarel*. In traversing holy ground Melville may have hoped, like his fictive seeker Rolfe, to "Slip quite behind the parrot-lore / Conventional, and—what attain?" (*WHM* 12:1; 31:37-38). If he wished to vivify or confirm his faith, he came to what appeared not only to him but to many Protestant travelers the very worst place to do it. "No country will more quickly dissipate Romantic expectations than Palestine," he observed in his journal (*WHM* 15:91). Jerusalem, ruled by the declining Ottoman Empire and close to the nadir of its fortunes, was shabby and venal, while the Church of the Holy Sepulchre (built around Jesus' tomb) was "a sickening cheat" (*WHM* 15:88), to which he nonetheless returned almost daily. The Judean desert was, in every sense, awful—like the ocean or the prairie, an image for Melville of the blank face of God in creation yet resonant at nearly every step with the recorded acts of the Old Testament Jehovah.

In short, Melville found in Palestine precisely what he brought to it: a sense of the bankruptcy and blight of the Judeo-Christian tradition which at once deepened his skepticism and whetted his spiritual hunger. The unanticipated discovery came on his homeward journey as he visited Athens, Naples, Rome (for nearly four weeks), and Florence. The sculptures in the Italian galleries combined with other evidence of ancient grandeur—the Acropolis, the Coliseum, the Baths of Caracalla, the ubiquitous ruined columns and aqueducts—to suggest a dignity and scale of life that dwarfed modern civilization with its vaunted triumphs of technology and its impoverishment of spirit. Bitter about the course of his career and inspired by the achievements of the classical world, Melville projected his feelings into a revised sense of history that qualified American meliorism with evidence of cultural cyclicalism, even of decline. If on one side Melville retained a faith in American possibility, on another he came increasingly to scorn the materialism, diminutiveness, complacency, and pretension he associated with modernity in general and America in particular. As the expatriate American Ungar would say in *Clarel*, "the Phidian marbles prove / The graces of the Grecian prime" and "declare / A magnanimity which our time / Would envy, were it great enough / To comprehend" (*WHM* 12:4, 10:142–43, 146–49).

Returning to America in May 1857 and resolved that he was "not going to write any more at present," as his brother-in-law Lemuel Shaw, Jr., reported in Bartlebyesque words (*Log* II:580),

Melville decided to try the winter lecture circuit, which had rewarded traveler-raconteurs like Bayard Taylor and George William Curtis. Rather than piece together a lively anecdotal account of his journey, Melville chose to sift his impressions of the Mediterranean in a discourse on past and present civilization titled "Statues in Rome." Reflective, aloof, undemonstrative, and occasionally inaudible, Melville earned a grudging respect for his bookish gravity but was not the kind of performer that audiences in Chillicothe, Ohio, or Clarksville, Tennessee, wanted to hear. Lectures in sixteen cities between November 1857 and February 1858 netted him $423.70—about the income of a productive winter's magazine work but hardly the "fame & fortune" his mother had predicted (*WHM* 9:517, 516). The following winter's lecture on "The South Seas" did slightly better, but Melville had little enthusiasm for it. A third winter's tour ("Traveling: Its Pleasures, Pains, and Profits") was brief and apparently unsuccessful, with more pains than pleasures and with scarcely any profits at all.

Reports vary about Melville's health and spirits during this period, but by 1859–1860 there was apparently cause for deep concern. Visiting him in Pittsfield in April 1859, two students from nearby Williams College, John Thomas Gulick and Titus Munson Coan, found him, in Gulick's words, "a disappointed man, soured by criticism and disgusted with the civilized world and with our Christendom in general and in particular. The ancient dignity of Homeric times afforded the only state of humanity, individual or social, to which he could turn with any complacency" (*Log* II:605). To Coan, who would befriend Melville in the 1880s and write a short biographical sketch after his death, Melville seemed to be "one who has suffered from opposition, both literary and social," and whose attitude toward his townsmen was "something like that of an Ishmael" (*Log* II:605). As early as mid-1857 Melville had sought to leave Pittsfield for New York City and employment in the customs house, but neither the position nor the sale of the property came through, and it would be more than six years before he could escape an environment in which, as Lemuel Shaw, Jr., said, he was "solitary, without society, [and] without exercise or occupation except that which is very likely to be injurious to him in over-straining his mind" (*Log* II:634).

Sometime during this period Melville began studying poetry and secretly undertaking to write it. By May 1860, when he hurriedly decided to accompany his captain brother, Thomas, on a voyage to San Francisco and beyond, Melville had enough poems to entrust a carefully arranged manuscript to Evert Duyckinck to circulate among New York publishers. None were interested and the simply titled "Poems by Herman Melville" was never published, nor are its contents known beyond the supposition that some or most of the poems grouped under the heading "Fruit of Travel Long Ago" and published in *Timoleon* may be revisions of the 1860 poems, along with short pieces dealing with Pittsfield life included in Melville's final poetry collection, *Weeds and Wildings*. For reading on his voyage Melville carried editions of Dante, Spenser, Milton, Chapman's Greek translations, and Wordsworth's *Excursion*, among other epic works, a choice that prompted Hershel Parker to speculate that Melville was intending to use the long seclusion to write "an American epic poem" of his own,[33] though he may simply have been settling in with comfortable traveling companions as later readers might with *War and Peace*, *Remembrance of Things Past*, and *Ulysses*. More tantalizing is Parker's other conjecture that in immersing himself in great poets who were also vitally involved with their times Melville may have been moving beyond the alienation of "Statues in Rome"—and, perhaps, the aesthetic miniaturism of the 1860 poems —and considering how as a poet he might constructively influence his world.

"To produce a mighty book," Ishmael said, "you must choose a mighty theme" (*WHM* 6:456). If Melville were indeed casting about for an epic subject and an epic occasion, he found them five months after his return to America in the outbreak of the Civil War. When the war began, Melville was forty-one years old and felt himself prematurely aged by the physical and psychological attrition of the preceding years. His practical involvement with the war, including a visit to his cousin Henry Sanford Gansevoort at the Virginia front in April 1864 (during which he rode with a cavalry scout in territory haunted by Confederate raider

John S. Mosby) is traced in Stanton Garner's exhaustive *The Civil War World of Herman Melville*. His attitudes, for want of primary evidence, are harder to determine other than from *Battle-Pieces* itself, read carefully in its aesthetic context and against the backdrop of family and region that Garner establishes as a probable gestalt. Politically, Melville was a moderate Democrat dating back to the mid-1840s when the chief legacy of Jacksonianism was still resistance to aristocratic privilege; most of his family and friends were also Democrats, often of a more conservative stripe, a circumstance that inclined him, Garner believes, to see "the events of the war largely through the Democratic eyes"[34] and that put a partial brake on his abhorrence of the "atheistical iniquity" of slavery.[35] Like Lincoln during the early years of the war, Melville understood the motive of the "Union" as precisely that—the preservation of the American nation against southern secession rather than the abolition of slavery. Even as the war ended, he regarded the initial challenge facing the victors as one of national reconciliation. The values of magnanimity and compassion he saw as the common legacy of the war extended across racial as well as regional lines; yet, given the established temper of the South, he believed that full and immediate justice for freed slaves could be enforced, if at all, only at the price of a bitterness that would aggravate sectional tensions and provoke the South to an "exterminating hatred of race toward race" (*Battle-Pieces* 202). The Union had won the war; whether it also won the peace in the sense of spiritually reuniting the nation depended on its "forbearance" toward the vanquished and its trust in "the graduated care of future legislation" to ameliorate the condition of the emancipated (*Battle-Pieces* 201, 200). All of this is to say that Melville was a pragmatist committed to what he regarded as the highest ethical and political resolution within the terms of the possible rather than according to the ideal. His vision of Reconstruction was closer to the one imagined by Lincoln than to the program enacted after his death by the Radical Republican Congress.

By Melville's own account, nearly all of the poems in *Battle-Pieces and Aspects of the War* (1866) were written after the fall of Richmond on April 3, 1865, though they assume the form of a polyphonic verse journal of events beginning with the execution of John Brown and extending through the imagined speech of Robert E. Lee addressing Congress to save "the flushed North" from the vindictiveness of the triumphant ("Lee is the Capitol"). A sign of Melville's political engagement is his decision to append to the volume, against "all literary scruples" (*Battle-Pieces* 196), a thoughtful and moving prose "supplement" whose closing lines reinforce the poems' implied vision of the war as national catharsis: "Let us pray that the terrible historic tragedy of our time may not have been enacted in vain without instructing our whole beloved country through terror and pity; and may fulfillment verify in the end those expectations which kindle the bards of Progress and Humanity" (*Battle-Pieces* 202).

It is as tragedian, or tragic moralist, that Melville constructs *Battle-Pieces* to reach beyond vignettes of the war and counter the dominant northern myth of America's exorcism of the crime of slavery and its return to covenantal status as a favored nation. In this respect Melville redefines the tradition of the American jeremiad, the declamatory sermonic and literary form that interpreted the trials of the New World community as punishments for apostasy from the terms of its divine "errand" but also as a promise that those terms might still obtain if the community cleansed itself and repented.[36] For Melville, national salvation depended on Americans' recognizing not their *exemption from* but their *common liability to* incursions of the catastrophic—"Tempest[s] bursting from the waste of Time" ("Misgivings")—and upwellings of the irrational and brutish. Milton is Melville's literary model for treating the war as military crusade (Confederates as Luciferian rebels, Unionists as Godly host) and as symbolic fall from Edenic innocence into historical experience. Yet, finally, the vision of *Battle-Pieces* is not Miltonic and providential, but Shakespearean and existential. The war is an initiation into a horrific blackness always subterraneously present beneath earth's "crust" of "solidity" and "pastoral green" ("The Apparition"). Where the exultant North imagined a threat providentially overcome and a nation restored to its immunities, Melville, as he had in "Hawthorne and His Mosses" and *Moby-Dick* but with greater urgency, sought to destroy the illusion of American exceptionalism and refound the nation on the secular, nonconvenantal bases of unexampled wisdom, generosity, and human respect operating in an anarchic world.

The extraordinary virtues that Melville asked from his countrymen were more easily maintained in literature than in life. In coming forward so undisguisedly in *Battle-Pieces* as the nation's would-be instructor, Melville left the cocoon of isolation and apparent indifference he had woven around himself as protection from the humiliations of his literary career. Reconstruction was a betrayal of his hopes; so was the popular and critical failure of *Battle-Pieces*—the volume was indifferently received and sold scarcely more than 500 copies in a decade despite good-faith efforts by its publisher[37]—which shattered whatever dream of cultural influence Melville may still have nourished.

When *Battle-Pieces* was published in August 1866, Melville had been living at 104 East 26th Street, New York City, for nearly three years. In December 1866, he assumed the position of inspector in the New York Customs House (salary: $4 a day) that he would hold until his retirement in 1885. Family members spoke of his improved spirits, and biographers generally followed their lead until the publication in 1975 of two newly discovered letters to New York Unitarian minister Henry Whitney Bellows—one from Melville's brother-in-law Samuel Shaw, the other from Lizzie Melville, both dated May 1867.[38] According to Shaw, Lizzie believed that Melville was insane, and family members—Gansevoorts and Melvilles, apparently, as well as Shaws—were pressing her to initiate at least a temporary separation. Lizzie's trials were evidently long-standing (in Shaw's eyes, at least), but she could not, would not, or at any rate did not consent to leave Melville. Four months later the civil war within the Melville household was overshadowed by a deeper family tragedy: on the night of September 10, eighteen-year-old Malcolm locked himself in his bedroom and the following morning shot himself in the head.

Was Melville insane? Did he vent his career frustrations in domestic tyranny? Was he a harsh, distant, or self-preoccupied father? Did he abuse Lizzie physically or psychologically? No one knows. The case for physical abuse rests on a story of "Herman's drinking, coming home smashed on brandy, beating up on Lizzie, throwing her down the back stairs, etc.," which great-grandson Paul Metcalf reported he heard from poet Charles Olson, who claimed to have heard it from Metcalf's mother, Eleanor Melville Metcalf, whom Paul Metcalf doubts would have told Olson even if it were true. "All this," Paul Metcalf adds, "has been filtered through so many ears and mouths, and minds of such diverse motivation, it is impossible of verification" (*Winding Way* 21–22). Tense and irritable when he was writing, prone to depression when he was not, Melville could not have been an easy man with whom to live, and Lizzie's particular form of well-meaning ineffectuality seems almost uniquely calculated to have called forth his impatience and anger, followed by self-loathing contrition. Even in the best of times Melville was only fitfully domestic; though he missed his family deeply on his travels, his most intense life was intellectual, and except for relationships with a very few intimates (brother-in-law John C. Hoadley, for one) he lived it largely alone. It seems almost inevitable that those around him would have suffered under the moodiness and irascibility that followed from his isolation and sense of failure; beyond that, virtually everything is rumor or speculation. *Battle-Pieces* includes a long section of epitaphs, inscriptions, commemorations, and requiems for the fallen on both sides, as the living gather around the dead and reunite in their common grief. Malcolm's death seems to have performed a comparable function for the Melvilles. The marriage would continue to have its strains, but henceforth there would be no serious thought of separation. As for guilt over Malcolm, Melville may have carried it to his grave, with or without reason; the tableau of filial forgiveness he dramatized in *Billy Budd* seems, among other things, a gesture of self-absolution.

As he had after the psychic crisis of *Pierre*, Melville overcame his depression by reconceiving himself as a writer yet again, this time as the author of an epic narrative and philosophical poem he had grounds to expect would be unsalable, if publishable at all, and very possibly unwriteable, given his duties at the customs house six days of the week, fifty weeks of the year. Walter E. Bezanson believes that Melville may have begun *Clarel: A Poem and Pilgrimage in the Holy Land* (1876) in 1867; Hershel Parker dates its inception "around the start of 1870" (Parker II:687). In either case, "working slowly and deliberately, with time for reading and meditation as he pondered the predicament of modern man, [Melville] filled in the margins of his daily life with the steady act of creation."[39] His journal of a decade earlier, with the Old and New Testaments behind it, was his prime resource for imagining the physical and symbolic terrain of the Holy Land, but in the early 1870s he began supplementing his impressions with travel books on the Near East. He also read widely in Hawthorne's fiction and published notebooks as he set about fashioning the Hawthornesque character Vine and imaginatively revisiting his still highly charged relationship to Hawthorne, now dead for more than a decade. Important in a more pervasive way were the poetry and criticism of Matthew Arnold, not only for their rendering of the Victorian spiritual crisis but for their broad contextualization of the present age within 2,000 years of Western history, which helped Melville to pattern the thoughts on civilization and progress he had first explored in "Statues in Rome." Working secretively on his poem, Melville finished it late in 1875 in what Lizzie called "a frightfully nervous state" (Metcalf 237) and, thanks to a legacy from his uncle Peter, succeeded in placing it with G. P. Putnam's Sons at his own expense. Apparently he did not care either for recognition—his first thought was to publish the book anonymously—or for remuneration, about which he had no illusions. It was enough for him to have written *Clarel* and sent it forth into the world, "content beforehand," as he said in his brief prefatory note, "with whatever future awaits it" (*WHM* 12:xiv).[40]

Virtually none did. A poem of 18,000 lines chiefly in terse octosyllabic couplets may well be "eminently adapted for unpopularity" (*WHM* 14:483), as Melville later wryly observed. Barely noticed in its own time, it did not (with a few exceptions) fare markedly better during the New Critical hegemony after World War II when the model for poetry was the short lyric and the touchstones for epic were the sonorous iambic periods of Milton and Wordsworth. *Clarel* is not only a great intellectual achievement; it is also in many of its 150 cantos a great poem, but it requires its readers to retrain their ears and their imaginations in what epic poetry can be.

For Americanist critics *Clarel* labors under the further disadvantage of seeming, as Lawrence Buell said, "more a western or Victorian than an American poem."[41] Though most of its major characters are expatriate Americans, they wear their nationality lightly and, for the most part, negatively as an absence of strongly marked local and historical peculiarities (the ex-Confederate soldier Ungar is the exception). At its highest, as in Melville's idealized alter-ego Rolfe, "Americanism" in *Clarel* signifies a questing independence of mind turned against all complacent or narrowing orthodoxies, those of America included. Without losing its defining idealism, America in *Clarel* has been incorporated into the postlapsarian world; its spiritual problems are those of ossified Christianity at large, while its formerly distinctive cultural problems of materialism, leveling democracy, and an unquestioning faith in progress have become European problems as well. In spirit the most "American" character in *Clarel* is the meliorist Anglican clergyman Derwent, against whose rosy view of the liberalization of society and culture Melville sets Ungar's nightmare vision of the impending "Dark Ages of Democracy": "Myriads playing pygmy parts— / Debased into equality: / In glut of all material arts / A civic barbarism may be: / Man disennobled—brutalized / By popular science—Atheized / Into a smatterer" (*WHM* 12:4; 22:139, 127–33). While Melville is not Ungar, he is intent that Ungar's viewpoint should be heard as a self-congratulatory America approaches its centennial; as he later wrote to English admirer James Billson, "altho neither pessimist nor optomist [*sic*] myself, nevertheless I relish [pessimism] in the verse if for nothing else than as a counterpoise to the exorbitant hopefulness, juvenile and shallow, that makes such a bluster in these days—at least, in some quarters" (*WHM* 14:486).

Aside from the tensions created at home by "this dreadful *incubus* of a *book*," as Lizzie Melville called *Clarel*, "because it has undermined all our happiness" (Metcalf 237), the 1870s were a trying decade for Melville. Reminders of mortality were everywhere; Melville's mother and younger brother Allan died in 1872, his favorite sister Augusta and uncle Peter Gansevoort in 1876, his cousin Henry Sanford Gansevoort in 1871, and Evert Duyckinck in 1878. As his circle of intimates shrank and with it his already

diminished relish for society, Melville channeled his impulse toward geniality into a prose/verse composition about a fictional
group of bon vivants, the Burgundy Club (Major Jack Gentian,
presiding), much as a solitary child might invent imaginary play-
mates. Melville still occasionally shone at family gatherings, but
as age and confirmed isolation took their toll, his interior life increasingly became a dialogue with books. "A few friends felt at
liberty to visit the recluse and were kindly welcomed," wrote
Arthur Stedman, one of the privileged, "but he himself sought
no one" (*Early Lives* 110). Invited to join the Authors Club in 1882,
Melville at first accepted, then declined on the ground that "he
had become too much of a hermit" and that "his nerves could no
longer stand large gatherings."[42] The episode is symptomatic of
the deep ambivalence with which he received all such overtures.
Still taunted by a dream of reputation but acutely sensitive to real
or imagined slights, he chose to armor himself with an air of
quiet indifference, declining as Stedman said, "to speak of himself, his adventures or his writings in conversation" (*Early Lives*
106), while guardedly encouraging English admirers like James
Billson and sea novelist W. Clark Russell, whose homage gave
promise of a belated recognition while exacting no risks. A
legacy to Lizzie in 1878 eased the family's outward situation, but
Melville's incalculable debt to Lizzie during these years of obscurity and creative anticlimax following *Clarel* was for her solicitude
and sustaining devotion.

An inheritance from Lizzie's stepbrother Lemuel Shaw, Jr., enabled Melville to retire from the customs house on December 31,
1885, after nineteen years of service. Of his children, Malcolm
was long dead but hardly forgotten; Stanwix, who never found
himself, would die of tuberculosis in San Francisco in 1886;
Bessie was an invalid and spinster living at home; and Frances
was comfortably married to Henry B. Thomas. Melville and
Lizzie had apparently weathered their storms and attained a sort
of peace. Melville's final verse collection, *Weeds and Wildings*,
would begin with an elaborate dedication "To Winnefred"
(Lizzie), a gift of love and perhaps of belated reparation.

Retirement commonly means ease, and Melville did savor the
pleasures of his books, his engravings, his rose garden, and the

generally placid tenor of his domestic life, though he was still subject to "moods and occasional uncertain tempers" (*Early Lives* 180), as one granddaughter reminisced. Despite his attraction to a refined aesthetic hedonism, his bedroom was austere, even forbidding, and posted on a side wall by his desk, visible only to himself, was a copied line from Schiller, "Keep true to the dreams of thy youth" (Metcalf 284). This Melville did, if the dreams of his youth can be said to have centered on a consecration of mind and spirit to a life journey toward no confidently postulated celestial city. As he wrote in the late poem "The Enthusiast" (from *Timoleon*), "Though light forsake thee, never fall / From fealty to light." The achievement of Melville's final years was to live for the light guided only by spiritual instinct, as an underground shoot might grope its way toward the sun. Practically, this meant resisting the downward pull of illness and exhaustion and devoting himself to four substantial projects despite the fact that he had no contemporary audience and may even have ceased to desire one. Two of these works—*John Marr and Other Sailors* (1888) and *Timoleon, Etc.* (1891)—he printed privately in editions of twenty-five copies and distributed himself. The other two—*Weeds and Wildings Chiefly: With a Rose or Two* (post. 1924) and *Billy Budd, Sailor (An Inside Narrative)* (post. 1924; standard edition 1962)—were left on his desk in near completion when he died on September 28, 1891, after what Lizzie called "two years of failing health" (*Log* II:836).

Writing essentially for himself, Melville gave concerted thought to the arrangement of the poetry collections and, as surviving manuscripts suggest, to details of prosody and diction. The poems are significant partly because Melville wrote them, or rather because they extend and redefine the trajectory, and therefore the meaning, of his long career. But each of the volumes includes poems deeply interesting in themselves and thematically more ambitious than nearly all American poetry between Whitman and Dickinson, on one side, and Robert Frost and the early modernists, on the other. *John Marr* is notable for four dramatic monologues that revisit the sailing-ship days and voice Melville's nostalgia for a lost world of camaraderie and largesse. The complementary "Sea Pieces," particularly "The Aeolian Harp," "The Berg," and "Pebbles," are testaments to a bleak naturalism, *Moby-*

Dick without Ishmael's picaresque delight, *Clarel* without traces of the storied footprints of God. Metaphysically, *John Marr* seems a bottoming out, as if Melville had to confront universal emptiness once again and be "healed" by nature's "pitiless breath" ("Pebbles") before he could reconstitute spirituality on the ground of an agnosticism raised to the emotional tenor of religion by an arduous fidelity to the highest in himself. *Timoleon* shares the world view of *John Marr* and, in its best poems (including two longer ones with figurative autobiographical references, "Timoleon" and "After the Pleasure Party"), explores the ethical question of how to live—whether aspiringly for truth and art or accommodationally for sensual pleasure and mental repose.[43] Several of the rose poems in *Weeds and Wildings* also elaborate this theme, with a complexity of language and symbol that is itself an index of Melville's own choice. In view of the uncertain dates of individual poems and their fluid arrangement in collections, it would be a mistake to read the successive volumes as phases in an unfolding spiritual autobiography. The collections are governed by decorums of theme, genre, tone, and occasion; together, however, they do indicate many of the concerns of late Melville and as such are an important context for considering his major effort of these years, *Billy Budd, Sailor.*

Billy Budd developed over the length of Melville's retirement and was chronologically complete but not fully revised when he died. The tale originated with the poem "Billy in the Darbies," a sailor monologue like those in *John Marr.* Initially, Billy was "an older man, condemned for fomenting mutiny and apparently guilty as charged,"[44] but as Melville expanded and revised the manuscript through what its editors describe as "nine major stages of inscription with their substages,"[45] its narrative emphasis shifted from Billy (now an Adamic innocent) to Claggart to Vere and its thematic emphasis from theology to politics to psychology. Its mode of presentation also changed from reportage to dramatized scene, from authorial pronouncement to ascribed opinion, and from a relative simplicity of meaning to a density of verbal and structural irony which, together with loose ends that Melville may or may not have resolved had he lived, make it susceptible to almost limitless interpretation. For some readers, *Billy*

Budd represents Melville's deathbed acceptance, whether of God, of the universe, of the avoidable or unavoidable tragedies of sublunary life, or of the indeterminacy of truth and the vagaries of worldly reputation. For others, it is a final uncompromised protest against one or another or all of these things. There will never be critical agreement about *Billy Budd* partly because it is an evolving text of shifting emphases, partly because it presents an infinitely nuanced and resonant dramatic situation frayed with truth's "ragged edges,"[46] and partly because its themes appeal to core political and philosophical commitments that divide readers into constitutionally warring parties of the mind.

Even as he labored on *Billy Budd* in the final months of his life, adding the late pencil revisions of the surgeon's role that questioned Vere's sanity and gave the tale yet another turn of the screw, Melville was working on the pastoral *Weeds and Wildings* with a mind to his enabling practical and emotional debt to Lizzie. On or about June 13, 1891, Lizzie's sixty-ninth birthday, he "gratefully and affectionately" inscribed *Timoleon* "To Her— without whose assistance both manual and literary Timoleon &c could not have passed through the press" (*Log* II:835). On August 4, he returned to Lizzie in his flowery as well as flower-strewn dedication to *Weeds and Wildings*. Eight weeks later, he was dead. The obituary in the *New-York Press* called him "once one of the most popular writers in the United States." "Probably, if the truth were known," the *Press* continued, "even his own generation has long thought him dead, so quiet have been the later years of his life" (*Log* II:836). Had Melville left instructions for his own obituary, he might have included the lines he marked in Schopenhauer in the last year of his life: "the more a man belongs to posterity, in other words, to humanity in general, the more of an alien he is to his contemporaries; since his work is not meant for them as such" (*Log* II:832–33).

NOTES

I would like to thank Richard Ruland, Donald Yannella, Richard Cook, and Gail Milder for their helpful comments on this chapter.

1. Arthur Stedman, introduction to *Typee* (New York: United

States Book Company, 1892), in Merton M. Sealts, Jr., *The Early Lives of Melville* (Madison: University of Wisconsin Press, 1974), p. 157. In text as *Early Lives*.

2. Herman Melville, *Correspondence*, vol. 14 of *The Writings of Herman Melville*, ed. Harrison Hayford, Hershel Parker, and G. Thomas Tanselle (Evanston and Chicago: Northwestern University Press and Newberry Library, 1968–), p. 193. All references to Melville's writings (with the exception of those to *Collected Poems*, *Battle-Pieces and Aspects of the War*, and *Billy Budd, Sailor*) are to this edition, hereafter cited in text as *WHM*.

3. Virginia Woolf, "The New Biography," in *Collected Essays*,vol. 4, ed. Leonard Woolf (London: Chatto & Windus, 1967), p. 229.

4. Allan Melvill, quoted in Hershel Parker, *Herman Melville: A Biography*, 2 vols. (Baltimore, Md.: Johns Hopkins University Press, 1996, 2002), I:35. In text as Parker. Maria Melvill would add an *e* to the family name after Allan's death.

5. Newton Arvin, *Herman Melville* (New York: Sloane, 1950), p. 23.

6. Nathaniel Hawthorne, in Jay Leyda, ed., *The Melville Log*, 2 vols. (New York: Harcourt, Brace, 1951), I:208. In text as *Log*.

7. See Sigmund Freud, *Civilization and Its Discontents*, trans. James Strachey (New York: Norton, 1962), and Herbert Marcuse, *Eros and Civilization* (Boston: Beacon, 1955).

8. D. H. Lawrence, *Studies in Classic American Literature* (New York: Viking, 1964), p. 137.

9. J. E. A. Smith, "Herman Melville," in Sealts, *Early Lives*, p. 128.

10. John Bryant, introduction to Melville, *Typee: A Peep at Polynesian Life* (New York: Penguin, 1996), p. xxii.

11. Eleanor Melville Metcalf, *Herman Melville: Cycle and Epicycle* (Cambridge, Mass.: Harvard University Press, 1953), p. 55. In text as Metcalf.

12. Maria Morewood, as quoted by her daughter Margaret, in Metcalf, *Herman Melville*, p. 259.

13. Warner Berthoff, *The Example of Melville* (Princeton, N.J.: Princeton University Press, 1962), p. 15.

14. William Charvat, "Melville and the Common Reader," in *The Profession of Authorship in America: The Papers of William Charvat*, ed. Matthew J. Bruccoli (Columbus: Ohio State University Press, 1968), p. 268.

15. Richard H. Brodhead, "*Mardi*: Creating the Creative," in *New*

Perspectives on Melville, ed. Faith Pullin (Kent, Ohio: Kent State University Press, 1978), p. 48.

16. F. O. Matthiessen, *American Renaissance* (New York: Oxford University Press, 1941), p. 400.

17. Evert A. Duyckinck, quoted in Luther S. Mansfield, "Glimpses of Herman Melville's Life in Pittsfield, 1850–1851: Some Unpublished Letters of Evert A. Duyckinck," *American Literature* 9 (1937): 32.

18. For a consideration of the Melville-Hawthorne relationship with reference to homoeroticism, see Edwin Haviland Miller, *Melville* (New York: Braziller, 1975), and Robert Milder, "Melville, Hawthorne, and Homoeroticism," *ESQ* 46 (2000): 1–49.

19. Howard P. Vincent, *The Trying-Out of "Moby-Dick"* (Carbondale and Edwardsville: Southern Illinois University Press, 1949), p. 37.

20. As Parker observes of the extant record, "Melville could not be relied upon to excite himself about whatever cause the nation was exciting itself about" (Parker II:220).

21. James Duban, *Melville's Major Fiction: Politics, Theology, Imagination* (DeKalb: Northern Illinois University Press, 1983), p. 83.

22. Walt Whitman, "A Backward Glance O'er Travel'd Roads," in *Leaves of Grass*, ed. Sculley Bradley and Harold W. Blodgett (New York: Norton, 1973), p. 564.

23. Evert A. Duyckinck, review of *Moby-Dick*, in *Literary World* 251 (November 22, 1851), reprinted in *Moby-Dick*, 2d ed., ed. Hershel Parker and Harrison Hayford (New York: Norton, 2002), p. 612.

24. See Leon Howard, "Historical Note to *Pierre*," *WHM*, vol. 7:365–79.

25. E. L. Grant Watson, "Melville's *Pierre*," in *Critical Essays on Herman Melville's "Pierre; or, The Ambiguities"*, ed. Brian Higgins and Hershel Parker (Boston: Hall, 1983), p. 183.

26. Hershel Parker, individually and with Brian Higgins, has argued that Melville's anger over the reviews of *Moby-Dick* caused him to disrupt a potentially brilliant psychological novel intended for a popular audience and use it as a vehicle to express his bitterness toward his readership. See, for example, Higgins and Parker, "The Flawed Grandeur of Melville's *Pierre*," in Pullin, *New Perspectives on Melville*, pp. 162–98. Parker's theory has led him to edit *Pierre* according to what he believes (without manuscript evidence) to have been

Melville's original book. See *Pierre; or, The Ambiguities* by Herman Melville, the Kraken Edition, ed. Hershel Parker (New York: HarperCollins, 1995). For the theory of Allan Melvill's illegitimate daughter, see Amy Puett Emmers, "Melville's Closet Skeleton: A New Letter about the Illegitimacy Incident in *Pierre*," *Studies in the American Renaissance* 1 (1977): 339–43; and Henry A. Murray, Harvey Myerson, and Eugene Taylor, "Allan Melvill's By-Blow," *Melville Society Extracts* 61 (1985): 1–6. Surveying the existing evidence, Parker concludes that "there is, as of now, no way of knowing" whether Allan Melvill had an illegitimate daughter or, if so, who the daughter might have been (Parker I:65). For a reading of *Pierre* in light of the psychosexual dynamics of the Melville-Hawthorne relationship, see Milder, "Melville, Hawthorne, and Homoeroticism," pp. 13–29 especially.

27. Fitz-James O'Brien, "Our Young Authors—Melville," in Higgins and Parker, *Critical Essays on "Pierre"*, pp. 75–76.

28. Charvat, "Melville and the Common Reader," p. 279.

29. Walter E. Bezanson, "Historical Note to *Israel Potter: His Fifty Years of Exile*," *WHM* 8:174.

30. Kay Redfield Jamison, *Touched with Fire* (New York: Free Press, 1993), pp. 216–19. I am indebted to conference papers by Wendy Stallard Flory on Melville and manic-depression.

31. Nathaniel Hawthorne, *The English Notebooks, 1856–1860*, the Centenary Edition of *The Works of Nathaniel Hawthorne*, vol. 12, ed. Thomas Woodson and Bill Ellis (Columbus: Ohio State University Press, 1997), p. 163. In text as *English Notebooks*.

32. For a discussion of the journey of 1856–1857 and its influence upon his writing, see Walter E. Bezanson, "Historical and Critical Note to *Clarel*," pp. 508–24; Howard C. Horsford, "Historical Note to *Journals*," *WHM* 15:178–94; and Robert Milder, "An Arch between Two Lives: Melville in the Mediterranean, 1856–57," *Arizona Quarterly* 55 (1999): 21–47.

33. Hershel Parker, "The Lost *Poems* (1860) and Melville's First Urge to Write an Epic Poem," in *Melville's Evermoving Dawn: Centennial Essays*, ed. John Bryant and Robert Milder (Kent, Ohio: Kent State University Press, 1997), p. 273; and Parker II:428–53.

34. Stanton Garner, *The Civil War World of Herman Melville* (Lawrence: University Press of Kansas, 1993), p. 24.

35. Herman Melville, supplement to *Battle-Pieces and Aspects of*

the War, in *The Battle-Pieces of Herman Melville*, ed. Hennig Cohen (New York: Barnes, 1963), p. 200. All references to *Battle-Pieces* are to this edition, hereafter cited in text.

36. For discussions of the jeremiad, see Perry Miller, *Errand into the Wilderness* (New York: Harper & Row, 1964), pp. 1–15; and Sacvan Bercovitch, *The American Jeremiad* (Madison: University of Wisconsin Press, 1978).

37. See Lawrence Buell, "American Civil War Poetry and the Meaning of Literary Commodification: Whitman, Melville, and Others," in *Reciprocal Influences: Literary Production, Distribution, and Consumption in America*, ed. Steven Fink and Susan S. Williams (Columbus: Ohio State University Press, 1999), p. 127.

38. See Walter D. Kring and Jonathan S. Carey, "Two Discoveries concerning Herman Melville," *Proceedings of the Massachusetts Historical Society* 87 (1975): 137–41. The Kring and Carey article is reprinted, along with an introduction by Kring and commentaries by eleven Melvilleans, in *The Endless, Winding Way in Melville: New Charts by Kring and Carey*, ed. Donald Yannella and Hershel Parker (Glassboro, N.J.: Melville Society, 1976). Cited in text as *Winding Way*.

39. Bezanson, "Historical and Critical Note to *Clarel*," *WHM* 12:532.

40. Parker ascribes Melville's overwrought condition as he completed *Clarel* and saw it through the press to his hope "that he might after all gain respectful attention or even admiring recognition during the high solemnities of the American Centennial" (Parker II:794). This seems unlikely given Melville's preference for anonymous publication, his severe criticisms of America in *Clarel*, and his painfully won understanding of the tastes and capacities of American readers and reviewers.

41. Lawrence Buell, "Melville the Poet," in *The Cambridge Companion to Melville*, ed. Robert S. Levine (Cambridge: Cambridge University Press, 1998), p. 148.

42. Charles De Kay, quoted in *Log* II:781.

43. Parker suggests that "After the Pleasure Party" may have belonged to the unpublished 1860 *Poems* (Parker II:421–22), but a fledgling poet seems unlikely to write a poem so thematically and technically accomplished. Parker also believes that "much of the 1891 *Timoleon* may have consisted of older material (however much re-

vised) than much of *John Marr*" (II:879). This is probably true for most of the poems included in the section "Fruit of Travel Long Ago"; otherwise, Parker's "may have" speculation about dates seems arguable on both aesthetic and psychobiographical grounds.

44. Harrison Hayford and Merton M. Sealts, Jr., editors' introduction, *Billy Budd, Sailor (An Inside Narrative)*, ed. Hayford and Sealts (Chicago: University of Chicago Press, 1962), p. 2.

45. Hayford and Sealts, *Billy Budd, Sailor*, p. 239.

46. Melville, *Billy Budd, Sailor*, Hayford-Sealts Edition, p. 128.

MELVILLE IN
HIS TIME

Romantic Answers, Victorian Questions

Cultural Possibilities for Melville at Midcentury

Leon Chai

Normally, we go from question to answer. For Herman Melville, however, the story of his relation to European Romanticism and what followed it is somewhat different. Instead of a movement from question to answer, he experienced, you might say, the reverse: a movement from answer to question. His exposure to European culture began at a moment when Romanticism was at its zenith. The generation born around 1770, most of whom were now recently deceased, had begun to make their way into the pantheon reserved for the great dead. In England: Wordsworth, Coleridge, Scott, and others of their circle, as well as the latecomers who died early: Byron, Keats, and Shelley. In France: Chateaubriand and Mme de Staël. In Germany: Goethe and Schiller, but also a host of thinkers who had radically transformed many fields of intellectual inquiry: Friedrich Schlegel, Schleiermacher, Fichte, Schelling, and Hegel. As a movement, Romanticism offered a lot of answers, and no one circa 1850 was in a good position to question its authority. That would come only later. Perhaps we might see Matthew Arnold's *Essays in Criticism* (1866) as indicative of a crucial turn or shift. There, Arnold put forward his famous assessment of Romantic verse: "In other words, the English poetry of the first quarter of this century, with plenty of energy, plenty of creative force, did not know enough" (*Lectures & Essays in Criticism* 262). To know more, Arnold says, the Romantics "should have read more books." What he really meant by that, I think, is that if they had done so, they would've learned to doubt, to question.

Like the Romantics, Melville began in a posture of hope. His early works reflect that sort of outlook. Like Arnold, however, he gradually read more books (a great deal of Arnold himself, among others), and as he read, came increasingly to doubt and to question. Unlike Arnold, though, he didn't stay in that position. Instead, he moved on: to what we might describe as a kind of transcendental irony. Simply put, it amounts to a belief that there's more reality than Horatio ever dreamt of in his philosophy. In this way, Melville returns at the end of his quest to the Romantic framework from which he began. And yet, at the same time, what he returns to is a Romanticism that ultimately looks beyond itself.

Subjectivity / Consciousness / Self

In recent years, we've become progressively more aware of what the Romantics themselves were always very much aware: the Gothic mode. To some extent, the eruption of subjectivity on the European cultural scene goes back to a time before the Romantic era. In England especially, it goes back to the Gothic novel. Here we might think of Horace Walpole, *The Castle of Otranto* (originator of the genre); William Beckford, *Vathek* (most fantastical); M. G. Lewis, *The Monk* (most sensational); and perhaps its most exemplary expression, Ann Radcliffe, *The Mysteries of Udolpho*. Walpole was fascinated by the portrait. In his work, a portrait (typically of a long-dead ancestor) can not only talk but even step down out of its picture frame and interact with people. What Walpole did with the portrait underwent further development in *The Monk*. This lurid novel looks at the possibility of spectral selves: a self, in other words, that doesn't pertain to any living individual but that nonetheless seems just as real, and that may be simply a projection or creation of some individual consciousness. In *The Monk*, Ambrosio is tempted and ultimately seduced by a ravishing nun (Rosario/Matilda) who turns out to be Satan in disguise. Can you have sex, though, with an illusory other? What makes *The Monk* uncanny is that its sense of otherness is real, and yet the other isn't. The power of subjectivity is even more apparent, in some ways, in *The Mysteries of Udolpho*. The protagonist, Emily St. Aubert, has the capacity to imagine events and personal relationships that turn out to be completely untrue. Yet the point Radcliffe wants to make isn't, I take it, merely about how fallible our subjectivity is, but equally about its creative energy, as a form of libidinal energy.

In *Pierre*, Melville puts all his knowledge of the Gothic novel to creative use. From various bits of evidence, we can infer that he probably had read virtually all of the works I've mentioned. But if they do in fact pervasively inform his novel, we might see *Pierre* as an extended meditation of those sources. Thus *Pierre* takes over the portrait motif from Walpole. The closet portrait of Pierre's father as a young man offers an equivalent to the Gothic Portrait of an ancestor. At the same time, it does more: whereas the portrait in Walpole merely acts, the portrait in *Pierre* can even reflect on the question of Pierre's sister. In this fashion, it achieves authentic otherness, by its ability to engage Pierre in a dialogue that forces him to a new level of awareness. Its autonomy prompts him to think about the portrait itself. As an instance of the uncanny, it surpasses the Rosario/Matilda figure of *The Monk*. To some extent, Rosario/Matilda could embody the libidinal energy of Ambrosio, intent on a form of narcissistic gratification. What makes the portrait of Pierre's father so unusual is the fact that it harks back to a real other. But that other is dead. Yet the state of mind captured by the portrait persists, regardless of the fate of its subject. And that state of mind is the essence of a subjectivity. So the sense of otherness is real because the subjectivity experienced is real, even though its source no longer exists. Moreover, subjectivity in *Pierre* comes across even more powerfully than in *The Mysteries of Udolpho*. Emily St. Aubert had only imagined conditions or events. By the time his story nears its end, Pierre wonders if he hasn't simply created Isabel and her whole situation within his own mind.

Besides its tendency toward subjectivity, Romantic literature also stressed the link between consciousness and self. We arrive at a sense of otherness through the medium or element of consciousness. And, as a result of our awareness of others, we become conscious, by a process of reversion, of self. So the phenomenology of consciousness, the process by which it takes in the world, achieves a new importance in the Romantic era. For the authors who define that period, it isn't just a matter of what we apprehend. How we apprehend it is now equally crucial, since our awareness of that is what produces, ultimately, our sense of self. Here we might think of the famous episode from Book I of *The Prelude* where the protagonist tries to steal a boat. Moored lightly to a willow tree beside a lake, it tempts him to take it for a spin. But as he does so, Wordsworth depicts the process by which he becomes aware of other presences and, consequently, of himself as a force distinct from Nature:

I dipped my oars into the silent Lake;
And, as I rose upon the stroke, my boat
Went heaving through the Water like a swan:
When, from behind that craggy Steep, till then
The horizon's bound, a huge peak, black and huge,
As if with voluntary power instinct,
Upreared its head.—I struck, and struck again,
And, growing still in stature, the grim Shape
Towered up between me and the stars, and still,
For so it seemed, with purpose of its own
And measured motion, like a living Thing
Strode after me. With trembling oars I turned,
And through the silent water stole my way
Back to the Covert of the Willow-tree;
. . . .
                              but after I had seen
That spectacle, for many days, my brain
Worked with a dim and undetermined sense
Of unknown modes of being; o'er mu thoughts
There hung a darkness, call it solitude
Or blank desertion. No familiar Shapes
Remained, no pleasant images of trees,

Or sea or Sky, no colours of green fields,
But huge and mighty Forms, that do not live
Like living men, moved slowly through the mind
By day, and were a trouble in my dreams. (*The Fourteen-Book*
   Prelude 38–39)

We witness a similar process at work in the "Counterpane"
episode from *Moby-Dick*:

At last I must have fallen into a troubled nightmare of a doze;
and slowly waking from it—half steeped in dreams—I opened
my eyes, and the before sun-lit room was now wrapped in
outer darkness. Instantly I felt a shock running through all my
frame; nothing was to be seen, and nothing was to be heard;
but a supernatural hand seemed placed in mine. My arm hung
over the counterpane, and the nameless, unimaginable, silent
form or phantom, to which the hand belonged, seemed
closely seated by my bedside. For what seemed ages piled on
ages, I lay there, frozen with the most awful fears, not daring
to drag away my hand; yet ever thinking that if I could but stir
it one single inch, the horrid spell would be broken. I knew
not how this consciousness at last glided away from me; but
waking in the morning, I shudderingly remembered it all, and
for days and weeks and months afterwards I lost myself in
confounding attempts to explain the mystery. (*Moby-Dick* 26)

In both instances, the shock comes from our sense of otherness.
The reversion from that shock is what produces an awareness of
self. Like Wordsworth, Melville seems to feel that we only arrive
at a sense of self indirectly. As for Wordsworth, moreover, consciousness forms the crucial link. We become aware of others
through the medium of consciousness because we can't control
what we take in. Consciousness, in other words, amounts to our
window of vulnerability. But vulnerability is fearful, hateful.
Hence the reversion: we instinctively shy away from the trauma
caused by our sense of vulnerability, and as we do so, we discover
that that vulnerability is what we are. Neither Wordsworth nor
Melville, however, knows what to do about it. The result is that,

by a kind of reflexivity, consciousness itself becomes what consciousness elects to brood on.

Intersubjectivity

Romantics worry about subjectivity, Victorians worry about intersubjectivity. Intersubjectivity is what happens when one subjectivity meets another. Typically, subjectivity wants to objectify whatever it comes across. Intersubjectivity begins when that fails to happen. It isn't as if our failure to objectify another subjectivity will automatically yield a clear perception of what that subjectivity is. Instead, we simply become aware of a force that resists our own tendency to objectify. But, precisely because that force has managed to resist our tendency to objectify, we feel compelled to define ourselves by our relation to it. In fact, we don't necessarily come to know the other any better. The only real gain is that we arrive at a different relation to ourselves. Whereas we began wholly absorbed by our own subjectivity, we can now apply our tendency to objectify to ourselves, rather than to others. And that, from a Victorian perspective, points to the possibility of our own moral transformation.

The classic example of this is Dickens. In *David Copperfield*, the protagonist marries Dora well before the end of the novel. But we know their marriage can't last. The problem is that it's too easy for David Copperfield to objectify Dora: as he sees it, she's only a "child-wife" rather than a proper marriage partner, a truth she herself admits on her deathbed. At the same time, we see how differently he looks at Agnes Wickfield. The reason he can't objectify her is that she knows him, and what he might be, even better than he could possibly hope to know himself. So he does, at the end, the only thing he can do: marry her. *Little Dorrit* follows a similar course, but in a slightly more complicated way. To some extent, Arthur Clennam is even less perceptive than David Copperfield. As a result, he falls in love with various women before he meets Amy Dorrit. But, unlike Copperfield, he never seems quite able to discover their defects by himself. Consequently, he can't objectify them as Copperfield does Dora. For

Clennam to reach this point, they have to marry themselves off to other men and take a turn for the worse. Only then, when he meets them again, is he forced to objectify. And very reluctantly at that. Of course, he can't objectify Amy Dorrit. On the contrary, she helps him to objectify himself, as the source of his best resolutions. Still, he can't initially marry her because, ironically, she's too wealthy. Her wealth, in other words, would allow her to be objectified in a different way. So he can only marry her once her family has lost its fortune. Then there can't even be any pretext that would permit him to objectify her.

If *Pierre* offers Melville an opportunity for his most extreme venture into the problems of subjectivity, "Bartleby" might mark his first effort to come to terms with Victorian intersubjectivity.[1] It is, obviously, much more than that. At the same time, in its unique fashion, it gives us his comment on a Victorian ideal. At first, the narrator tries to objectify Bartleby. From his perspective, the newest addition to his office staff is merely a copyist, someone who ought to fit well into the human machinery of his establishment. The narrator has already managed to objectify the rest of his staff, as a result of their predictability. Initially, he even fears his new scrivener will prove too mechanical. But Bartleby turns out to be different. Increasingly, the narrator finds himself unable to predict what Bartleby will do in a given situation. It begins with the scrivener's famous response to various normal office requests: "I prefer not to." It doesn't, however, end there. As the narrator discovers to his dismay, Bartleby isn't predictable in his preferences. On some level, no doubt, he prefers not to be. Because of his disruption of office routine, Bartleby forces the narrator to recognize that his scrivener can't be objectified. The narrator gradually becomes obsessed about Bartleby, to the point where he begins to think of himself primarily in terms of his relation to his scrivener. Nevertheless, his new self-definition as caretaker of his scrivener doesn't result in his moral transformation. Here, then, the Victorian blueprint for intersubjectivity breaks down. The narrator can only be morally transformed if Bartleby wants to be helped in ways the narrator can understand. But Bartleby doesn't want to be helped. At the end, consequently, the narrator can only disengage. Thus what seemed to promise the possibility of genuine intersubjectivity fails, in the final analysis, to materialize.

In "Benito Cereno," Melville takes the process of intersubjectivity to its natural limit. The ultimate form of intersubjectivity is slavery. In this sort of intersubjective relation, no disengagement is possible. Instead, as Melville shows, master and slave are locked together in a perpetual nightmare of intersubjectivity. The master/slave dynamic has only one rule: objectify the other at any cost. Within its deadly framework, you either objectify or you get objectified. And the crucial determinant is whether you're afraid to die. Because whoever is afraid to die will at some point give up in his/her struggle with the other for mastery. At that point, the other will take over. And both participants know it. So the whole game is to find out who will blink first.

Once Babo gains control of the *San Dominick*, he has to kill the owner, Don Alexandro Aranda, to demonstrate to Benito Cereno what his own fate will be if he tries to regain control. Yet the murder of the slave owner isn't by any means sufficient. More important, Babo has to demonstrate constantly to Benito Cereno that he himself isn't afraid to die, and that, in any situation that involves the possibility of it, Benito Cereno will blink first. Hence the charade of submission with Atufal, enacted for the visitor, Captain Amasa Delano. Babo knows that if anyone is even slightly off, the ruse will be discovered and he'll die. But he banks on the fact that Benito Cereno will himself be so afraid that he'll play his part perfectly. His performance, in turn, will signal his submission to Babo, the true master. So the charade of submission becomes, in a hidden but very real sense, the enactment of a different kind of slavery. Babo proves to Benito Cereno, by his acceptance of his role, that he deserves to be a slave. Later, the game becomes even more openly sadistic. Babo brandishes his razor in Don Benito's face as he shaves him, and then, when the other flinches, nicks him slightly as a reminder of his power. Not content with that, however, Babo then cuts himself savagely, to show his captive that he himself isn't afraid of the razor at all. In "Benito Cereno," then, intersubjectivity displays its most nightmarish aspect. The Victorian concept of it had been founded on a belief that the other's refusal to be objectified would lead to an awareness of otherness and, eventually, recognition of another subjectivity. "Benito Cereno" shows why that might fail to happen. More, perhaps, than any other Melville text, it reveals what's at stake in the game of intersubjectivity.

Secular Religion

The impulse toward a more secular form of religion surfaces late in the Romantic period. For many, Coleridge became the figure to whom they looked. His *Aids to Reflection* put its finger on the spiritual need of a generation. In that work, Coleridge spoke of the anxiety he sensed in those who lived in the troubled years after the French Revolution and its Napoleonic sequel: "There is an aching hollowness in the bosom, a dark cold speck at the heart, an obscure and boding sense of a somewhat, that must be kept *out of sight of* the conscience; some secret lodger, whom they can neither resolve to eject or retain" (*Aids to Reflection* 24). For those who felt this kind of anxiety, Coleridge realized, traditional forms of worship could no longer suffice. Instead, they would need to turn inward. What he tried to give, in *Aids to Reflection*, was an analysis of their situation that led to the necessity of religion, as the only viable answer to their questions. His perspective, however, was psychological rather than doctrinal. He centered his attention on the various stages of mind by which we finally arrive at a religious outlook. He described conversion in terms of a journey, with all its attendant uncertainty. He spoke of metanoia as "passing into a new mind" (*Aids to Reflection* 132). Most of all, he focused on the Will, and on how Original Sin or the Fall might be understood psychologically. He defined Reason and Understanding in relation to religion and described in detail the crucial functions they fulfill. By means of this psychological perspective, then, he effected a renewal of interest in religion. Those who could no longer accept traditional dogma could now return to it from a new, more inward viewpoint that spoke to their individual circumstances. Most important, Coleridge stressed that the core of religion was experiential. In order to know what it was really about, you had to try it yourself. And what you felt when you did so defined the essence of religion.

In *Moby-Dick*, the impact of this new psychological or experiential perspective on religion can immediately be felt. In the desolate waters near Antarctica, Ishmael worships the albatross because it induces in him a kind of emotion he can only describe as one of sublimity:

> At intervals, it arched forth its vast archangel wings, as if to embrace some holy ark. Wondrous flutterings and throbbings shook it. Though bodily unharmed, it uttered cries, as some king's ghost in supernatural distress. Through its inexpressible, strange eyes, methought I peeped to secrets which took hold of God. As Abraham before the angels, I bowed myself; the white thing was so white, its wings so wide, and in those for ever exiled waters, I had lost the miserable warping memories of traditions and of towns. (*Moby-Dick* 190)

Like Hamlet face to face with his father's ghost on the ramparts, Ishmael feels himself in the presence of what is in some sense unspeakable, which marks (as for the Ark of the Covenant) the essence of the holy. Subsequently, he compares himself to Abraham at Mamre. The comparison is significant. At first, Abraham doesn't know that the men he sees at Mamre are in fact Yahweh. What they really are emerges only gradually in the course of their stay. For Ishmael, the crucial point is that since they don't announce they're Yahweh, the only way Abraham can become aware of it has to be purely experiential. But if Abraham can detect God experientially, it should be possible for anyone else to do so in the same way.

Besides the experiential perspective introduced by Coleridge, secular religion had by 1850 assumed other forms as well. In *Sartor Resartus*, Carlyle had espoused a sort of pantheistic belief: even the ordinary, the everyday could reveal some trace of the ineffable, or divinity. But by 1850, his "Natural Supernaturalism" was no longer the latest word. Dickens was now in the ascendant, both in England and in America. And Dickens didn't care about pantheism, or any other form of belief in supernatural presences. Instead, the kind of secular religion he wanted to promote consisted of an ideology that focussed primarily on the moral, rather than the metaphysical. Based on the notion of a religion of the affections, it harked back to second-generation Romantics like Keats and Shelley. The source of this religion was a belief that our sense of what is moral ought to come from our affections, or what we feel. For Dickens, it all lay in what he called the "mind of the heart" (*David Copperfield* 532). But, unlike Pascal, who had employed a similar motif to talk about the deep, instinctive movement by which we turn to religion, Dickens believed that the "mind of the heart" would dictate the right moral choices, even though we might not be able to justify these rationally. Thus Copperfield doesn't know why Steerforth is bad company. Nor does he ever really arrive at a full character assessment. But somehow, on some deep emotional level, he eventually manages to discern the self-destructive tendency Steerforth harbors.

Despite the cogency of this belief in the heart for many readers in mid-nineteenth-century America, Melville didn't buy it. What happened if the heart were influenced by forces it wasn't fully aware of? *Pierre* is his attempt to enter a sceptical critique. It begins with a very Dickensian premise: Pierre is appealed to by a young woman, Isabel, who claims to be his half sister. As she turns out to be extremely attractive, Pierre feels himself irresistibly engaged. His thoughts about the matter are properly Dickensian. To himself he says: "The heart! the heart! 'tis God's anointed; let me pursue the heart!" (*Pierre* 91). But if all the initial moves look a lot like Dickens, the sequel distinctly doesn't. To support Isabel's claim, Pierre destroys the happiness and, ultimately, even the sanity of his mother. On top of that, he breaks his engagement to Lucy, only to plunge into incestuous sex with Isabel. Many of these events ensue because Pierre isn't aware of how influenced he is by his sexual attraction to Isabel. Nonetheless, Melville also wants to argue that for many ethical situations, the sort of emotional intuitionism advocated by Dickens simply doesn't suffice. The point of the plot in *Pierre*, then, is that it's difficult to apply any kind of moral rule to one's acts.[2] The reason Pierre goes astray isn't merely that he fails to follow his emotional intuition sufficiently. Instead, what Melville seems to imply is that for any complicated ethical situation, no amount of moral intuition can save you.

The Bildungsroman

In many ways, the Bildungsroman (or novel of self-development) might be described as the favorite Romantic genre. On some deep level, the Romantic era was attracted to development in general. From a Romantic perspective, development meant fluidity. It worked against rigidity because it set all definitions and concepts into flux. It meant that all concepts could now be perceived merely as moments of a development, which implied the primacy of change over stasis. In addition to change or movement, the Bildungsroman was also about fulfillment. It wasn't just interested in change per se. Instead, it saw change as movement toward a particular end. And that end was the fulfillment of an individual through a process of growth informed by a teleology. In other words, the Bildungsroman was about the process by which an individual came to be what he or she was. As an example, we might take the way Wordsworth perceives his own evolution if *The Prelude*. To him, the real subject of the poem was "the growth of his own mind" (*The Fourteen-Book* Prelude 5). From his standpoint, then, the process of his development was an organic one. Each incident or episode in it was linked in a vital, necessary fashion to all the rest. His early childhood in the Lake district, his education at Cambridge, his experience of the sublime in the Alps, his presence in France at the outbreak of the Revolution, had all contributed to the process by which his mind was formed. Moreover, the process had its own internal teleology. Somehow, by means that lay beyond his capacity to fathom or explain, it had moved toward a definite fulfillment, marked by his intellectual development. That was how Wordsworth saw his growth process. It worked under the eye of a higher agency, which had arranged every moment, every incident, toward a predestined end.

For different reasons, Victorian literature was equally fond of the Bildungsroman. Unlike the Romantics, however, it didn't subscribe to the belief that development invariably turned out well. Quite often, in fact, the weight of evidence seemed to indicate that it didn't. Nonetheless, Victorian authors were equally convinced that circumstances of origin, the way an individual began his or her development, was crucial. Even more than its Romantic counterpart, the Victorian Bildungsroman lays a lot of stress on childhood and adolescence. From a Victorian perspective, this interval constituted a critical formative time. During our early years, we're especially subject to what might be termed moral influences. The Victorian Bildungsroman, then, is all about how moral influences (especially in our formative period) makes us what we are. David Copperfield turns out well because at various important moments in his development, the right moral influences (his Aunt Betsey Trotwood and, later, Agnes Wickfield) come into play. The task of the Bildungsroman is to show us how to discern the right moral influences. So its role is, above all, a salutary one. By its capacity to point out the distinctive aspects of good or bad moral influences, it works to shape our moral education. For the Victorians, these influences were personal. They consisted of particular people, whose specific personalities or traits caused them to act on others in a definite way. Nor were these people perceived merely as instruments that enacted the will of some higher agency. Instead, as Dickens, Thackeray, and others saw it, they did what they did because they wanted to do it, and they wanted to do it because they liked it. But if the moral influences represented by various characters in a novel merely expressed some sort of personal inclination or tendency, that meant they didn't have to be submitted to passively. Whether one submitted to them or not now became very much a matter of choice. If one made the right choices, one turned out well. So the process by which the protagonist of a novel sifts the data he or she has about people, in order to make choices, becomes crucial. Thus, whereas Romantic ideology looked at the process by which an individual becomes what he/she is as determined by a higher agency, the Victorian perspective viewed it as almost wholly dependent on that individual's will.

In *Pierre*, Melville combined the Romantic and Victorian perspectives in a way that was bound to cause trouble. He begins with the notion that we are what we are because of factors over which we have no control: our genetic makeup, if you like. So if we happen to feel strongly attracted to a particular person at first sight, well, we can't help it. That's just the way we are. Moreover, Melville says explicitly that these genetic factors over which we have no control have to be traced, ultimately, to some sort of divine agency. If so, however, we presumably can't help to shape the trajectory of our development: a higher agency puts particular influences in our path, and how we react to these is determined by our genetic makeup, which we can't control. Like Wordsworth, then, we can only hope (or so it would seem) that our development somehow turns out well. But what if it doesn't? Romantic pietism would dictate that we simply accept it. Somehow, it wasn't meant to be (Wordsworth, "Michael"). But here, for Melville, the Victorian perspective kicks in. Which is to say: we have moral responsibility for the choices we make and hence, finally, for how our development turns out. In other words, even though we didn't determine our genetic makeup, we still have to feel responsible for our acts, regardless of how these may have been influenced. The result: a no-win situation. Unlike the Victorians, Melville doesn't pretend to believe we can really control our own acts. But, unlike the Romantics, he can't quite fob off the responsibility for these acts on some higher agency.

On a concrete level, what this means is that Pierre gets a cryptic message from someone named Isabel Banford, who purports to be his half sister and who wants his help in her efforts to establish some sort of viable financial/social situation for herself. So Pierre does his best to help out. Since he can't acknowledge her as his half sister (because it would expose his father's scandalous liaison with a young Frenchwoman), he commits himself to an even more extreme position: he pretends to marry her secretly. Unfortunately, their consequent and unavoidable physical closeness to each other leads to intimacy of another kind. And Pierre can't help it. After all, he didn't create himself. His liaison with Isabel, though, produces disastrous consequences. First, he has to break off his engagement to Lucy Tartan. Second, as a result of her violent reaction to his commitment to Isabel, his mother dies. Because these consequences come about due to a process he himself initiated, Pierre can't simply refuse to look at what's happened from a moral / ethical perspective. What he sees when he considers his own development from that perspective, however, is problematic. Within a Victorian framework, he appears morally culpable for the wrong choices. At the same time, he can't help but feel that the ultimate cause of those choices wasn't within either his knowledge or control, that it lay in his very makeup and hence is attributable to the force or agency responsible for that. Still, since he feels the moral or ethical import of what he's done, he believes it really does have moral / ethical significance. But if he's responsible (as he thinks he is), he wants to say that the higher force or agency that made him is finally responsible for his responsibility. His take on his own Bildungsroman, then, puts the burden of blame on the higher agency that shaped his development, but in a way that makes it morally imperative for him to resist its scheme. His position is aptly if somewhat cryptically expressed by the Enceladus episode at the end of the novel:

> So Enceladus was both the son and grandson of an incest; and even thus, there had been born from the organic blended heavenliness and earthliness of Pierre, another mixed, uncertain, heaven-aspiring, but still not wholly earth-emancipated mood; which again, by its terrestrial taint held down to its terrestrial mother, generated there the present doubly incestuous Enceladus within him; so that the present mood of Pierre—that reckless sky-assaulting mood of his, was nevertheless on one side the grandson of the sky. For it is according to eternal fitness, that the precipitated Titan should still seek to regain his paternal birthright even by fierce escalade. (*Pierre* 347)

Symbolics

Perhaps the most remarkable aspect of Romantic symbolics is its notion of transparency. Unlike traditional allegory, a symbol was supposed to convey what it meant in a direct, immediate way.

Above all, it was supposed to give a glimpse of the divine presence vouchsafed by concrete or material objects. For England, Coleridge probably summed it up best in his *Statesman's Manual* when he spoke of the symbol as a "translucence of the Eternal through and in the Temporal" (*Lay Sermons* 30). Whereas allegory only hinted at what it wanted to signify, a symbol disclosed it fully, wholly, completely. As a result, it virtually placed us in the presence of the thing itself. Put in this way, we might see it as related to the desire for personal transparency voiced by French Revolution ideology. A state of society where all of us are completely known to each other might seem ideal, compared to one in which we struggle to guess each other's motives or plans. But Romantic symbolics was after even more: it wanted to break through the epistemological impasse of unknowability that had haunted late eighteenth-century philosophy. A theory of transparency could provide an answer to the problem posed by the noumena of Kant. If you looked at material objects as ultimately transparent, it didn't matter whether you were able to grasp their noumenal essences, since you could see beyond those essences. Finally, Romantic symbolics represented a form of apocalyptic. What Charles Lamb said of his friend Coleridge could be said, with equal justice, of the Romantic theory of the symbol: that it expressed a hunger for eternity. Initially, Blake and other supporters of the Revolution had believed its advent would signal an end to time. When that hope gradually faded in the wake of the Reign of Terror, temporal hope was transformed into a transtemporal perspective that allowed the object of that hope to be preserved conceptually.

Nonetheless, even by the outset of the Victorian era, the reasons for belief in symbolic transparency no longer seemed so evident. Thus in his *Sartor Resartus* Carlyle already felt impelled to sound a note of caution. "All visible things," he says, "are emblems." And subsequently: "Matter exists only spiritually, and to represent some Idea, and *body* it forth" (*Sartor Resartus* 55–56). Yet, increasingly, his emphasis falls on material manifestations of the spiritual. To be sure, he later asserts (in typically Romantic fashion) that a symbol is the embodiment and revelation of the Infinite. But now even the Infinite is merely symbolic: collectively, the Infinite + Finite Universe only amount to a symbol of God (*Sartor Resartus* 162–63). More significantly, Carlyle isn't content just to obtain a glimpse of the Eternal. Instead, he stresses what would become the Victorian gospel: work. The shift toward praxis or activity is even more pronounced in Dickens. And the corollary of his increased emphasis on activity, I would argue, is a different attitude toward symbolism. For Dickens, symbolism no longer possessed the kind of apocalyptic quality it had for the Romantic era. Instead, its role becomes almost purely functional: it offers a premonition of what will happen later in the novel. "Shadows" is a favorite Dickensian term. Although its origin is typological, Dickens gives it a wholly secular, more limited scope. In *Dombey and Son*, at the farewell party given by his school, Paul Dombey hears the sound of waves, which subsequently turns visual in the "golden water" motif on his bedroom wall that forecasts his death. Later, James Carker feels the ground tremble as he flees from Dombey, a hint of how he'll later meet his end by means of a train. In *David Copperfield*, Dickens gets into the symbolism of places: the blackness of the Thames River with its refuse sets the stage for Martha's attempted suicide, while the symbolism of other appearances heralds the recovery of Emily by Mr. Peggotty. Throughout, then, symbolism expresses what we might describe as the foreknowledge that the novel has about itself.

By contrast, the sort of symbolism Melville employs in his fiction after *Moby-Dick* expresses no such foreknowledge. Even in *Pierre*, we find doubts about the notion of symbolic transparency. Toward the end of the novel, the narrator observes: "Say what some poets will, Nature is not so much her own ever-sweet interpreter, as the mere supplier of that cunning alphabet, whereby selecting and combining as he pleases, each man reads his own peculiar lesson according to his own peculiar mind and mood" (*Pierre* 342). What we obtain from Nature, then, would no longer seem to be a glimpse of the eternal nor of a divine presence within material objects. Nor does it even yield the sort of limited foreknowledge of events we've learned to associate with Dickens. Instead, what we receive from Nature is now perceived as determined wholly by our own subjectivity. To be sure, Co-

leridge had already admitted in his "Dejection" Ode that "we receive but what we give, / And in our life alone does Nature live"
(*Poetic Works* 365). But the kind of subjectivity *Pierre* has in mind
is somewhat different. Here the specific mention of mood hints
at the most extreme form of individual subjectivity.

We get a sense of what the new symbolism is all about from
The Piazza Tales, which appeared just a few years later. As an example of how it works, the set-piece description presented at the
outset of "Benito Cereno" is particularly suggestive:

> The morning was one peculiar to that coast. Everything was
> mute and calm; everything gray. The sea, though undulated
> into long roods of swells, seemed fixed, and was sleeked at the
> surface like waved lead that has cooled and set in the smelter's
> mould. The sky seemed a gray surtout. Flights of troubled
> gray fowl, kith and kin with flights of troubled gray vapors
> among which they are mixed, skimmed low and fitfully over
> the waters, as swallows over meadows before storms, Shad-
> ows present, foreshadowing deeper shadows to come. (*The
> Piazza Tales* 46)

The passage starts off in very realistic fashion: a lot of specificity,
a lot of detail. Almost immediately, detail turns into analogy. A
Sea marked by long swells is likened to waved lead. Then, the
first faint hints of a mood: the sky a gray surtout (constraint) and
flights of fowl compared to swallows over a meadow before a
storm (anxiety). In our present context, the summary remark at
the end is quite nifty. It makes use of a favorite Dickensian term
(shadows), only to give it a very different turn: whereas for Dickens shadows forecast the future, here they lead only to deeper
perplexity. All in all, the passage is exemplary of the new symbolic mode: no revelation of the eternal, nor even of specific future plot developments, but only a vague sense of mood that
can't even be ascribed to any one individual, but only to a kind of
collective consciousness.

By his use of this new symbolic mode, Melville aligns himself
with literary fashion in the later nineteenth century. Almost at
the same time that *The Piazza Tales* appeared, a young Parisian

poet named Charles Baudelaire astonished the French literary world with a volume entitled *Les Fleurs du Mal*. One of its recurrent motifs was that of the sky as a *couvercle* (lid, cover). A decade and a half later, Gustave Flaubert would have a character in his *L'Education sentimentale* spot a casket in the street below her apartment and feel a momentary shudder, not for some future plot event, but as a reinforcement of her momentary mood. We might attribute these psychologically inflected symbolic instances to the loss of a teleological framework. In any case, they point to a concentration of libidinal energy within the novel, which would later culminate in the symbolic epiphanies of a work like Joyce's *Portrait of the Artist as a Young Man*.

Technology

From a literary standpoint, technology begins in the Victorian era. In fact, the Romantic period had already witnessed a great deal of technical innovation. But only in the Victorian era do we find a literary awareness of it as technology. Balzac was perhaps the first prominent author who really celebrated technology. *Les Illusions perdues* contains a detailed description of printing-press machinery (of which Balzac had firsthand knowledge). A similar interest in machinery appears in Dickens: on this point, I suspect, he took his cue from Balzac. *Little Dorrit* displays excitement over the prospect of new inventions, from which Arthur Clennam hopes to profit. Likewise, Elizabeth Gaskell chose to set half of *North and South* in a factory town. Although she doesn't discuss machinery in detail, the economics of the factory figures importantly into the plot. All these instances of the presence of technology in literature point to a sense of its power to affect human life in manifold ways. As a social force, it had to be defined, in order to be controlled. That was the task Victorian fiction set for itself. It saw technology as a form of energy, hence as a quantity that had to be understood by study of its activity. In that respect, Victorian fiction adopted an accommodationist posture: by its assimilation of the technical, it hoped to harness the massive power of machinery as a social influence.

Melville took a radically different position. It comes out in a relatively little known masterpiece from *The Piazza Tales*: "The Bell-Tower." The story begins with several epigraphs, all presumably by Melville himself. One is of particular interest: "Seeking to conquer a larger liberty, man but extends the empire of necessity." I see this epigraph as doubly suggestive. Unlike some Victorian authors, Melville doesn't regard machinery as an alien force: instead, he perceives it as an extension of the human. At the same time, he views its activity as a form of expression of necessity. For him, in other words, what characterizes mechanical activity isn't its massive force (he doesn't deny it) but rather its necessary aspect or quality. The story focuses on Bannadonna, a master "mechanician" commissioned by some Italian city at the time of the Renaissance to construct a bell tower that will also serve as a clock tower. Babel-like, his tower gradually begins to rise toward the sky, and as it does, so does his ambition. When he comes to design a mechanical substitute for the watchman who's supposed to strike the bell at the appropriate moment, he envisions the possibility of a much grander invention. In the words of the narrative:

> He still bent his efforts upon the locomotive figure for the belfry, but only as a partial type of an ulterior creature, a sort of elephantine Helot, adapted to further, in a degree scarcely to be imagined, the universal conveniences and glories of humanity; supplying nothing less than a supplement to the Six Days' Work. . . . All excellences of all God-made creatures, which served man, were here to receive advancement, and then to be combined in one. (*Piazza Tales* 183–84)

In contrast to other Renaissance thinkers, however, Bannadonna doesn't believe in the need to approximate mechanical forces to vitality. From his standpoint, a knowledge of mechanics alone is sufficient for his purpose:

> However marvelous his design, however apparently transcending not alone the bounds of human invention, but those of divine creation, yet the proposed means to be employed were alleged to have been confined within the sober forms of

sober reason. . . . A practical materialist, what Bannadonna had aimed at was to have been reached, not by logic, not by crucible, not by conjuration, not by altars; but by plain vice-bench and hammer. In short, to solve nature, to steal into her, to intrigue beyond her, to procure some one else to bind her to his hand;—these, one and all, had not been his objects; but, asking no favors from any element or any being, of himself, to rival her, outstrip her, and rule her. He stooped to conquer. With him, common sense was theurgy; machinery, miracle; Prometheus, the heroic name for machinist; man, the true God. (*The Piazza Tales* 184)

Nevertheless, like other Melville questers, he overreaches himself. As he works to perfect his horological device, his own mechanical helot strikes him down by inevitable necessity, as it moves to sound the first bell at the appointed hour.

As a comment on technology, the story has a lot to say. Unlike Ruskin (or, for that matter, Marx), it clearly doesn't see the mechanical as a source of alienation. On the contrary: Bannadonna obviously considers the mechanical helot he's fashioned merely as an extension of himself. Moreover, what the text tells us about the genesis of the idea points to its inspiration as distinctly defined by a human framework: Bannadonna gets the idea of a mechanical watchman from his observation of human watchmen at a distance. But perhaps the most significant reflection that the story has to offer about technology concerns its relation to necessity. For Melville, necessity is the hallmark of mechanical activity. At the same time, the subtlest form of necessity in the story isn't that of Bannadonna's horological machinery. It involves, rather, the impulse by which the master "mechanician" is moved to create it. What Melville wants to say, then, is that the source of all mechanical necessity is ultimately the mind itself. To that extent, the creation of technology would seem to be unavoidable. So even if the creation of technology is fraught with fateful consequences for its creator, the fact of its unavoidability means that it remains an indispensable aspect of his self-assertion. In this way, like other aspects of the story, and of Melville's later fiction as a whole, it looks beyond the Victorian era to the possibility of a different kind of story about our development, and how we come to be what we are.

NOTES

1. To my knowledge, the first study to think seriously about the link between the American Renaissance and Victorian literature was Jonathan Arac, *Commissioned Spirits: The Shaping of Social Motion in Dickens, Carlyle, Melville, and Hawthorne* (New Brunswick, N.J.: Rutgers University Press, 1979).

2. I owe my sense of this topic to an unpublished manuscript by Thomas Hove, "Melville and Ethical Knowledge." It offers a superb analysis of *Pierre* (and other Melville texts) within a framework of contemporary moral philosophy.

SOURCES

Arnold, Matthew. *Lectures & Essays in Criticism*, ed. R. H. Super. Ann Arbor: University of Michigan Press, 1962.

Carlyle, Thomas. *Sartor Resartus*, ed. Mark Engel and Rodger Tarr. Berkeley: University of California Press, 2000.

Coleridge, Samuel Taylor. *Aids to Reflection*, ed. John Beer. Princeton, N.J.: Princeton University Press, 1993.

———. *Lay Sermons*, ed. R. J. White. Princeton, N.J.: Princeton University Press, 1972.

———. *Poetical Works*, ed. E. H. Coleridge. London: Oxford University Press, 1967.

Dickens, Charles. *David Copperfield*, ed. Nina Burgis. Oxford: Clarendon, 1981.

Melville, Herman. *Moby-Dick*, ed. Harrison Hayford et al. Evanston, Ill.: Northwestern University Press, 1988.

———. *The Piazza Tales and Other Prose Pieces, 1839–1860*, ed. Harrison Hayford et al. Evanston, Ill.: Northwestern University Press, 1987.

———. *Pierre*, ed. Harrison Hayford et al. Evanston Ill.: Northwestern University Press, 1971.

Wordsworth, William. *The Fourteen-Book* Prelude, ed. W. J. B. Owen. Ithaca, N.Y.: Cornell University Press, 1985.

Melville and Class

Myra Jehlen

O ne of the most cited passages in *Moby-Dick* celebrates the common people and declares them equal to any and all, unto the highest born. The passage closes a chapter devoted to the description of Starbuck, the *Pequod*'s chief mate and a man so morally upright that, were he ever to falter, the narrator says he could not bear to relate the event. The fall of an ideal man is a spectacle terrible to contemplate, for "man, in the ideal, is so noble and so sparkling, such a grand and glowing creature." Here, Melville, or the narrator, Ishmael, uses "noble" and "grand" provocatively, implying the currency of a notion that greatness necessarily has an aristocratic component. But no,

> this august dignity I speak of is not the dignity of kings and robes, but that abounding dignity which has no robed investitures. Thou shalt see it shining in the arm that wields a pick or drives a spike; that democratic dignity which, on all hands, radiates without end from God; Himself! The great God absolute! The centre and circumference of all democracy! His omnipresence, our divine equality!
>
> If, then, to meanest mariners, and renegades and castaways, I shall hereafter ascribe high qualities, though dark; weave round them tragic graces; if even the most mournful,

perchance the most abased, among them all, shall at times lift himself to the exalted mounts; if I shall touch that workman's arm with some ethereal light; if I shall spread a rainbow over his disastrous set of sun; then against all mortal critics bear me out in it, thou just Spirit of Equality, which hast spread one royal mantle of humanity over all my kind! Bear me out in it, thou great democratic God! who dist not refuse to the wart conflict, Bunyan, the pale, poetic pearl; Thou who didst clothe with doubly hammered leaves of finest gold, the stumped and paupered arm of old Cervantes; Thou who didst pick up Andrew Jackson from the pebbles; who didst hurl him upon a war-horse; who didst thunder him higher than a throne! Thou who, in all Thy mighty, earthly marchings, ever cullest Thy selectest champions from the kingly commons; bear me out in it, O God![1]

Describing the commons as "kingly" has the revolutionary effect of reversing the established order wherein it is the king and generally the nobles who bestow identity onto a kingdom's ordinary folk. In this case, it is kings and noblemen who are derivative beings, while ordinary folk are the ones to distill the best and most interesting features of the race.

This passage has been the key to a number of readings of Melville's fiction as an indictment of mid-nineteenth-century ways of class and social hierarchy. The readings suggest that the author's caustic denunciations of the conduct of his own middle class carried the positive charge of advocating not just the rights but the values of the lower classes, the kingly commons whom, according to this interpretation, Melville considers to be the central protagonists of American civilization, the real, the important Americans. The fervent rhetoric of this ode to the wielders of picks and drivers of spikes, the writing's uncharacteristic lack of ironic distance, is evidence for this view, and suggests that Melville himself shared it. Invoking "our divine equality," he does seem to embrace a democracy undivided by rank or prestige. Only, it was less an embrace than a quick hug. The rest of *Moby-Dick* and, more immediately, the pages that precede the invocation of equality, propose a different view of the ideal American, one whose relation to the kingly commons is quite ambiguous. I will try, in this chapter, to trace out this relation and some of its implications for Melville's view of class.

The invocation concludes the first of two chapters with the same title, "Knights and Squires." The sketch of Starbuck being the first chapter's entire content, he is the proximate inspiration for the celebration of democratic man. The trouble with this, or at any rate, the hitch in its logic, is that Starbuck is not a mean mariner, renegade, nor a castaway. Although not highborn (not lowborn either), he has distinguished himself both personally and professionally. Not only a man of superior character and moral reputation, he is also at the top of the ship's social hierarchy since, as chief mate, he is the second in command in a political system which, the title "Knights and Squires" reminds us, is hardly even republican, let alone democratic, but instead feudal.

The two "Knights and Squires" chapters strike a feudal note not only in their title but in the way they unfold. The title, which seems at first ironic and which the passage on the Spirit of Equality would certainly seem to gloss as ironic, is and then is not ironic. At a first take, it suggests that the *Pequod* is hardly Camelot nor would any modern American reader want it to be; its crew and command are all stout fellows. At the same time, the feudal appellations are fully functional and descriptive, for the *Pequod*, like any ship at sea, is organized in strict feudal order.

And so the second "Knights and Squires" chapter continues the sketch of a feudal pyramid. The first chapter dealt with the first mate, the second moves to the second mate, Stubb, then, in turn, to the third, Flask. These three, Ishmael explains, ensure that everything goes in an orderly fashion. They "were momentous men . . . who by universal prescription commanded three of the *Pequod*'s boats as headsmen. In that grand order of battle in which Captain Ahab would presently marshal his forces to descend on the whales, these three headsmen were as captains of companies" (919–20). All this then leads to a chapter called "Ahab" devoted solely to the man at the pinnacle of the pyramid, Captain Ahab, in which the *Pequod*'s functional king appears for the first time, though the ship is already far out to sea and the novel more than a hundred pages along. By that time, Ishmael has observed that the mates, though ostensibly in command, often emerge from the ship's cabin "with orders so sudden and peremptory, that after all it was plain they but commanded vicariously." He concludes that the mates' "supreme lord and dictator was there, though hitherto unseen by any eyes not permitted to penetrate into the now sacred retreat of the cabin" (923). Here once more, as when Melville described the mates and their lieutenants as "knights and squires," his dubbing Ahab a "supreme lord and dictator" is more accurate than ironic. The tone is a little mocking but the joke is finally on Ishmael, because Ahab is in fact, not metaphorically, the lord of the *Pequod*.

None of the three mates, nor Ahab, are aristocrats on land. But the invocation of democracy in the passage with which I began spoke of mean mariners and workmen, convicts and paupers. Starbuck, before becoming first mate of the *Pequod*, was a solid middle-class citizen of Nantucket, a Quaker endowed with all of the mercantile implications of that denomination, and he has risen to his command through merit. Stubb, the second mate, has risen less high and is proportionately less heroic; Flask still less. The other worthies whose credentials the chapter summarizes are the ship's harpooners, and chief among them is Queequeg, who is Starbuck's "squire." Back home on his South Seas island, Queequeg is the son of a high chief, nephew of a high priest, and he finds himself aboard the *Pequod* because he is traveling the world for his education prior to taking his own place at the top of a tribal hierarchy. Next below him and described next is the harpooner Tashtego, an "unmixed Indian from Gay Head" with a distinguished lineage: "Tashtego's long, lean, sable hair, his high cheek bones, and black rounding eyes— for an Indian, Oriental in their largeness, but Antarctic in their glittering expression—all this sufficiently proclaimed him an inheritor of the unvitiated blood of those proud warrior hunters, who in quest of the New England moose, had scoured, bow in hand, the aboriginal forests of the main" (920). Tashtego is attached to Stubb, second in rank to second in rank. The third harpooner, properly assigned to the third mate, is Dagoo, an "imperial negro" of exceptional size and strength. All of these characters, in sum, are extraordinary people. If they represent democracy, it is not in an egalitarian sense but in the sense that democracy proffers equality of opportunity to rise above the commons.

The "Knights and Squires" chapters are not the first to broach the issue of social equality. It comes up in the very first chapter, "Loomings," in relation to the most important character in the novel besides Ahab: the narrator, Ishmael. If the three knights and their squires, with the captain, constitute at once the high society of the *Pequod* and the novel's chief protagonists, Ishmael, who as narrator wields the most power of all, belongs to the lowest social class on board the ship; moreover, this status, or lack of it, is the crux of whom he is. The first chapter, which begins with probably the best first sentence in any novel, "Call me Ishmael," moves almost at once to the matter of Ishmael's social position. Explaining why, as the story opens, he finds himself in Nantucket in search of employment aboard a ship, he says it is his policy, whenever he feels on the verge of depression or worse, to go to sea. He sails not as a passenger, which he could not afford to do, but neither as "a Commodore, or a Captain, or a Cook." No, he goes as "a simple sailor, right before the mast, plumb down into the forecastle, aloft there to the royal mast-head" (797, 798).

Since he is the apparent author of the paean to "divine equality," Ishmael's rejection of all social distinction could be taken as glossing the Spirit of Equality, rather than in the meritocratic terms associated with Ahab and his lieutenants, in the terms of the meanest mariners after all. While this would make the "Knights and Squires" chapters more or less incoherent, incoherence, in a literary work, is not necessarily fatal. In the event, however, there is no incoherence. As Ishmael unfolds his own story, his simplicity grows complicated. It turns out that the humble life is his neither by social rank nor by nature; in fact, it requires considerable self-discipline for him to live humbly. Humility for him is quite a philosophical thing:

> True, they rather order me about some, and make me jump
> from spar to spar, like a grasshopper in a May meadow. And at
> first, this sort of thing is unpleasant enough. It touches one's
> sense of honor, particularly if you come of an old established

family in the land, the Van Rensselaers, or Randolphs, or Hardicanutes.² And more than all that, if just previous to putting your hand into the tar-pot, you have been lording as a country schoolmaster, making the tallest boys stand in awe of you. The transition is a keen one, I assure you, from a school-master to a sailor, and requires a strong decoction of Seneca and the Stoics to enable you to grin and bear it. But even this wears off in time.

What of it, if some old hunks of a sea-captain orders me to get a broom and sweep down the decks" What does that in-dignity amount to, weighed, I mean, in the scales of the New Testament" Do you think the archangel Gabriel thinks any-thing the less of me, because I promptly and respectfully obey that old hunks in that particular instance" Who aint a slave" Tell me that. Well, then, however the old sea-captains may order me about—however they may plump and punch me about, I have the satisfaction of knowing that it is all right; that everybody else is one way or another served in much the same way—either in a physical or a metaphysical point of view, that is; and so the universal thump is passed around, and all hands should rub each other's shoulder-blades, and be content. (798)

"Who aint a slave?" is neither a political nor a social nor even a cultural question. You can tell that it is none of these because it is rhetorical: the implied answer is "no one," when we know that, in reality, certainly in the reality of mid-nineteenth-century America, some people are decidedly not slaves in that they en-slave others who are. In other words, "Who aint a slave?" is an ontological query that does not and cannot connect to the politi-cal/social/cultural nature of democracy as a working political system, but, rather, connects to that of transcendent individual identity.

Here lies the central issue in Melville's treatment of class: how to reconcile the romance of individual self-creation with the po-litical narrative of class. In *Moby-Dick* and in other writings, Melville frequently takes up the subject of inequality in America and is generally harshly critical of the nation's ways with the poor, the manual workers, and the nonwhite, who are dispropor-

tionately poor manual workers.³ At the same time, not only in
Moby-Dick, he expresses this criticism through a series of disillu-
sioned or defiant heroes who are all, in the context of their stories, at the top, not the bottom, of the social pyramid. Ishmael,
who though no Van Rensselaer is, as he tells us, even more distinguished in being a schoolmaster, is no simple sailor, quite the
contrary. By choosing to ship out before the mast, he actually
places himself, by dint of refusing his rightful elevated position,
above even the captain. The one in a hierarchical society who
chooses not to climb the ladder when he could reach the top is
special and superior. There is no incongruence to Ishmael's distinction as narrator and possessor of the largest vision and deepest understanding in the novel. Ishmael is no low-class sailor but,
literally, *declassé*, unclassed; he transcends class altogether, which
is the highest status of all. Narrator and commander/creator of
the story, he is also an arch self-creator.

Ahab comes next in class status, being captain of the ship and
the story's prime mover and having determined, since he can
conceive of self-creation only in terms of engagement (Ishmael
conceives of self-creation in the still loftier terms of disengagement), to die rather than to accept the universe's power over
him. Starbuck, the third in status, defines it as the ideal fulfillment of engagement; Stubb and Flask do their jobs uncom-
monly well. No one in this company embodies the Spirit of
Equality, unless the Spirit of Equality is somehow without
equals. This is what Melville hints at, in fact, when he praises the
democratic God for distinguishing John Bunyan despite his years
in prison for unlicensed preaching, for distinguishing Cervantes
in spite of his poverty, and for making Andrew Jackson the president, though he was born in the backwoods.⁴ The authors of
Pilgrim's Progress and *Don Quixote*, along with an American
president, incarnate the Spirit of Equality as the choosiest of
meritocrats.

The worst aspect of finding oneself among the poor and the
manual workers, in Melville's account, is that one is robbed of individuality and made to be just another representation of a
group identity. His short story "The Paradise of Bachelors and
the Tartarus of Maids" is one of the few accounts in American

fiction of life inside a factory.[5] The story is divided, as its title suggests, into two parts, the first of which is about a dinner taken with a group of barristers in their snug quarters at the Temple, an ancient cloister made over into a club.[6] The second, in explicit and pointed counterpart, describes women and girls working in a paper mill.[7] This paper mill is a hell in which the workers suffer the torments of the damned. The story begins with a narrator, who is also the main protagonist, on his way to the mill, located, he says, in a deep valley "not far from Woedolor Mountain in New England."[8] The name Woedolor echoes the legend over the gate to Dante's hell ("I am the way into the city of woe, / I am the way to a forsaken people, / I am the way into eternal sorrow."),[9] and a few lines later the narrator makes the reference explicit by describing the entrance to the road leading down to the mill as a "Dantean gateway." The local people have dubbed the hollow in which the mill stands the "Devil's Dungeon." The narrator piles on allusions to death and hell: the Dantean gateway is also called the Black Notch; following the road past this notch, he descends "among many Plutonian, shaggy-wooded mountains"; he advances accompanied by the sounds of torrents that eventually come together in a stream known locally as Blood River; he passes by the ruin of an old sawmill around which tumbled ancient logs seem to hark back to the Dark Ages; at last, "not far from the bottom of the Dungeon," the paper mill stands out against the black background "like some great white sepulchre" (1266). In the distance, the shrouded mountains form "a pass of Alpine corpses" (1268).

The narrator is a seed merchant and since, to make envelopes for his seeds, he needs great quantities of paper, he has decided to do away with the middlemen and buy directly from the Devil's Dungeon paper mill. It is a sound business decision, and the merchant is manifestly a man of solid judgment and abundant energy who does not shirk from a difficult journey in the dead of winter. Arriving at the mill in a snowstorm, he looks about for a shed to shelter his horse and, seeing a young girl run by, asks her whether such a thing can be had. Then, strangely, he at once withdraws the question (" 'Nay,' faltered I, 'I mistook you. Go on; I want nothing' ") when, "[P]ausing, she turned upon me a face pale with work, and blue with cold; an eye supernatural with un-related misery." He tries again, knocking at the door of the mill, whereupon "[a]nother pale, blue girl appeared, shivering in the doorway as, to prevent the blast, she jealously held the door ajar." Again, he cannot put his question ("Nay, I mistake again. In God's name shut the door") but this time adds, "is there no man about?" A "dark-complexioned well-wrapped personage" passes by and directs the seedsman to a woodshed.

His horse provided for, the narrator now enters the factory and finds himself in a large room where "[a]t rows of blank-looking counters sat rows of blank-looking girls, with blank, white folders in their blank hands, all blankly folding blank paper" (1270). The symbolism trades subtlety for fierceness. In this inferno of a fac-tory, at the bottom of a black chasm, women, or rather girls of various ages—the narrator so defines them upon learning that all are virgins, no married women ever being hired for fear they might prove intractable—do work that leaches them of all vitality and color. Those in command of this terrible process are men, dark with the excess of color drained from the girls. The male principle here is also the industrial principle and vice versa, for Melville views the paper mill, where women work twelve hours a day all year "excepting Sundays, Thanksgiving, and Fast-days," as not just socially but naturally perverse.

This perversity is represented by a monstrous mimicry of na-ture. The mill owner sends the narrator on a tour of the plant guided by a red-cheeked boy dubbed Cupid. The paper is made of rags. The bleached rags that the girls shred, by dragging them across giant scythes, are not a natural raw material. These rags are no longer connected to their origins in the cotton plant, but are the stuff of still other mills, textile mills, Blake's "dark Satanic Mills" which, both in the new England and the old, were the first indubitable signs of the industrial revolution.[10] Shredded and boiled, the rags resolve into a pulp "not unlike the albuminous part of an egg," which, pouring out of two vats into one channel, is guided into a great machine which generates "a strange, blood-like, abdominal heat as if, true enough, were being finally devel-oped the germinous particles lately seen." From this machine, the paper emerges to pass through constructions of rollers and cylinders that give it more and more the appearance of paper, until the end product is received as a fully-fledged sheet of paper by an older woman who was once a nurse but, from too little business in that profession, has taken up employment in the paper mill. The process takes exactly nine minutes.

There is no doubting Melville's anger at the travesty of nature perpetrated by the dark Satanic mill. It is a Moloch consuming life and producing nothing, a blank. Standing before the infernal machine, the narrator has a horrible vision: "Before my eyes— there, passing in slow procession along the wheeling cylinders, I seemed to see, glued to the pallid incipience of the pulp, the yet more pallid faces of all the pallid girls I had eyed that heavy day. Slowly, mournfully, beseechingly, yet unresistingly, they gleamed along, their agony dimly outlined on the imperfect paper, like the print of the tormented face on the handkerchief of Saint Veronica" (1277). To work in the mill is to be crucified; girls and women, the latter frozen into an abortive girlhood, are so many Christs, the martyrs of the industrial age.

Melville was not the only one in his time horrified by the situation of the working class in an emerging industrial economy. The depictions in other writings are often as bleak and were widely read. Somewhat later, in 1861, Rebecca Harding Davis published *Life in the Iron Mills* in the influential *Atlantic Monthly*, but contemporary with Melville's tale, Maria Susanna Cummins's *The Lamplighter* became one of the bestselling of the popular sentimental novels. *The Lamplighter* appeared in 1854, the same year as Charles Dickens's *Hard Times* which was, along with all of his novels, much pirated in the United States. However, Melville's American peers were more circumspect. Hawthorne took no evident interest. Emerson did, and warned that labor under present conditions, instead of enhancing, actually reduced whole human beings to "walking monsters" incarnating the required functions:

> Man is thus metamorphosed into a thing, into many things. The planter, who is Man sent out into the field to gather food, is seldom cheered by any idea of the true dignity of his min-

istry. He sees his bushel and his cart, and nothing beyond, and sinks into the farmer, instead of Man on the farm. The trades-man scarcely ever gives an ideal worth to his work but is rid-den by the routine of his craft, and the soul is subject to dol-lars. The priest becomes a form; the attorney, a statute-book; the mechanic, a machine; the sailor, a rope of a ship.[11]

Thoreau in *Walden* complained of the same process whereby work, instead of enabling, precluded living:

Most men, even in this comparatively free country, through mere ignorance and mistake, are so occupied with the facti-tious cares and superfluously coarse labors of life that its finer fruits cannot be plucked by them. Their fingers, from exces-sive toil, are too clumsy and tremble too much for that. Actu-ally, the laboring man has not leisure for a true integrity day by day; he cannot afford to sustain the manliest relations to men; his labor would be depreciated in the market. He has no time to be any thing [*sic*] but a machine.[12]

In both of these passages, the criticism attaches to those who allow themselves to be diminished, rather than to those who em-ploy them with that result: the sailor becomes a rope of a ship by not rising to a larger sense of himself; ignorance and mistake are the reasons men become preoccupied by coarse labor. Whitman has an opposite account of man at work:

I hear America singing, the varied carols I hear,
Those of mechanics, each one singing his as it should be blithe and
    strong,
The carpenter singing his as he measures his plank or beam,
The mason singing his as he makes ready for work, or leaves off
    work,
The boatman singing what belongs to him in his boat, the deck
    hand singing on the steamboat deck, The shoemaker singing as
    he sits on his bench, the hatter singing as he stands,
The wood-cutter's song, the ploughboy's on his way in the morn
    ing, or at noon intermission or at sundown.[13]

These people are all at work individually: each mechanic sings his song independently, as does the carpenter, the mason, the boatman, the ploughboy, so that, while they have little individuality, they are not members of a class but ideal incarnations of transcendent entities: America, Work, Song. They are classic Romantic figures. Melville's angry sympathy with "girls [who] did not so much seem accessory wheels to the general machinery as mere cogs to the wheels" (1271) differs from all three of these criticisms of the conditions of American labor by being addressed to a class of persons in the aggregate and postulating their individual humanity.

Then again, the humanity of the mill workers, in Melville's tale, is no more than a postulate. In retrospect, it is important that neither of the two pale, blue girls, who are the first people the narrator encounters at the mill, responds to his question about sheltering his horse. The pity out of which the narrator forbears to press them for an answer is of a kind inspired by those who are not only weak but inferior. None of the women speak; all of the conversation in the story is among the male figures: the mill owner, Cupid, the merchant-narrator. There are two kinds of people at the mill: one set is female, pale, silent; the other set is male, dark, ruddy, vocal. A cultural typology makes each set plausible. It does not seem unlikely that men are the active defining voices in a story, nor that women are pale and silent. The story works well in projecting a vision of an industrial hell inhabited by captive innocents. It works well in eliciting the reader's sympathy for these innocents. It does not work to give these innocents a place in the literary sun, a voice in the literary chorus. The paradise of bachelors, described in the first half of the diptych tale, is a heavenly mix of "good living, good drinking, good feeling, and good talk" (1264). In this stuff out of which their story is woven, talk is the most vivid strand. In the fabric of the tartarus of maids, the maids' silence is one of the most vivid strands.

Silence does not inevitably diminish characters. In another Melville story, "Benito Cereno," the silence into which a character lapses preserves a last modicum of his power. Refusing speech, in that instance, bespeaks an unbowed self. The character, Babo, is not innocent but guilty, killer more than victim (though in having been enslaved, he is also a victim), and not devoid of understanding but, on the contrary, a man whose scheme to take power has required that he understand better than anyone the situation in which he finds himself. In "Benito Cereno," it is the narrator who is the unconscious innocent, and the counterpart of the paper-mill owner is a wasted victim. This story forms an interesting contrast to "The Paradise of Bachelors and the Tartarus of Maids."

Briefly told, the plot turns on the total misunderstanding by Captain Amasa Delano of the situation aboard a Spanish merchantman that puts in one day at a South American port where Delano's ship is also lying at anchor. The Spanish ship carries a cargo of African slaves and appears to be in distress. The conscientious Delano boards to offer his assistance and finds the ship in disarray and its captain, Don Benito Cereno, nearly incapacitated. A Massachusetts man, Delano brings to the meeting with the Spanish captain a set of preconceptions about Latin indolence and human nature in general. These will prove nearly catastrophically false.

The true situation aboard the ship is that the slaves, led by the exceedingly intelligent Babo, have seized control and are holding the Spanish captive. Babo, pretending to be Don Benito's faithful servant, in fact guards him, threatening instant death if he reveals the mutiny. In one scene, Babo shaves the captain, who trembles beneath the razor held at his throat, while Delano sentimentalizes about the beauty of a servant's fidelity. At the last instant, when the deluded American captain is already seated in the boat that will take him back to his own ship, Don Benito leaps desperately into the boat, followed by three of his sailors and the insidious Babo. Persuaded that the Spaniard intends to murder him, the remarkably obtuse Delano first takes Babo to be trying to save his master. Then, at long last, "with the scales dropped from his eyes, [he] saw the negroes, not in misrule, not in tumult, not as if frantically concerned for Don Benito, but with mask torn away, flourishing hatchets and knives, in ferocious piratical revolt."[14]

Disabused, the American captain belatedly comes to the aid of the Spanish, and the slave rebellion is put down. This is not easily done. Delano's men have been promised the booty of the Spanish ship if they can capture it, and they charge with all the enthusiasm of greed. But their first assault proves costly:

> The negroes giving too hot a reception, the whites kept a more respectful distance. Hovering now just out of reach of the hurtling hatchets, they, with a view to the close encounter which must soon come, sought to decoy the blacks into entirely disarming themselves of their most murderous weapons in a hand-to-hand fight, by foolishly flinging them, as missiles, short of the mark, into the sea. But ere long perceiving the stratagem, the negroes desisted, though not before many of them had to replace their lost hatchets with handspikes; an exchange which, as counted upon, proved in the end favorable to the assailants (736).

The final battle goes to the whites. Having boarded the ship, the "unflagging sailors" are evidently the better fighters: "Exhausted, the blacks now fought in despair. Their red tongues lolled, wolf-like, from their black mouths. But the pale sailors' teeth were set; not a word was spoken; and, in five minutes more, the ship was won" (738).

The remarkable thing about this description, as about the whole of the story, is how evenly the two sides are matched. In the first part, the blacks are superior in both brain and muscle. In the second part, things are reversed: the whites are both the better strategists and the better fighters. But even then, the white advantage is not overpowering. The blacks initially repel the whites, and they are only momentarily tricked into wasting their hatchets. In the end, though, they are doomed, and this not only by a history that has delivered them to the cupidity of whites, but by their race. Melville was adamantly antislavery and, in characters like the regal Queequeg, could well imagine a black consciousness equal to the white. Still, the horror of those lolling red tongues in black mouths is not Delano's but the narrator's, that is, Melville's. He does not champion Babo, the author of the rebellion, as an emancipator. But if he is not the righteous hero of

the tale, the mutinous slave is, nonetheless, a fully fledged protagonist, an actor, one of those who creates the tale. In *Moby-
Dick*, Babo would belong formally among the knights, higher
than a squire, a man who could be imagined ultimately as a captain. His blackness is against him, but it does not preclude the author's investing him with an interior life. While he is free, this interior life expresses itself in speech. He gives commands, asks
questions, speculates, is seen conversing with his co-rebels. He
speaks not only his own language but Spanish as well. In the former, he harangues his men; in the latter, he threatens the whites.
He is eloquent. In the presence of the deluded Delano, he speaks
deceptively.

The token that this interior life survives after he is returned to
captivity is his refusal ever to speak again. After leaping into the
departing Delano's boat in pursuit of Don Benito, Babo is
quickly overpowered: "Seeing all was over, he uttered no sound,
and could not be forced to. His aspect seemed to say, since I cannot do deeds, I will not speak words" (755). This refusal to speak,
which resembles the scrivener Bartleby's refusal to write, is the
negative expression of an utterly frustrated self-consciousness.
Babo turns into a sort of black hole of consciousness. The conditions in which the man finds himself baffle any implementation
of selfhood; he preserves selfhood by refusing to participate in
those conditions. At that cost, however, Babo does preserve selfhood: "Some months after [the trial at which he is condemned],
dragged to the gibbet at the tail of a mule, the black met his
voiceless end. The body was burned to ashes; but for many days,
the head, that hive of subtlety, fixed on a pole in the Plaza, met,
unabashed, the gaze of the whites" (755).

Also a study in black and white, the cast of "Benito Cereno"
is, like that of "The Tartarus of Maids," divided between the free
and the enslaved. If "Benito Cereno" is a vastly different take on
this division, it shares, with the tale of the exploited women, a set
of organizing terms among which the link between speech and
effective action seems primary. The girls of "The Tartarus of
Maids" work unendingly, but they never act nor speak. The men
in the tale speak about them and the narrator speaks on their be-
half, protesting the death-in-life to which they have been con-

signed. But this implicit advocacy for the betterment of their lives does not impart life to them. Rather than embodiments of the Spirit of Equality, they are casualties of class.

What is lacking in the lowly and oppressed of "The Tartarus of Maids" is evident in "Benito Cereno?: interiority. The oppressed of "Benito Cereno" have interiority, which the American captain is too deafened by his own assumptions to overhear in a myriad conversations. In this story about African slaves, in contrast to the story about women workers in a paper mill, the oppressed possess selves; they are self-possessed in the modern sense. Nonetheless, at the moment of truth, black mouths gape uncontrollably open, while the whites set their teeth. Within the story, this ultimate inferiority is as much the reason that the blacks are defeated as the preponderance of force on the white side: witness the contrary example of the exceptional black, the undefeated Babo who, even after his death, unabashedly meets the gaze of his white killers.

Still, Babo is not wholly exceptional. His savagery ties him to his race; more intelligent than his peers, he is commensurately more savage. The description of the murders that launch the rebellion, contained in depositions at the trial that concludes the story, include an account of how Don Alexandro Aranda, the owner of most of the slaves on the ship, was dragged on deck "yet half alive and mangled," and how Babo stopped the rebels from throwing Aranda overboard, "bidding the murder be completed before him, which was done, when by his orders, the body was carried below, forward" (743). Four days later, it reappeared, a skeleton mounted as the ship's figurehead in place of its predecessor, a carved image of Christopher Columbus. "Babo took by succession each Spaniard forward, and asked him whose skeleton that was, and whether, from its whiteness, he should not think it a white's" (744). Don Benito, a broken man when we first see him, had been before the rebellion, on the whole, honorable and even gentle. Melville, writing in the 1850s, opposed slavery but was ambivalent about the enslaved. The specter of slave rebellion that haunted the whole of the nation was animated by a vision of African savages, and those who have terrified the Spanish captain are a terrifying horde. Babo, more intelligent than the other slaves, is rendered by his intelligence not less but more terrifying. For this reason, despite the justification of fighting for his freedom, he cannot really be added to the company of Bunyan, Cervantes, and Andrew Jackson. In the chapter of *The Confidence-Man* titled "The Metaphysics of Indian-Hating," Melville did draw a portrait of an Indian-hater for which Jackson could have posed. But there is no aura of such judgment in the way that the "Knights and Squires" passage invokes the general hurled upon a war-horse and thundered higher than a throne. In that representation, Jackson's brutality against the Indians is not active, while Babo's brutality against the Spaniards is always active.

However, the African's moral failing is not his most disabling feature. It is more important that, in the passage which pronounces him an incarnation of the Spirit of Equality, Jackson appears as a triumphant individual, like Bunyan and Cervantes, while Babo, for all his superiority to those he leads, is always seen as one of them. Babo, in short, suffers from a mild case of the same disability as the maids of the paper mill: they are all members of a class, and this membership, all by itself, disqualifies them from representing the necessarily individually transcendent Spirit of Equality.

The women are indistinguishable from one another. The narrator encounters one, then a second, then a whole group: except for the old ex-nurse, he discerns no difference among them. Their voicelessness is the expression of a lack of individuality. They are at the bottom of the ladder to democratic transcendence. Babo, the leader of his band of rebels, is near the top. But to reach the top, he would have had to step away from the band altogether, to become someone who can be defined wholly in his own terms— as Andrew Jackson is in the passage that celebrates his career as a general, without invoking his army. Each of the knights and squires in the two "Knights and Squires" chapters of *Moby-Dick* are sufficient unto their definitions. Starbuck, Stubb, and Flask are each his own man. They could be plucked out of the positions they occupy on the *Pequod* and would not appear different in another setting. The same is true for Queequeg, Tashtego, and Dagoo.

Ahab offers the most telling contrast to Babo. The captain of the *Pequod* is also necessarily a leader of other men, but he is unlike any of them, in fact unlike any living man: "He looked like a man cut away from the stake, when the fire has overrunningly wasted all the limbs without consuming them, or taking away one particle from their compacted aged robustness. His whole high, broad form, seemed made of solid bronze, and shaped in an unalterable mould like Cellini's cast Perseus" (924). Ahab commands not by example but by singularity. The court deposition describes Babo as "the ringleader" backed by "six Ashantees who were his bravoes." In addition, on board the ship, "four aged negroes" keep such order as is needed to fool the gullible Delano (746). A necessity for concerted action may be blamed for Babo's failure to transcend. For instance, he does not have an a priori scheme but forms one in response to the report of a young African named Jose that the organization of the ship has left the whites vulnerable. According to the court depositions at the trial that ends the story, Jose later kills his master "without being commanded to do so by the negro Babo" (749). The deposition states further that "the negro Babo was the plotter from first to last; he ordered every murder, and was the helm and keel of the revolt; that Atufal was his lieutenant in all; but Atufal, with his own hand, committed no murder; nor did the negro Babo"(749–51). Babo is the head of a gang, but the others complete him. Ahab, in Ishmael's term, is a man of "singular posture"(925) who, in a memorable scene in which he rallies the crew to his mad purpose, does not so much persuade them as reveal to them the quest on which they have already departed. That Starbuck, in that scene, is not rallied, seems not to subtract from the wholeness of Ahab's sway, as Ishmael's survival to tell the tale somehow does not mitigate the cosmic fatality of its ending.

For all that his final absolute silence expresses an absolute self-possession, Babo cannot be imagined as a transcendent narrator on the order of Ishmael either. The account he can be imagined giving of the tragedy aboard the Spanish ship would be one-sided. He cannot know the story as Benito Cereno lives it, the way Ishmael knows the story lived by Ahab, so that a reader does not question Ishmael's account nor think to wonder what Ahab might have added to it. Babo remains locked inside the limits of his own perspective: this is another way of defining his nontranscendence.

The implied assumption that enables Ishmael's question "Who aint a slave?" to make sense, is that slavery is a state of mind. The assumption that social bondage is finally an affair of nontranscendence is implicit in "The Tartarus of Maids" as well. The women of the paper mill suffer grievously but incidentally from the ways their class is exploited by the mill owner. They suffer fundamentally from just belonging to a class. Democracy, in the passage about the Spirit of Equality, means being able to escape class. Those who do not, because they cannot or because they will not (out of ignorance or mistake, as Thoreau puts it) are lesser beings. In short, class is what defines those who do not define themselves. The workers of the Devil's Dungeon paper mill are not members of "our divine equality." Mute in their lack of individual interiority, they are not members of the republic of modern fiction. We can measure the inadequacy of Babo to embody the Spirit of Equality by the extent to which being free is essential to being who he is. Free or slave, Ahab (who is completely himself even minus a leg) and Ishmael would anyhow always be fully themselves. The Spirit of Equality resides only in the class-transcendent—in whole individuals, Ishmael, Ahab, the individual knights and individual squires, in Bunyan, Cervantes, and Andrew Jackson. The Spirit of Equality is an avatar of the self-created Self whose romance, generally doomed to tragedy by democracy's shortfalls, is Melville's great theme. Class in Melville is the mark of inferiority, of a defeated being or a failed one. In the instances I have cited, there is, to underline the fatality of the flaw of class, no instance of class mobility. No one rises in social position over the course of *Moby-Dick*, "The Tartarus of Maids," or "Benito Cereno." If Melville *were* to tell a story of mean mariners, renegades, and castaways, it would be a story of how they ceased being any such thing and turned into captains and narrators.

NOTES

1. *Moby-Dick*, in *Herman Melville: Redburn, White-Jacket, Moby-Dick*, ed. G. Thomas Tanselle (New York: Library of America, 1983), 916–17. All further citations are from this edition.
2. The following note is taken verbatim from the Bobbs-Merrill

edition: *Moby-Dick or, the Whale*, ed. Charles Feidelson Jr. (New York, 1964), 27n13: "The first two were aristocratic families of New York and Virginia; Hardicanute was an eleventh-century king of Denmark and of England."

3. The most important reading to make this point is still C. L. R. James's *Mariners, Renegades, and Castaways* (New York: James, 1953), which James published himself with a cover on which he reprinted most of the passage I cited at the beginning of this chapter, beginning "If, then, to meanest mariners" and ending "thou just Spirit of Equality, which hast spread one royal mantle of humanity over all my kind!"

4. Feidelson has notes on all three, p. 161.

5. Rebecca Harding Davis's *Life in the Iron Mills* is another example. Davis tries hard to grant consciousness to the lower-class characters in her story. Her hero is a mill worker who is also an artist and who dies in the attempt to procure the means to practice his art in a society that denies his class the capacity for the consciousness of art. Theodore Dreiser's *Sister Carrie* is another rare example in its depiction of the inside of a clothing factory. The heroine, Carrie, rejects such work as deadening, and all of her growth as a character is dependent on her escape from the factory.

6. This is based on an actual experience of Melville's, when he was invited to such a dinner by one Robert Francis Cooke in December 1849. See note to 1259.9 in the Library of America edition, p. 1472.

7. Making all of the mill workers women is mostly a poetic conceit. Overall in the country, in the 1850s and 1860s, around 40 percent of the workers in paper mills were women, though it may have been higher in New England, and in some mills that produced fine paper women could have been in the majority. (In the 1850s and 1860s, women made up about 20 percent of the nonagricultural workforce.) But the machinery in the mills was almost always worked by men. Paper making first became an industrial process in 1817 in the Delaware mill of Joshua and Thomas Gilpin, but the decisive mechanization of the industry did not happen until the 1830s and 1840s with the establishment of the Fourdrinier machine. Women did the hand work of preparing the materials for the machines and then cutting and sorting the finished product. Melville visited the Dalton, Massachusetts, paper mill in January 1851, but in depicting what he

saw there he probably had in mind not only the plight of paper makers but the general situation of women workers in New England, especially the situation of workers in the textile mills who did handle heavy machinery. This is suggested as well by the fact that women in the paper mills tended to be older than those in the textile mills and also in Melville's story, were often married, and had families.

8. "The Paradise of Bachelors and the Tartarus of Maids," in *Herman Melville: Pierre, Israel Potter, The Piazza Tales, The Confidence-Man, Uncollected Prose, Billy Budd, Sailor*, ed. Harrison Hayford (New York: Library of America, 1984), 1265. All further citations are from this edition.

9. Dante Alighieri, *The Inferno*, trans. by John Ciardi (New York: New American Library, 1954), 42.

10. William Blake, "And did those feet in ancient time," *Selected Poetry and Prose of William Blake*, ed. Northrop Frye (New York: Modern Library, 1953), 244: "And did the Countenance Divine, / Shine forth upon our clouded hills? / And was Jerusalem builded here / Among these dark Satanic Mills?"

11. "The American Scholar," in *Emerson, Essays and Lectures* (New York: Library of America, 1983), 54.

12. From Henry David Thoreau, *A Week on the Concord and Merrimack Rivers; Walden; or Life in the Woods; The Maine Woods; Cape Cod* (New York: Library of America, 1985), 327.

13. "I Hear America Singing," "Inscriptions," *Leaves of Grass (1891–1892)* (New York: Library of America, 1982), 174.

14. "Benito Cereno," in *Herman Melville: Pierre, Israel Potter, The Piazza Tales, The Confidence-Man, Uncollected Prose, Billy Budd, Sailor*, ed. Harrison Hayford (New York: Library of America, 1984), 734. All further citations are from this edition.

Melville and the Marketplace

Sheila Post

At this point in our critical understanding of the relation between writers and their cultural moments, it should come as no surprise that Herman Melville, as well as a host of his contemporaries, shaped their works in accordance with the trends of the mid-nineteenth-century literary marketplace. What may seem unusual, however, was the particular set of marketplace conditions that characterized this period in American literary history.

American authors at midcentury, unlike the majority of their more wealthy literary predecessors, who approached writing as a leisure activity, attempted to profit from their publications. In so doing, they necessarily faced the challenge of combining personal visions with the complexities of literary production at midcentury. Due to international copyright laws, which failed to protect royalties for American books published solely in America, American authors were forced to publish their writings first in England or risk the pirating of their works by European publishers. Since American publishers tended to gauge the response of British readers before publishing an American edition, American authors needed to craft their writings to cater simultaneously to British and American tastes. While English reading habits were segmented along socioeconomic lines, American authors faced the additional challenges in America of writing for divergent readerships within the middle class and negotiating the critical debates over genre and style that raged in the literary magazines of the day.

From the start of his writing career, Melville demonstrated a keen understanding of these marketplace conditions. While he incorporated the interests of particular groups of readers into his books and shorter fiction, thereby aiming specific works at particular readerships, he also creatively combined popular forms and styles to reach multiple audiences simultaneously.

More unexpected is the fact that Melville discovered a creativity that emerged from his deliberate reliance upon popular literary trends. The rationale for suggesting a permeability between the works of this "classic" male writer and his culture originates in Melville's own formulation of artistry. This line from the author's 1850 review of Nathaniel Hawthorne's *Mosses from an Old Manse* articulates the relation between individual creativity and cultural practice: "Whereas great geniuses are parts of the times,they themselves are the times, and possess a correspondent coloring."[1] This formulation underscores the role of marketplace trends as a foundation to Melville's own writings.[2]

The Literary Marketplace

From 1842 to 1860, the number of books (both literary and nonliterary) published in the United States increased dramatically. In 1835, 64 new books were published; by 1842, the number had increased only to 100. The year 1855, however, witnessed the publication of 1,092 novels. Improved public education, diminishing illiteracy, increased population, and especially innovative methods both of publishing and the mass distribution of printed materials contributed to the rise of large-scale audiences during the 1840s and 1850s.

Perhaps more than any other single factor, the shift in demographics shaped new readerships at midcentury as antebellum America witnessed the emergence of an urban middle class. Yet within this socioeconomic group, the purposes for reading differed considerably, resulting in a heterogeneity of readers. Contemporary cultural speakers referred to the multiplicity of audiences. "General," "common," or "popular" readers referred to those middle-class audiences of both sexes who read largely for entertainment. It is this group of "fireside readers," for example, whom Melville identifies as his audience in *Typee: A Peep at Polynesian Life* (1846).

Other individuals attempted to regulate literary production as well as the aesthetic tastes of general readers; such reviewers, literary critics, clergymen, particular authors, and other people of high social standing represented a separate audience usually referred to by their contemporaries (and themselves) as "intellectual" or "cultivated" readers. With their desire to shape literary production—and by extension, American culture—cultivated readers tended to be quite opinionated on issues concerning genre and tended to be more conservative than general readers in outlook. These attributes offer a context for understanding the differences in style and genre between Melville's first two books since the author incorporated the demands of this second group into *Omoo: A Narrative of Adventures in the South Seas* (1847).

A third group, referred to as "literary" readers, represented a midpoint between general and cultivated readers, groups that differed occasionally on matters of style, tone, and subject but differed frequently on attitudes toward family, work, individuality, gender, and morality. Literary readers blended the receptiveness of general readers to progressive political and social views with the particularly formulated aesthetic standards demanded by cultivated readers. Reading Melville's third novel, *Mardi: And a Voyage Thither* (1849) in the context of the interests of literary readers goes far in recovering the author's method and use of narrative conventions of the day.

These varied audiences within the middle class stood apart from and occasionally opposed an even larger readership commonly referred to as the "masses," or "the people." This almost exclusively working-class audience, which came into its own during the mid-1850s, sought literature that was, among other attributes, more secular, more liberal, and even more openly defiant of middle-class values. The interests of this audience served as a mine for middle-class writers who frequently borrowed from working-class literary forms, themes, and styles when writing for both middle-class and working-class readers. It was at this combined audience that Melville targeted his much-misunderstood *Pierre; or, The Ambiguities* (1852), whose publication linked the author to the bestselling female novelists of the 1850s.

The interests of particular groups of readers can be readily identified through their commitment to specific genres. Suspicious of fiction, American cultivated readers of the 1840s considered nonfictional works aesthetically more pleasing than fiction and poetry, a bias also common among cultivated English readers of the period. Anthony Trollope recounted the conventional attitude toward fiction held by the upper classes: "The families in which an unrestricted permission was given for reading of novels were very few, and from many they were altogether banished."[3] Even as late as 1851, Susan Warner, in her successful bestseller *The Wide, Wide World* presented the strong bias against fiction through her portrayal of John Humphreys, the exemplar of cultivated middle-class attitudes. Journals ranging from the elite *North American Review* to the more popular middle-class monthlies *Graham's Magazine* and *Godey's Lady's Book* featured reviews of biographies, histories, essays, and travels in addition to poetry and stories, and antebellum readers suspicious of fictional taints included all of these various genres in their formulation of the term *literature*.

The demand for truthful, realistic narratives partially accounts for the decade's interest in particular genres, such as pseudoscientific literature. Well-attended Lyceum lectures on science, together with their wide coverage in daily papers such as the *New York Tribune*, attest to the interest of antebellum readers in scientific and, more generally, nonfictional topics. The immense popularity, for example, of Edgar Allan Poe's purportedly authentic accounts prompted an unprecedented 300,000 readers to buy "The Gold Bug," though a number of reviewers for general magazines and papers located much of the popularity of Poe's scientific tales in the author's deliberate strategy of challenging the reader to detect the stories' essential fictiveness.

Such popular interest in the scientific and in the assessment of the veridical by general readers provides a context for understanding Melville's use of cetological information, naturalistic observation, and realistic details of whaling ships as well as of his subtle portrayal of the limitations of scientific truth. In this light, *Moby-Dick; or, The Whale* (1851) played into the culture's fascination for pseudoscientific writing. As two reviewers proclaimed of Melville's mighty new work of 1851, "In one light [it is] romantic fiction, in another statement of absolute fact," while another jested, "[W]ho would have thought to look for philosophy in whales and poetry in blubber?"[4]

This combination of fact and fiction may explain the success of two of the most widely reviewed (and perhaps also read) genres of the period: travel adventures and domestic narratives. Travel writers as well as authors of domestic life greatly appealed to middle-class general and cultivated readers. Travel accounts that related interesting facts of native lives and cultures intrigued literal-minded readers and catered to the decade's demand for realistic portraiture. These expectations played a large role in both the revisions to *Typee* and the composition of *Omoo*.

Likewise, what the decade fondly called "hair-breathed 'scapes"—sensational tales of escape from native or marginal peoples—particularly fascinated general and mass (working-class) readers, and the sensational mode, among other rhetorical appeals to the emotions, such as the sentimental mode, represented styles that permeated all levels of antebellum society.[5] Although these modes of writing vied with biographies, histories, and geographers' expeditionary accounts, the domestic and travel genres increased in popularity as the 1840s progressed. By midcentury, these two styles represented the most frequently published literary genres in middle-class circles. The heterogeneous reading habits of antebellum middle-class audiences provided a creative challenge for writers to combine forms and styles that appealed simultaneously to different readerships.

Taking up this challenge, Melville discovered through such mixtures a site for creativity as well as a new niche in the literary marketplace. The ingenious balance between sentiment and sensation in *Typee* accounts for Melville's extraordinary success

among American general readers. Reviewers of the day ex-
claimed that the author's first book of adventures was read by
"every man, woman, and child in the Union who undertakes to
keep pace at all with the current literature," while others proclaimed *Typee*, to be "the most successful hit in bookmaking."[6]
By combining in his next work, *Omoo*, the various elements and
genres that won different readerships for his first book with the
preference of cultivated readers for narrative accuracy, Melville
displayed a sophisticated understanding of the literary marketplace. In his third work, *Mardi*, Melville's engagement in a daring
(some say, reckless) attempt to reach all three reading audiences
in middle-class circles proved moderately successful. As one reviewer proclaimed:

> Here are points of interest for every mind. The scholar can
> feast upon its classical illusions, the man of erudition can add
> to his story, the divine food for thought and discussion, the
> poet luxuriate in scenes of pure fancy, the little child find en-
> tertainment, and genius salute the author as the rising sun.[7]

This uncanny ability to reach various audiences simultaneously
through the creation of specific narrative and thematic mixtures
provided the foundation to the author's next two books; *Redburn:
His First Voyage* (1849) and *White-Jacket: or, The World in a Man-of-
War* (1850), in which the author endorsed the reigning cultural
values placed on social responsibility and civic duty through a reliance upon popular narrative forms. But it was in planning what
was to become his masterpiece, *Moby-Dick; or, The Whale* (1851),
that the author discovered within existing literary trends a specific narrative form conducive to his particular creativity.

The heterogeneity of *Moby-Dick*—often attributed to the author's "soared ambition," "fluid consciousness," "shifting . . .
conceptions," and even "lessons of craft from Shakespeare"—
actually reflects a narrative license of the times.[8] The metaphysical discussions, genre shifts, use of Shakespearean conventions,
and mixture of facts and romance, typically considered Melville's
improvisations, also appear in "Mixed-Form" narratives, a genre

(in)famous at midcentury, but now largely overlooked. Through this heterogeneous form, Melville linked his work to a popular yet radical trend in both English and American antebellum literary cultures. Indeed, Melville's debt to "Mixed Form" is central to understanding both the narrative form and the author's method in *Moby-Dick*.

"Mixed-Form" Narratives

The genre of the "Mixed-Form" novel emerged in transatlantic literary circles as a response to early nineteenth-century critical strictures on literary realism. Radically multiple, "Mixed-Form" novels simultaneously presented different perceptions of experience through mimetic and intuitive modes. Often referred to as "metaphysical" narratives, they depict the "truth of causes" and deliberately mix levels of approach thus appearing to be, in the words of Edward Bulwer-Lytton, one of the first serious literary theoreticians and practitioners of "Mixed Form" in England, "neither wholly allegory, nor wholly matter-of-fact, but both at times."[9]

Yet the very nature of their mixture suggests an alternate view to the world of facts. This was achieved by combining a Lockean positivistic world view—the belief that there is a "definite complement of truths related to human procedure which may be ascertained by reason, experience, and a scientific study of the natural laws"—with a reflective, mystical, often visionary, Kantian point of view. As such, these novels stress the necessity of "a deeper faith, a faith metaphysical, in which these very truths must be rooted out ere they can function so powerfully as they might."[10] The need for metaphysical truth within the world of facts informs the structure of "Mixed-Form" narratives and helps to explain this mixture.

Narratives based upon this genre tended to chronicle the individual's "progress through the very blackness of darkness, with only natural reason, or the revelation that can come through reason, as his guide":

There is the mind preying on its own metaphysical roots; there is the parting, piece by piece, of the old hereditary faith, and yet all the remaining torture of the ceaseless interrogation which that faith satisfied. . . . there is the burden of sin and the alternate sullenness and madness of despair. . . . Sometimes the mind under probation is made to ascertain for itself that its perpetual metaphysical self-torture, its perpetual labour on questions which cannot be answered, is a misuse of its faculties, and so take rest in the philosophic conclusion that man was not born to solve the problem of the universe, but to find out where the problem begins, and then to restrain himself within the limits of the comprehensible.[11]

This description of the conventions of this genre could serve as a description of the existential struggles of the major characters in Melville's *Moby-Dick*.

While facts supported the veridical orientation of the genre in travel, historical, and nautical narratives, in metaphysical narratives they were used to suggest alternative possibilities to the materialist world. Presenting the world bound by regular laws, the metaphysical writer then contradicted that world and its facts from an idealist point of view. Although the linear plot depicted the empirical approach to experience, the nonlinear digressions, multiple genres, and interpolations elucidated the preferred, idealist view.

A glance at a few of Melville's contemporaries depicts some of these commonalities. In *St. Leger; or, The Threads of Life* (1850), Richard Burleigh Kimball cleverly juxtaposes his chronicle of the cognitive and philosophical journey of his hero and an essentially historical narrative. By providing extensive genealogical facts, Kimball represents the traditional position of realist writers, yet these facts offer an epistemology and perspective different from the protagonist's search for intuitive knowledge. Kimball ultimately challenges the thematic value of realistic narration through his philosophical, intuitive account of the metaphysical discoveries of his protagonist. The understanding gained in the realistic narrative through studying family tradition is spurned by the narrator for the visionary insights gained through philosophical inquiry.

To portray the alternate world views signaled by either a narrative of facts or one of inspiration, philosophy, or vision, metaphysical writers employed various stylistic devices, including using different literary genres to depict alternate perspectives of reality. Sylvester Judd, in *Margaret: A Tale of the Real and Ideal, Blight and Bloom* (1845), relied on poetry and Native American oral traditions, while Kimball interpolated poetry and soliloquies in the Shakespearean style into his narrative. In Melville's era Shakespeare was truly a popular playwright with all audiences and not the icon of highbrow culture, a status assigned to him only in the late nineteenth century. Melville shares with others of his day lessons from Shakespeare. Though resembling Melville's Ahab, the following soliloquy comes not from Ahab, but rather from the narrator of Kimball's *St. Leger*:

> Be still, rebellious temper. Dare not disturb the calm current of my thoughts. Down, ye mocking suggestions. Away, ye dark, thick, brooding fancies—hence, all! all! At any rate, your time is not *yet*. The mysterious union of body and spirit still is, though faintly indeed does Vitality in me perform her office; but the wheel is not yet broken: I am at the helm still! therefore, Doubt, thou supple, coward slave of evil, avaunt!
> I *WILL* that I believe.
> I *DO* believe! [12]

This work, like *Moby-Dick* after it, also utilizes the different genres of poetry and drama. Shakespearean conventions share textual space with decidedly less-classical materials in Kimball's book, just as they do in *Moby-Dick*.

Most writers who relied on the "Mixed-Form" narrative combined scientific observation and facts with fictional narratives. In the historical romance *Kaloolah* (1849), William Starbuck Mayo provided ethological accounts of ocean birds, fish, and dolphins. In *The Berber*, Mayo combined geographical information and romance, a technique hailed by a *Harper's* reviewer:

The scene is laid in Morocco, affording the writer an occasion for the use of a great deal of geographical and historical lore, which is introduced to decided advantage as a substantial back-ground to the story, which, in itself, possesses a sustained and powerful interest.

The reviewer then located that powerful interest specifically in the narrative's "Mixed Form": "These sudden and decided transitions [of *The Berber*] form a striking feature of the volume. . . . They constantly pique the attention of the reader, keeping curiosity alive, and presenting the combined charm of surprise and alternation."[13] Mayo's descriptions grounded his romances in the world of science—a contrast that satisfied readers who required realistic depictions.

Some writers mixed scientific and literary genres as a way of presenting different epistemological schemes. Judd's *Margaret*, whose title blends the scientific ("blight and bloom") with the philosophical ("real and ideal"), juxtaposes polytheistic, Native American forest lives and a Christian, Anglo-Saxon village. Village life dramatizes the philosophical, whereas forest life portrays the natural world of geology, botany, and biology. Here the "real," natural world offers an epistemology represented variably through Native American and other non-Christian world views which, in turn, serve as an alternative to the "ideal." Through a lesson in geology (anticipating the anatomy lessons of *Moby-Dick*), Judd compares the geological formation known as a *geode* to the human head:

Man like this stone is geodic. . . . expressing all men collectively viewed in their better light. . . . Much depends upon this light, phase, or aspect. . . . an Indian head in one position . . . If I could crack any man as I do this stone, I should lay open beautiful crystals.[14]

Again anticipating Ishmael, who contrasts different philosophical views in the "Whale's Head" chapters (74–75), Judd underscores here the relativism inherent in philosophical perspective.

In this light, the cetological center of *Moby-Dick* reflects both the mid-nineteenth-century interest in natural science and the necessary empirical realism of the "Mixed-Form" novel. *Moby-Dick* correspondingly abounds in statistical, historical, economic, and anatomical facts which, are interspersed throughout the philosophical chronicle of Ishmael's developing metaphysical insights. As a codified form within this tradition, cetological and whaling information is an integral element of the narrative form in *Moby-Dick*. In terms resembling the *Harper's* review of *The Berber*, the *New Haven Daily Palladium* praised the mixture of forms in *Moby-Dick*: "The work possesses all the interest of the most exciting fiction, while, at the same time, it conveys much valuable information in regard to things pertaining to natural history, commerce, life on shipboard, and etc."[15]

While Melville innovated the genre of "Mixed Form" by reshaping it to portray the necessity, in the words of Ishmael, to advocate for a multiplicity of views, that is, to consider experience "in every light," the author's conscious alternation of facts with fiction concurs with the deliberate approach to narrative form by metaphysical writers. In *Moby-Dick*, Melville created for the "Mixed-Form" narrative a new metaphysical world which centered on the philosophy of "trying all things," an attitude central to the journey of his protagonist, Ishmael, and to himself—as exemplified in his engagement with marketplace trends. *Moby-Dick* remains a timely and timeless testimony to the creativity inherent in writing for the marketplace.

The Periodical Marketplace

As general readers turned to literary magazines, periodical literature increasingly dominated the market. By 1840, a year that produced approximately 40 new novels, the existence of more than 1,500 periodicals provided a significantly more extensive reading environment. Examining the reasons for the sudden surge in periodical readership during the 1840s, William Kirkland, a literary critic of the day, explained:

Though but a small part of what is *published* they [monthlies] constitute much of what is *read*. A large percentage of books published scarce finds a purchaser; numbers of those purchased are never read and many that *are* read, are read by one or two persons, while with periodicals the *un*-read are the exception. One has but to look into circulating libraries, reading-rooms and the like places to see that an extensive class of readers finds time or inclination for little else.[16]

This "extensive class"—a mixture of general middle-class and working-class readers—radically altered the literary marketplace through its increasing demand for magazine literature.

Eager for contributions from popular authors, magazines provided writers with ready outlets for their work. After nearly two decades of writing books, Washington Irving shifted over to the periodicals in 1839, with this explanation:

I am tired of writing volumes: they do not afford exactly the relief I require; there is too much preparation, arrangement, and parade in this set of coming before the public. . . . I have thought therefore, of securing myself a snug little corner in some periodical work, where I might, as it were, loll at my ease in an elbow chair, and chat sociably with the public.[17]

During the 1840s and 1850s, prominent writers such as Caroline Chesebro' (Maria Jane McIntosh), Fanny Fern (Sara Payson Willis Parton), Fanny Forrester (Emily Chubbuck Judson), Nathaniel Hawthorne, Caroline Lee Hentz, Herman Melville, Edgar Allan Poe, Catharine Sedgwick, Elizabeth Barstow Stoddard, E.D.E.N. Southworth, Harriet Beecher Stowe, Walt(er) Whitman, and N. P. Willis established their careers by contributing to the magazines.

Many writers found the periodical marketplace more critically receptive and economically rewarding than the book market. In a period when the annual income of many popular authors amounted usually to no more than $500–1,600, *Godey's Lady's Book*, in its first few years, paid the popular Lydia Sigourney $500 yearly—over $200 more than the average annual wage for skilled workers—just to add her name to its list of contributors without her actually writing anything. In the 1850s, Robert Bonner, founder of *the New York Ledger*, revolutionized the salaries of magazine writers. He boasted in his paper that he paid the popular Fanny Fern "by far the highest price that has ever been paid by any newspaper publisher to any author": $100 per column and, in the case of Fern's first serialized novel in the paper, $1,000 a story.[18]

Yet, as Irving pointed out, writing for the magazines differed significantly from writing to meet the demands of book publishers. Despite the existence of a "literary economics," which helped to shape the conditions of the book marketplace, authors experienced great leeway in writing novels. With the notable exception of the English publisher John Murray, who insisted upon "factual" works, houses on both sides of the Atlantic published a wide range of books and thus did not usually limit their authors to a particular genre. When Harper Brothers learned that the popular young author of *Typee* had a second manuscript, for example, Fletcher Harper instructed his employees to "take it at once" sight unseen, and indeed this publisher accepted other manuscripts by Melville without having read them. As long as a writer maintained his or her celebrity, publishers tolerated innovation. This freedom accounts for the "experimenting," as it was termed by various reviewers of the day, in different genres which many of these writers, such as Herman Melville, were so fond of doing.

Magazine writing, on the other hand, required a different kind of rigor. Periodicals aimed at audiences with specific demographic characteristics and tailored their editorial policies to satisfy their targeted readers. Due to stiff competition, periodical publishers attempted to capitalize on the uniqueness of their magazines. Thus, in the 1840s, a given reader would turn to *Godey's Lady's Book* for adventure and domestic stories, to the *Democratic Review* or the *American Review* for political and analytical essays, to the *North American Review* or the *Literary World* for literary discussions, and to *Graham's* for literary and "family circle" reading.

The changing conditions in the periodical marketplace of the 1850s provided environments which encouraged the kind of personal creativity that characterized the magazine writing of the best periodical writers of this decade: Fanny Fern, E.D.E.N. Southworth, and Herman Melville. During the 1850s, some magazines reached mass circulation. Harper Brothers started *Harper's Magazine* in June 1850 with an initial run of 7,500 copies; by December of that year its readership had increased dramatically to 50,000. And by January 1854, 130,000 issues reeled off the presses monthly. Robert Bonner created the bestseller of periodicals with his *New York Ledger*. By targeting both middle- and working-class audiences and by hiring bestselling women writers, most notably Stowe, Southworth, and Fern—whose *Fern Leaves* in 1853 and *Ruth Hall* in 1855 sold 70,000 and 50,000 copies, respectively—his circulation quickly surged to more than 400,000 readers *weekly*. Increasing dramatically within two decades, American periodical audiences now dominated the literary marketplace.

The enormous success of magazines stemmed from their particular—and heavily advertised—editorial policies. As long as the contributors to Bonner's *Ledger* adhered to the editor's demand for a style that was "pure in morals, honest and noble in sentiment, simple in diction, plain in construction, and thoroughly adapted to the taste and comprehension of the people," writers such as Fern and Southworth could freely treat a variety of topics, including crime, women's rights, adventure, and social issues.[19] Both Fern and Southworth creatively combined Bonner's editorial policy with their own literary concerns and styles, and consistently produced some of their best writing in the pages of the *New York Ledger*. Southworth's most popular—and, many would proclaim, her best—novel, *The Hidden Hand*, was serialized three different times in the *Ledger*, while the weekly articles of Fanny Fern produced a sensation almost unheard of among antebellum readers.

When we turn to Melville, we discover in his magazine fiction particularly instructive examples of a creative reliance upon editorial policies. Like Poe and Hawthorne before him, and alongside Fern and Southworth, who aligned their tales to specific magazine practices, Melville traded in this popular market by tailoring his submissions to adhere to the policies and stances of two middle-class monthlies that vied for top ratings, *Harper's Magazine* and *Putnam's Monthly*.

Magazine writing offered Melville the opportunity to earn a predictable and steady income, a reason commonly cited for his switch from the novel form. However, more than financial gain was at stake. For the first time in his career, he discovered large audiences receptive to his literary interests. When Melville turned to magazine writing in 1853, he participated in the two distinct literary environments of *Harper's* and *Putnam's*. Melville's magazine writing, together with his longer works of the 1850s exhibit the author's deep concern over a wide range of social issues, including poverty, homelessness, slavery, industrialization, and sexism. Yet the particular articulations of these themes reflect the author's deference to their publishing contexts, the stylistic conventions that distinguished *Harper's* and *Putnam's*.

Melville submitted seven tales, roughly half of his entire short fiction output, to one of the most politically conservative and sentimental monthlies of the decade, *Harper's Magazine*. Although periodicals such as *Putnam's* and even *Holden's Dollar Magazine* provided the author with more heterogeneous environments, and *Putnam's* paid him the same high rate per page ($5), Melville continued to submit to *Harper's*. The particular type of social critique found in tales such as "The Fiddler," "Jimmy Rose," "Cock-a-Doodle-Doo!" and "The Paradise of Bachelors and the Tartarus of Maids," all published in *Harper's*, was not limited to nor defined by a personal strategy of the author. The themes of social alienation and obscurity in Melville's *Harper's* stories form part of a larger tradition in *Harper's* fiction. The author's stylistic techniques in the seven tales published in *Harper's* are directly linked to the editorial policies and magazine practices of the popular sentimental monthly.

The deliberateness of Melville's practices and his keen awareness of the contrasting magazine styles become clear in the distinct fiction he wrote for *Putnam's*. The liberal philosophy of *Putnam's* editors encouraged Melville to include some of his most sophisticated formulations of political, social, and aesthetic themes in the fiction that he submitted to this magazine. Not solely a characteristic of Melville's prose, richly symbolic language and a heterogeneous style became the trademark of *Putnam's* essays and stories.

Melville carefully considered this stylistic approach and orientation when writing for *Putnam's*. Some of the author's best shorter works and indeed the stories included in his collection *The Piazza Tales* (1855), such as "Bartleby, the Scrivener: A Story of Wall Street," "Benito Cereno," "I and My Chimney," and "The Encantadas," were initially written for and published in *Putnam's Monthly*. These submissions contain unabashedly realistic appraisals of socioeconomic, racial, and gender inequities. While the stories in *Harper's* treat social issues through sentimental rhetoric that is suggestive, the author's stories for *Putnam's* criticize sentimental views that soften social and political realities.

Writing for these two major literary monthlies of the 1850s, which differed significantly in ideological perspectives and literary styles, required, from Melville, a stylistic heterogeneity and creativity that modern readers have come to associate with him. The author's continued submission to both monthlies indicates his interest in working within the different magazine policies. The challenge for *Harper's* contributors to empower the sentimental image with potentially different levels of meaning remained for Melville an artistic challenge, as Melville's later stories for *Harper's* demonstrate. At the same time, the task of *Putnam's* writers to directly criticize the pervasive uses of abstracted sentiment in literary narratives through the use of heterogeneous, multi-leveled texts represented a kind of writing intimately related to the style of the author of *Moby-Dick*.

Melville's tales became so popular with *Putnam's* readers that the author's work became the trademark for the magazine. The *American Publishers' Circular* pronounced that the author's stories were "instrumental in raising that journal to its present proud position—the best of all American monthlies."[20] Examining Melville's magazine fiction in its socio-literary contexts reveals how literary economics and marketplace realities informed the practices of both the writer and the literary magazines.

Non-Partisan Sentiment in *Harper's Magazine*

Started in 1850, *Harper's* became one of the century's most widely read magazines, with a circulation surpassing 100,000 by 1860. Its overwhelming popularity stemmed largely from its editorial policy of aiming to please all segments of the middle class—to reach "the great mass of the American people." Since the "great mass" of middle-class readers held different and at times opposing political views, the monthly discouraged controversy: "The Magazine . . . will provide . . . the most perfect freedom from prejudice and partiality of every kind" (June 1851). It accomplished this feat by strictly maintaining what it considered to be a nonpartisan stance on politics, social issues, and religious topics. *Harper's* catered to the taste of a mixed reading public through a stylistic mode that hoped to assuage more than to criticize. Forerunner of Saturday night radio programs listened to by American families nationwide a century later, the "parlor" literature of *Harper's Magazine* favored family-oriented, entertaining, and moralistic fiction.

With their determination to remain a magazine of "light" literature aimed at "parlor" readers, the editors preferred a sentimental style. This narrative mode, while employed in thematic treatments of an array of topics, including domestic, social, and political issues, subordinated analyses of events to an emphasis on the emotional responses of the narrators, characters, and readers. Sentimental fiction in *Harper's* cast the motifs of suffering, abuse, poverty, and exploitation—social problems that plagued American society in the 1850s—into stylized portraits of moral fortitude. This sentimental style was employed to emphasize the abilities of characters—always the poor, unempowered, and marginalized—to find contentment through the hardships they encountered by transforming the social problems their existence embodied, into a celebration of the moralistic principles of toleration and acquiescence. Such thematized messages, rather than focusing on the issues themselves, attempted to demonstrate that "difficulties are the tutors and monitors of men placed in their path for their best discipline and development" (January 1852, 212), as one character in a *Harper's* story proclaimed.

The emphasis on class in *Harper's* fiction reflects the larger social distancing that was occurring between working-class people and the burgeoning new middle classes. Aloof spectator-narrators representing the privileged middle class isolated themselves from the events they related and used their status to observe less-fortunate characters from above on the ladder of success. Celebrating the economic success of middle-class readers, *Harper's* tales relegated the stances of acquiescence and toleration to the lower classes, who were the subjects, rather than the narrators. In this way, middle-class narrators displaced in their fiction the very people whom the stories ostensibly chronicled. While narrators alluded to the misery of poverty and alienation, they deflected the reader's empathy from the despair vividly portrayed to themselves by disengaging themselves from the environments of their unfortunate characters. Instead of explicitly expressing opinions regarding misspent lives, *Harper's* narrators resorted to a conventional response, usually culminating in a final sentimentalized exclamation, such as the ending of "The Chateau Regnier": "May he die in peace!" Such endings indirectly lauded the good-willed nature of the narrator without directly grappling with the unresolved social problems that the stories raised. This abstract representation of social issues, coupled with an emphasis on the emotions, the philanthropy, or simply the good fortune of the narrator enabled writers to support the *Harper's* commitment to a perspective that supported raising timely issues, but that stopped at implication.

This process of displacing the working-class, immigrants, African-Americans, and Native Americans to the margins—and beyond—of society mirrored the actual displacement and subjugation that such peoples experienced as the new middle class empowered itself through a self-conscious centering of its new class base. Thus, in the case of *Harper's*, the cultural work in which the form engaged was work that reproduced itself culturally, reinforcing itself even though ostensibly focusing on the socially disadvantaged.

Contrasting different kinds of lifestyles, Melville's stories adhered closely to the magazine's stylistic demands. The author focused on social issues of the day, including reversed fortunes and economic status. Yet in the fashion of the magazine, Melville's narrators both chronicled and distanced themselves from their tales of the "unfortunate": "ruined" men ("The Happy Failure," "Jimmy Rose"), loss of fame ("The Fiddler"), poverty ("Cock-a-Doodle-Doo!" "Poor Man's Pudding and Rich Man's Crumbs"), and social inequities ("The Paradise of Bachelors and the Tartarus of Maids"). In addition, they supported the ideology that poverty and obscurity are ennobling virtues ("Cock-a-Doodle-Doo!" "The Happy Failure," and "The Fiddler").

Although Melville suggested horror in his titles and images and provided alternative possibilities to the ideological structures his tales seemed to support, his stories avoided the direct critical analyses of his earlier novels and the contemporaneous stories written for *Putnam's*. They ended on the same sentimental note found in the other pages of the magazine: "God grant that Jimmy's roses may immortally survive!" ("Jimmy Rose"); "Heaven save me equally from the 'Poor Man's Pudding' and the 'Rich Man's Crumbs'"; "COCK-A-DOODLE-DOO!—OO!—OO-OO!" "Praise be to God for the failure!" ("The Happy Failure"); and "Oh! Paradise of Bachelors! and oh! Tartarus of Maids!" While Melville creatively employed this formula, as did female domestic novelists, his reliance on the sentimental mode also supported the tastes and expectations of his readers.

A central point in understanding Melville's particular compositional strategies here is that his *Harper's* tales differ significantly from the methods employed in contrasting the lives of the slaves and the Spanish sailors in "Benito Cereno," for example, or of Bartleby and the attorney in "Bartleby, the Scrivener." In these stories, oppositional perspectives fully participated in the drama. In writing for *Harper's*, Melville necessarily restrained the thoughts and actions of his narrators. In his *Harper's* tale "The Paradise of Bachelors and the Tartarus of Maids," for example, the worlds of the bachelors and the maids remained fragmented rather than interactive since the narrator offered only discordant slices. While these discordances may have seemed to challenge and criticize newly formed middle-class attitudes toward social stratification, they also simultaneously reflected those views. Although overlapping themes could be found in the stories written for *Putnam's* during the same period, this deference to a sentimental rhetoric that stops at implication clearly distinguished Melville's *Harper's* fiction from the stories submitted to *Putnam's*.

Liberal Language in *Putnam's Monthly*

Putnam's Monthly started in 1853 as a critical commentary on the times and as a direct contrast to the political conservatism and sentimentalism of *Harper's Magazine*. Rigorously analytical, *Putnam's* appealed to a more intellectual, aesthetically sophisticated, politically liberal, and thus smaller audience, which ranged from 2,000 to 20,000 subscribers, averaging around 16,000 readers monthly.

Putnam's promised American commentary on national and international affairs. In his first editorial, Charles Briggs asked, "In what paper or periodical do you now look to find the criticism of American thought upon the times?" (January 1853, 2). Answering his own question, Briggs promised to collect "the results of the acutest observations, and the most trenchant thought, illustrated by whatever wealth of erudition, of imagination, and of experience" that American writers possessed. By emphasizing "trenchant thought" and "erudition," rather than just the popularity of their writers as was the custom in *Harper's*, the editors conveyed the rhetorical style to which they aspired.

The monthly treated social, political, and literary themes from a perspective markedly different from the non-partisan, non-analytical stance of its competitor. Articles, essays, and stories analyzed—and evaluated—the variety of perspectives that comprised a particular issue. Unlike its competitor, *Putnam's* strongly condemned the popular rhetoric of sentiment, a mode of writing that, according to the editors, tried to assuage and cover more than it directly challenged and uncovered. *Putnam's* editors rejected sentimental rhetoric as a tool for representing the times, because it glossed over reality and "paints only the gentle, the grieving, the beautiful." The sentimental style of

Harper's fiction, argued *Putnam's* editors, severs the link between social problems and the teller's emotional response to them by highlighting abstracted sentiment. The anti-sentimental stance implied a dissatisfaction with the consistently "clear, true, and transparent" prose of sentimental writing and endorsed a deliberately ambiguous, multi-layered text.

A look at how editorial policies on sentimental rhetoric at *Putnam's* were articulated in fiction illustrates how closely Melville's strategies reflected the general practices in the magazine. George William Curtis, a best-selling author in addition to being one of the magazine's editors, undermined sentimental conventions in "The Potiphar Papers." Creating a setting commonly employed in domestic fiction, the author reinforced this domesticity by including a traditional activity, home decorating. While in the conventional sentimental tale, the adventures of the decorator would dominate the story, the male narrator, disturbed at the refurbishing attempts of his wife and family, determined to subdue their efforts. Melville's story "I and My Chimney" reproduces a similar situation. The similarity of these two tales helps to explain Curtis's thorough enjoyment of Melville's story. It is central to note that the narrators in these two stories contrast strongly with the sentimentalizing bachelor who dreams of domesticity in *Reveries of a Bachelor,* written by a leading writer for *Harper's,* Ik Marvel. While the *Putnam's* stories adhered to a common rigorous antisentimentalism, Marvel's bachelor—highly praised by the sentiment-loving reviewers of *Harper's*—epitomized the sentimental rhetoric.

The common stance of *Putnam's* writers against sentimental rhetoric and their commitment to challenging middle-class values goes far in accounting for the strategies that Melville employed in "Bartleby, the Scrivener," one of his best and most stylistically challenging stories. In "Bartleby, the Scrivener," the author employed a sentimental style as a methodological weapon against itself and, in doing so, reinforced the *Putnam's* editorial stance. Partially sentimental, this story portrayed the devastating effects of Wall Street on those "pallidly neat, pitiably respectable, incurably forlorn" individuals like Bartleby, and yet the overall manner was more in keeping with the heterogeneity of *Putnam's* than with the sentimentalism of *Harper's*.

In order to represent the sentimental perspective, Melville created a narrator who resembled the detached narrators of *Harper's*. Yet the narrative method in "Bartleby" differed significantly from Melville's fiction in *Harper's*. By examining the methods of social involvement and retreat adopted by individuals in the workplace, Melville allied his tale with the editorial concerns of *Putnam's*. This subject was of particular interest to the monthly since, from its first issue, it encouraged analyses of the world of work. Passages such as the following, by George William Curtis in his story "Andrew Crabelly: Attorney at Law," portrayed the despair of the industrial worker: "I knew that men had been hard at work since sunrise—since daybreak—toiling heavily at labor that should not end until their lives ended; confined in close and noisome places, in which the day was never very bright, and their hopes grew daily darker" (*Putnam's*, January 1853, 18). Curtis's depiction of the dehumanized worker anticipated Melville's chronicle of Bartleby's attitudes toward survival in the world of business.

Melville conflates the magazine editors' concern for the effects of industrialization on the individual worker with their—and his own—arguments for a narrative style that represented individual perspectives. The narrator assumed the dual role of lawyer and narrator and his relation to his literal and narrative subject, Bartleby, conveyed a double story: the tale of the lawyer's involvement with his employee Bartleby and the tale of the narrator's relation to his subject. Through this paradigm, Melville cleverly employed the magazine's concerns about Wall Street's exploitation of the individual worker as a means to examine the periodical marketplace demands on the writer for a sentimental style.

By conflating the attitudes of *Putnam's* editors toward the problems of industrialization and toward narrative method, Melville represented and yet innovated on magazine conventions. The more favorable policies of *Putnam's* provided this author with a context that encouraged creativity. "Bartleby, the Scrivener" blended sentiment and social critique in such an effective manner that it rekindled the writer's popularity with flagging supporters. His depiction of the power struggles involved in the complex relations between employer and employee, narrator and narrative, contributed to the story's popularity and fascination for *Putnam's* readers. In a letter to Evert Duyckinck, Richard Henry Dana proclaimed that "'Bartleby' . . . shows no common insight."[21] Indeed, Melville's insights into the literary uses of magazine conventions and their impact on readers' perspectives of society, as well as into the nature of narrative itself, produced one of the most widely read and discussed tales in American literary history.

The act of placing Melville's "Benito Cereno," written for one of the most intellectual and politically progressive magazines of mid-nineteenth-century America, into its original publishing context reveals its link to magazine practices. The political opinions debated by *Putnam's* editors throughout numerous articles, essays, and stories on the questions of racial equality, the institution of slavery, and expansionism find thematic and ideological analogues in "Benito Cereno." A clear affinity existed between Melville's probing study of the nature of American political dominance in the Americas and the editorial politics of the monthly.

Putnam's promised American commentary on both national and international affairs. The publisher, George Palmer Putnam; the chief editor, Charles F. Briggs; and the contributors were closely aligned to the antislavery movement. Briggs, popularly known as Harry Franco, was an outspoken critic of slavery and a staunch supporter of various abolitionists. Writers such as Richard Burleigh Kimball, Parke Godwin (from the radical *Democratic Review* of the 1840s), and Frederick Law Olmsted (one of the founders of the still-extant, liberal weekly paper *The Nation*) consistently spoke out against poverty, slavery, racial bigotry, and expansionism. Godwin proclaimed that *Putnam's* was "profoundly stirred by these agitations of the outer world. For the first time in the history of our higher periodicals, its managers had stepped down from their snowy pedestals to take part in the rabble and scuffle of the streets."[22]

The political views expressed in *Putnam's* were enormously influential. So powerful—and convincing—were these writers that they contributed significantly by the end of the decade to changing the political stance of their competitor, *Harper's*. George William Curtis, who eventually switched editorial positions to become the political editor of *Harper's*, was instrumental in changing the orientation of that politically conservative monthly to reflect the liberalism of the by-then defunct *Putnam's*. The political essays and articles on American interventionism and racial equality written by Kimball, Olmsted, and Godwin were referred to in popular literary culture through the end of the nineteenth century.

Yet *Putnam's* did not merely editorialize a particular stance. Articles, essays, and stories analyzed and evaluated the variety of perspectives that comprised a particular issue. Parke Godwin, author of more than thirty pieces in *Putnam's*, employed this analytical style in his political essays. For example, in "Our Parties and Politics," Godwin first described the different parties and platforms that were currently active in the mid-1850s. But in discussing the ideological implications of these platforms, he pointed out and often severely criticized the contradictions in, for example, believing in individual liberty but reserving it for whites only.

Putnam's editors established their progressive political stance by leading the first number of the magazine with a highly controversial plea against current American foreign policy. *Putnam's* followed this position with a series of articles that clearly denounced an American foreign policy that would support government intervention and expansionism, themes repeated in "Benito Cereno."

Melville continued the practices of Godwin, Kimball, Briggs, and Curtis by submitting a series of tales to the monthly, particularly "The Encantadas," "Benito Cereno," and "The Bell-Tower," which questioned, probed, and ultimately challenged sentimental depictions of political interventionism as brotherly assistance and slavery as paternal nurturing. In "Benito Cereno," the author subtly examines these pressing political and social issues that faced the United States in the mid-1850s by playing off sentimental views, represented in the character of Amasa Delano, against the political criticism of the progressive magazine. Melville portrayed and criticized an American ideology that was based on "piratical" appropriation of an enslaved people for "material gain," dramatized both through Benito Cereno's relation to the ship's "cargo" and Amasa Delano's sentimentalized attitudes toward slavery. The author's articulation of America's economic impetus for expansion corroborated the perspective offered by Kimball's articles on the Caribbean, editorials by Briggs, and essays by Curtis and Godwin. Melville's contributions to *Putnam's* represented and supported the positions of the monthly on social and political issues.

The anti-sentimental stance of *Putnam's* pervaded even the nonfictional contributions. While a frequent use of superlatives and exclamations marked *Harper's* sentimental travel literature, *Putnam's* travel writings provided acute political analyses of the places under discussion and questioned conventional views. A writer in *Putnam's* described *Harper's* travel writers as the "worn-out debauchees of Europe who travel to get rid of themselves or to find a new sensation." *Putnam's* travel writers, on the other hand, "estimate [all novelties] at their true value with an unerring practical sagacity."[23] While J. Ross Browne and others published travel pieces in *Harper's* that simply cashed in on readers' conventional expectations, Thoreau, Curtis, and others published in *Putnam's* acute analyses of the areas and people under their scrutiny. Far from being the islands of enchantment that their name suggested, Melville's "The Encantadas" participated in this critical tradition.

Another pressing national issue for the editors of the monthly concerned what they called the lack of a truly *American* novel. Responding to the lament that "our first novel of [American] society has yet to be written" (*Putnam's*, January 1853, 102), Melville shaped his next work to center what the editors at *Putnam's* called the "idea" and "pulse" of America through his use of American place, the Mississippi River, and the persona of what critics of the day referred to as "an original American idea"—the confidence man. While *The Confidence-Man* (1857) was hailed by a reviewer in *Putnam's* as a "thoroughly American story," the journal went bankrupt two weeks after the publication of Melville's latest work, which seriously affected the author's interest in writing for the periodical marketplace, opening the way to his thirty-odd-year interest in the "less traveled" path of poetry.

The mid-nineteenth-century literary marketplace provided a profitable, creative, and aesthetically rich framework for Melville's writing as shown by the large amount of work he published—over eighteen novels and short stories—in just one decade. Recovery of the conditions of the literary marketplace provides key insights not only into the motivations, compositional approaches, styles, and intended audiences of particular authors, such as Herman Melville, but into the nature of literary creativity itself. As his formulation of genius indicates, Melville was a master at reading and innovating forms. In this light, we can think of this author as a responsive genius who employed popular forms to create a "correspondent coloring" between his own literary interests and his cultural moment.

NOTES

1. Melville, Review of Nathaniel Hawthorne's *Mosses from an Old Manse*, *Literary World*, 17 August 1850, 126.

2. For a detailed study of the relation between marketplace conditions and the works of Herman Melville, see Sheila Post, *Correspondent Colorings: Melville in the Marketplace* (Amherst: University of Massachusetts Press, 1996). I am indebted to the University of Massachusetts Press for granting me permission to rely on material from my book for this chapter.

3. Quoted in Kathleen Tillotson, *Novels of the 1840s* (Oxford: Clarendon Press, 1954), 16.

4. Evert Duyckinck, *Literary World*, 22 November 1851; Review of Melville's *Moby-Dick*, *John Bull*, 25 October 1851.

5. Margaret Fuller, Review of Melville's *Typee*, *New York Tribune*, 4 April 1846.

6. Charles Briggs, Review of Melville's *Typee*, *Anti-Slavery Standard*, 27 May 1847; *Columbian Magazine*, June 1847.

7. *New York Mirror*, 13 April 1849.

8. Harrison Hayford, "Historical Note I," *Moby-Dick; or, The Whale*, 1851; rpt, (Evanston and Chicago: Norwestern University Press and The Newberry Library, 1968), 583; James McIntosh, "The Mariner's Multiple Quest," in *New Essays on Moby-Dick*, ed. Richard Brodhead (Cambridge: Cambridge University Press, 1986), 26; George R. Stewart, "The Two *Moby-Dicks*," *American Literature* (1954): 414–48; Larzer Ziff, "Shakespeare in Melville's America," in *New Perspectives on Melville*, ed. Faith Pullen (Edinborgh: Edinburgh University Press, 1978), 55.

9. Edward Bulwer-Lytton, "On the Different Kinds of Prose Fiction with Some Apology for the Fiction of the Author," in *The Disowned* (London: Bently, 1835), 1: i–ix; quoted in Edwin M. Eigner, *The Metaphysical Novel in England and America* (Berkeley: The University of California Press, 1978), 1–12.

10. David Masson, "British Novelists since Scott, Lecture IV," in Masson, *British Novelists and Their Styles: Being a Critical Sketch of the History of British Prose* (Cambridge: Macmillan, 1859), 214–27; partially reprinted in Edwin Eigner and George J. Worth, eds., *Victorian Criticism of the Novel* (New York: Cambridge University Press, 1985), 148–58; Masson, "British Novelists," 275–76.

11. Masson, "British Novelists," 287–88.

12. Richard Burleigh Kimball, *St. Leger; or, The Threads of Life* (London: Richard Bentley, 1850), 232.

13. "Review of Mayo's *The Berber*," *Harper's Magazine*, (December 1850).

14. Sylvester Judd, *Margaret: A Tale of the Real and Ideal, Blight and Bloom* (Boston: Jordan and Wiley, 1845), 240.

15. *New Haven Daily Palladium*, 17 November 1851.

16. William Kirkand, "British and American Monthlies," *Godey's Lady's Book*, June 1845, 271.

17. Washington Irving, "Editor's Column," *Knickerbocker*, March 1839.

18. Robert Bonner, "Editor's Column," *New York Ledger*, 19 May 1855.

19. Fred Louis Pattee, *The Feminine Fifties* (New York: Macmillian, 1940), 196; quoted in Susan Coultrap-McQuinn, *Doing Literary Business: American Women Writers in the Nineteenth Century* (Chapel Hill: University of North Carolina Press, 1990), 75.

20. *American Publisher's Circular and Literary Gazette*, 31 May, 1856.

21. Quoted in M. Thomas Inge, *Bartleby the Inscrutable*, (Hamden, Conn.: Archon Books, 1979), 31.

22. Parke Godwin, *George William Curtis: A Commerative Address Delivered before the Century Association, New York, December 17, 1892* (New York: Harpers and Bros., 1892), 29–30.

23. "Review of *The Homes of American Authors*," *Putman's*, January, 1853.

Without the Pale

Melville and Ethnic Cosmopolitanism

Timothy Marr

Served up à la Pole, or à la Moor, à la
Ladrone, or à la Yankee, that good dish,
man, still delights me; . . . I never
weary of . . . smacking my lips over
this racy creature, man, continually.
—*The Confidence-Man*

And thus, with our counterlikes and
dislikes, most of us man-of-war's-men
harmoniously dovetail into each other,
and, by our very points of opposition,
unite in a clever whole, like the parts of
a Chinese puzzle. But as, in a Chinese
puzzle many pieces are hard to place,
so there are some unfortunate fellows
who can never slip into their proper an-
gles, and thus the whole puzzle becomes a puzzle indeed, which is the
precise condition of the greatest puzzle in the world—this man-of-war
world itself.
—*White-Jacket*

Why, ever since Adam, who has got to
the meaning of this great allegory—
the world?
—Herman Melville to Nathaniel
Hawthorne, November 7, 1851

After four weeks at sea, nineteen-year-old Herman Melville
arrived in England on the Fourth of July 1839 to celebrate Independence Day on British soil. The real independence he experienced, however, emerged from the ways that the worldly vitality of Liverpool's docks contrasted with the confinement of
shipboard life and the conventional morality of his upbringing in
provincial America. Open-eyed Melville was struck by the numbers of the poor and the prostitutes who worked the streets of
the world's busiest maritime port. He was even more fascinated
by the freedoms enjoyed by dark-skinned sailors in a city whose
wealth had been generated from the slave trade. This comparative equality made Melville more aware of how the strict social
lines of his own homeland had preserved slavery in the South,
fostered poverty in the North, and established hierarchies that
separated Americans. When he wrote about this journey ten
years later in his novel *Redburn*, one long sentence defined the
process of how Melville's travels had inaugurated his cosmopolitan awakening to a greater vision of American allegiance:

> Being so young and inexperienced then, and unconsciously
> swayed by those local and social prejudices, that are the mar-
> ring of most men, and from which, for the mass, there seems
> no possible escape; at first I was surprised that a colored man
> should be treated as he is in this town; but a little reflection
> showed that, after all, it was but recognizing his claims to hu-
> manity and *normal equality*; so that, in some things, we Ameri-
> cans leave to other countries the carrying out of the principle
> that stands at the head of our Declaration of Independence.
> (202; emphasis added)

Melville grew up with Dutch roots on his mother's side in New York, a place that was developing—through industry, commerce, and immigration—into a maritime hub that would in his lifetime replace both Liverpool and London as the quintessential modern city. As a young New Yorker eager to experience the world, Melville was well situated to observe how an emergent transnational capitalism was drafting and mixing various peoples, including himself, into its system. Melville's later travels among the diverse crews of the whaling industry and the navy— as well as his exposure to Pacific cultures, European countries, and eastern Mediterranean societies—confronted him with a puzzling array of cultural practices that forever disrupted the sway of "local and social prejudices." Melville's father, Allan, was a man of the world of the post-Revolution generation who traveled widely in Europe and spoke fluent French in his business of importing fine goods. After Allan's economic and psychological ruin, however, his son rejected his commercial project of supplying the upper class. Herman Melville chose to profess a more critical cosmopolitanism: to expose through his prose the nakedness of aristocratic superiority and the hypocrisy of a nation founded on equality but thriving on slavery, exploitation, and dispossession. In a comment on the horrendous conditions that captains allowed in the steerage of ships bringing emigrants from Ireland to America, Melville noted what was a common refrain of his cultural criticism: "we may have civilized bodies, and yet barbarous souls" (*Redburn* 293).

Unlike many Americans of his time, Melville refused to repress his exposure to the enigma of human variety. Instead, he actively celebrated it as a fresh and original dimension of a new world literature that lay claim to a more global genealogy. Melville used the shipboard society of multicultural sailors and the phenomenon of the gam—the coincidental meeting of two ships at sea—to dramatize the continuing need for liberation from the conventions he called "King Common-Place" (*Clarel* 1.34.24). In one short chapter in *Moby-Dick* called "Midnight, Forecastle," Melville individualizes the crew of the *Pequod* by introducing Anglo, African, and Native American members from Connecticut, Nantucket, Long Island, and Martha's Vineyard, but he also includes sailors from England, Ireland, Denmark, Holland, France, Portugal, and Spain; from Iceland, Malta, Sicily, the Isle of Man, the Azores, the Cape Verdes, and Tahiti; and from China, India, and Africa (173–78). By accentuating the worldly diversity of his crew, Melville "federated" a broad latitude of literary characters that empowered his challenge to the ethnocentric claims of universality held by the supposedly civilized. Similarly, in the chapter "The Street," Melville portrays the world's seaports at mid-century as matrices of migration where startling intercultural encounters "make a stranger stare." Melville confounds the sight of cannibals in New Bedford with the arrival of green "bumpkins" from the interior of New England to destabilize this sense of strangeness, completing the circle by noting that "at Bombay, in the Apollo Green, live Yankees have often scared the natives" (*Moby-Dick* 31). Capitalizing upon such an exotic perspective, Melville wrote in the capacity of a citizen of the world to deconstruct the discriminations that Americans had devised to formulate the foreign. In a writing career that continued from the publication of his first novel in 1846 until his death forty-five years later, Melville registered a global affiliation with the ethnic, the alien, and the other as expansive and creative as that of any American author not only of his time but also of our own.

Melville's ethnic cosmopolitanism represented a world view at odds with the emergent "science" of ethnology that gained prominence in his time, a discourse that legitimated social conventions of religious and racial exclusion. The "American School" of Samuel G. Morton, Josiah C. Nott, and George R. Gliddon confidently asserted a system of polygenetic creation that circumscribed different peoples, especially Africans, as not only inherently unequal races but into spheres so separate in origin as to efface their common humanity.[1] Melville's deeper discrimination was to understand the social necessity of transcending the hierarchical categories that relegated other humans to subordinate positions. By figuring cultural difference as a disguise that obscured an essential human unity, Melville marked ethnicity itself as an ethical field through which he could test the allegiance of his readers and measure the sincerity of the new nation's ethos of equality.

In his progressive attempts to incorporate ethnic characters as essential elements of a new national literature, however, Melville remained hampered by limitations of intercultural understanding and political efficacy. The relatively short duration of his travels and his inability to speak the languages of many of the peoples he met during them were a measure of his lack of access to the interior cultural landscapes of others. "Sailors only go *round* the world, without going *into* it," he acknowledged in *Redburn* (133). The many proto-ethnographies and travel narratives in English that he read to educate himself were sometimes written to help subjugate the same people they set out to describe. Melville's philanthropy, therefore, suffered the disability of not being informed by reliable anthropology, a field whose problematic parameters had not yet been established. As a result, his commitment to human intersubjectivity was premised more upon strategic and philosophical desire than developed from actual intercultural dialogue. Melville's engagement with the ethnicities addressed in this chapter—Polynesians, Asians, Jews, Native Americans, and Africans—remained largely an imaginative one, and this reality rendered his characters into allegorical presences whose bodies were sometimes subject to the very acts of colonization that Melville had hoped to criticize. However, Melville found an epistemological escape from such bondage by portraying Americans themselves, including many of his own narrators, as ethnic creatures marked by the codes they had invented to malign others. Melville acknowledged, perhaps most fittingly in his characterization of the Cosmopolitan himself in *The Confidence-Man*, that human diversity was an ultimate condition that could never be ethically embodied in a literary character, nor imagined from one authorial or national perspective.

Melville's cosmopolitan imagination nevertheless remains instructive despite these limitations. The special courage of his creativity rests upon his literary attempts to bridge and ultimately to embody the alienation imposed by alterity. For readers approaching the complexity of Melville's representations of (and ruminations on) human multiplicity, it is important to understand that his symbolic use of ethnic difference served dual ends that were difficult to reconcile. On one hand, the democratic dignity of human diversity empowered him with rich resources for a romantic and redemptive philanthropy. But on the other hand, Melville also figured ethnicity as the embodied site of human strife that rehearsed the tragic misanthropy of how peoples emphasized their differences to the point of violating the sanctity of human unity. Such a double consciousness explains how Melville figured savagery not as an essential ethnic pedigree but rather as any ideological practice that willfully rejected a fundamentally human allegiance. In this complex way Melville salvaged ethnic difference as a primary resource for his cosmopolitan criticism.

"A Mutual, Joint-Stock World, in All Meridians"

When Nathaniel Hawthorne reviewed Melville's first novel, *Typee*, in 1846, he commented on Melville's "freedom of view—it would be too harsh to call it laxity of principle—which renders him tolerant of codes or morals that may be little in accordance with our own."[2] In fact, Melville's perspective of tolerance was a principle that challenged Hawthorne's smug propriety, which affirmed instead what he called "that firm creedless faith that embraces the spheres" (*Redburn* 291). Melville's principled cosmopolitanism was philosophically fostered by four major intellectual currents of his time: a Christian belief in the power of scriptural ethics, a classical tradition of Greek and Roman humanism, a republican ideology of democratic equality, and an Enlightenment philanthropy skeptical of any cultural claim to absolute truth. Melville drew on each of these resources to found a compelling vision of common human ancestry and destiny. He reserved the full measure of his skepticism and republicanism for exposing the fallacy of "fancied superiority" that led people to forget their fraternity (*White-Jacket* 277). As a "multiform pilgrim species" (*Confidence-Man* 9), humanity was understood by Melville to be both theologically connected in its creation and genetically unified in its evolution, and he railed against any uncharitable denial of another person's natural affiliation in that family. "For man, like God, abides the same / Always," Melville averred, "through all the variety / Of woven garments to the frame" (*Clarel* 4.21.71-3). Reading his religious lessons in the actions of the world, Melville hoped that literature might evoke a spiritual fellowship that might honor the potential of the human spirit by celebrating its rich cultural diversity.

Melville rooted this cosmopolitan ethos in the creation story of Adam and Eve. His world view was informed by the idea of monogenesis—that all humans are descended from one set of parents and therefore share the same race—and he therefore felt a kinship with the "billions of posterity" issuing from this common genealogy (*Piazza Tales* 141). "Like envoys from all Adam's race, / Mixed men of various nations pace," Melville wrote concerning the variety of worshipers he saw convened in Jerusalem (*Clarel* 1.41.49–50). The narrator of Melville's third book, *Mardi* (1849), assured by this essential unity of species, felt liberated to exhort his readers to rise above ethnic chauvinism:

> [I]n antediluvian days, the sons of God did verily wed with our mothers, the irresistible daughters of Eve. Thus all generations are blended: and heaven and earth of one kin . . . the nations and families, flocks and folds of the earth; one and all, brothers in essence—oh, be we then brothers indeed! . . . Away with our stares and grimaces. The New Zealander's tattooing is not a prodigy; nor the Chinaman's ways an enigma. No custom is strange; no creed is absurd; no foe, but who will in the end prove a friend. In heaven, at last, our good, old, white-haired father Adam will greet all alike, and sociality forever prevail. (12–13)

Melville's philanthropic vision here is simultaneously nostalgic and millennial. He resurrects a family reunion in Eden at which seemingly alien ethnicities are once again reassembled around the same social table. Melville erases the penalty of the Fall through a whole-hearted resumption of pleasures at once domestic, worldly, and heavenly, with Adam reinstalled as symposiarch. Refusing to believe in a "Temperance Heaven" (*Correspondence* 191), Melville often transfigured moments of genial leisure into emblems of celestial delight. For example, in his poem "Herba

Santa," the sociality of shared smoking gathers the "bristling clans of Adam" around "one hearthstone of the world."[3]

In his most optimistic moments Melville gloried in the belief that, despite the fall from Eden, humans remained divine in their pedigree and familial in their relation. In *Moby-Dick*, Melville praises the "Great Democratic God" whose "just Spirit of Equality . . . has spread out one royal mantle of humanity over all my kind!" (117), and he emphasizes in *Redburn* that "none of his [God's] children are without the pale of his care" (140). Melville's inclusive cosmopolitanism endowed him with a religious view of the consanguinity of human kind that underlay the "infinite fraternity of feeling" that he felt while laboring with fellow crew members or consorting with Nathaniel Hawthorne (*Correspondence* 212). In his long poem *Clarel*, published during the nation's centennial in 1876, Melville created an expansive cast of ethnic characters who enabled him to extend the biblical basis of his vision by affirming an "intersympathy of creeds" that incorporated all who held Adam as ancestor (1.5.207). Melville's cosmopolitan vision generated a process of ethnic creativity that was itself Adamic in its originality, one that helped him to loosen his attachment to more restrictive cultural norms.

Melville's emphatic and empathic humanism served as more than artistic inspiration alone. He also projected it as a millennial aspiration for the nation as he envisioned the redemptive role of democracy in recovering the primitive vitality of the species. In his famous review "Hawthorne and His Mosses," he noted: "This world is as young today as when it was created" and compared the Vermont dew on his feet with "Eden's to Adam's" (*Piazza Tales* 246).[4] Melville has been allied with the group of New York critics called Young America, who called for the emergence of the United States from its anxious postcolonial relationship with British culture. In doing so, Melville privileged the United States as the earthly location for a multicultural paradise that drew upon the whole world for an American legacy. "[O]ur blood is as the flood of the Amazon, made up of a thousand noble currents all pouring into one," Melville claimed in *Redburn*. "We are not a nation, so much as a world" (169). By imagining his own cosmopolitan vision as national destiny, Melville was complicit with the American expansionism of his age for, as Wai-chee Dimock has argued, Melville's "literary individualism is always imperially articulated."[5] Melville echoed the rhetoric of manifest destiny when he uncritically announced in *White-Jacket* that "national selfishness is unbounded philanthropy" (151). His aspirations for the nation, however, were not founded on defining the nation's promise through superiority or isolation. Melville was exuberant about the pull of this new world on immigrants and figured the Americas as the earthly field for the hybrid cultivation of cosmopolitanism, such as when he prophesied that "[o]n this Western Hemisphere all tribes and people are forming into one federated whole; there is a future which shall see the estranged children of Adam restored as to the old hearth-stone in Eden" (*Redburn* 169).

Melville's most renowned celebration of this restoration of the estranged takes place in a bed at an inn in New Bedford where Ishmael's engagement with Queequeg generates the very plot of *Moby-Dick*. Melville designs Queequeg to offend convention: he is a cannibal, an idolater, a Sabbath-breaker, and a man of such hideous appearance as to set any racial distinction in gentler relief. Yet underneath Queequeg's repulsive surface, Ishmael discovers "a bosom friend" who expresses kindness, charity, and heroism—virtues that render him a savior in savage form. Although Queequeg's cultural roots are in Polynesia, Melville announces his cosmopolitanism by his mythical native land of Kokovoko, his Congo idol, his ritualistic Ramadan, and his unearthly purple-yellow skin color (whose squares he compares to farms in the Andes). It is as the epitome of the alien, then, that Melville both ushers him into his text and makes him the symbolic bridegroom of his narrator. This collaboration is dramatized in a chapter called "The Monkey Rope," where Ishmael stands on the *Pequod* holding a rope tied tautly to Queequeg's waist as the harpooner perilously strips the shark-surrounded whale carcass on which he stands. The lines of Melville's prose affiliate the American and the alien in a "Siamese connexion" that links all people in a common destiny. Melville grasps the emergence of the great nineteenth-century development of evolutionary thought by figuring the monkey rope as a cord that unites all people in a system of complementary labor even as they all were umbilically linked to their mothers (319–20). Through the antic kinship of Queequeg and Ishmael, Melville enacts his hybrid philosophy, "It's a mutual, joint-stock world, in all meridians" (62).

"De God Wat Made Shark Must Be One Dam Ingin"

Highlighting these selective moments of interethnic unity, mostly expressed in Melville's early fictional works, emphasizes only his most manic realizations of romantic universalism. While humans ideally shared a noble genealogy, the grinding anguish of human strife and division were dark realities that Melville could never ignore for long. In Melville's view there were two Adams: the robust primitive in the garden exulting in the creative pleasure of progeniture and the fallen vagabond in earthly exile experiencing a world of woe ending only in death. As an outcast species, humans inherited the crushing dislocation that had been heaped upon Adam. With Eden's joys but a faint and fleshless fantasy, the dwellers of the earth became fragmented into "isolatos"—lost and poor "sons of Adam" who, like the forlorn Bartleby, can only inspire "fraternal melancholy" (*Piazza Tales* 28).

   Among the woes afflicting a lapsed humanity was the legacy of racism that splintered the species into antagonistic ethnicities. The mark of Cain and the curse of Babel were biblical markers of how Scripture had sectored the circle of human solidarity into separate camps. After an African and a Spanish sailor face off with knives on the forecastle during the midnight storm in *Moby-Dick*, the soothsaying Manx sailor can only bemoan the madness of creation: "Why then, God, mad'st thou the ring?" (178). Cain's curse—that humans were predisposed to violence against each other despite their divine "brotherhood"—was a central theological paradox that bedeviled Melville for his entire career. Melville testified that "we find the head-waters of our fraternity in nothing short of the great gods themselves" (363), but he knew that human suffering also sprang from the same "sourceless primogeniture" (464). It is through Ahab that Melville most fully charts this countergenealogy of earthly misery. Melville clearly noted in the margins of his copy of the works of Milton: "the fall of Adam did not so much prove him weak, as that God had made him so."[6] When Melville wrote that "the ineffaceable, sad birthmark in the brow of man is but the stamp of sorrow in the signers" (464), he testified that both the constitution of mankind and the Constitution of the nation seemed compromised by a lack of charity for fellow humans that left all "damned in the midst of paradise" (167). Melville's spiteful rage against this fate is dramatized in Ahab's tragically compassionate affiliation with Pip, the African American cabin boy driven insane after he fell out of a whaleboat and was abandoned by his fellow crew members in the middle of the ocean.[7] Ahab sees in Pip's desertion a living embodiment of how "the omniscient gods [are] oblivious of suffering man" and splices his hand with the mad lad in defiance of such heartless injustice (*Moby-Dick* 522).

Melville was unwilling to break the circle of unity and took on the burden of its contentious diversity as a central and inescapable conundrum of the human condition. He dismissed the "white man's burden" of uplifting the barbarian and replaced it with the ironic and critical mission of marking the whole world as ethnic in the barbarism of its fallen nature. The curse of Ham to labor for the benefit of others was not confined to Africans alone but afflicted all. "Who aint a slave?" (6) confesses Ishmael, himself named for the son of a bondswoman, who retorts "as though a white man were anything more dignified than a whitewashed negro" (60). He protested the Protestant missionary enterprise because he believed that Christianity rested on an unearned superiority and was itself in need of salvation. Hence, his cosmic supplication in *White-Jacket*: "Are there no Moravians in the Moon, that not a missionary has yet visited this poor pagan planet of ours, to civilize civilization and christianize Christendom?" (267). The crucifixion of Christ—Melville called him "the Second Adam" and "man's fraternal Lord" (*Clarel* 1.5.83; 2.6.36)—powerfully embodied the tragedy of how humans sacrificed their hopes for divine redemption to the idols of their own imaginations. "'Twas *human*, that unanimous cry," Melville wrote about such a universal betrayal. "'We're fixed to hate him—crucify!'"

(2.3.145–46). Melville's staged sacrifice of this second Adam in the form of his final protagonist, Billy Budd, epitomizes the fratricidal fate of humans who, in the service of some self-serving and limited cause or established social institution, choose violence against others over the affirmation of their human oneness.

"The Common Continent": Melville's Ethnic Federalism

On July 9, 1842, twenty-one-year-old Melville declared his own independence when he and a fellow shipmate abandoned ship and ran away into the groves of Nukahiva in the Marquesan islands. The Pacific Ocean was Melville's new world: it formed the matrix of his literary career and merits a prominent focus here because it transformed Melville's understanding of cultural difference. His journeys in the South Seas in 1841–1843 enabled him to experience not only a symbolic return to paradise envied by many of his contemporaries but, more important, to develop a critical latitude from which he assailed the claims of Western superiority. Melville was appalled by the "remorseless" cruelties (*Typee* 15) inflicted on Polynesians through the coming of "snivelization" (*Redburn* 101) and accused the white man in his first book of being "the most ferocious animal on the face of the earth" (*Typee* 125). His trenchant sarcasm is evident in this lecture from 1857 on why Polynesians possess an "almost instinctive hate of the white man:"

> This may of course be a mere prejudice of these unlettered savages, for have not our traders always treated them with brotherly affection? Who has ever heard of a vessel sustaining the honor of the Christian flag and the spirit of the Christian Gospel by opening its batteries in indiscriminate massacre upon some poor little village on the seaside—splattering the torn bamboo huts with blood and brains of women and children, defenseless and innocent? (*Piazza Tales* 415–16)

Written just prior to the California gold rush that drew the nation's attention to its western shores, Melville's first fictional works helped to orient critical attention to the effects of French, British, and American expansion into the islands of the Pacific. American commerce in the Pacific, which began during the China trade in the late eighteenth century, resulted in some of the earliest engagements in extraterritorial imperialism for the new nation, events that preceded by a century the annexation of Pacific islands as the spoils of the Spanish-American War. American captain Joseph Ingraham visited the Marquesas while en route to China in 1791 and appropriated them as symbolic American territory by naming them the "Washington Group." Commodore David Porter stopped for repairs in Nukahiva (which he named "Madison's Island") during the War of 1812 and initiated the first attempts by the U.S. Navy to subdue Pacific Asians with military violence, bloodying the very valley that Melville would visit in 1842. Thirty years later, Melville created a disenchanted veteran who ruthlessly indicted Anglo Americans for having inherited the colonial brutality of Spain:

The Anglo-Saxons—lacking grace
To win the love of any race;
Hated by myriads dispossessed
Of rights—the Indians East and West.
These pirates of the sphere! grave looters—
Grave, canting, Mammonite freebooters,
Who in the name of Christ and Trade
(Oh, bucklered forehead of the brass!)
Deflower the world's last sylvan glade. (*Clarel* 4.9.117–25)

Melville's exposure to this disgracing of indigenous peoples took place in the crucible of cross-cultural contact initiated by the emergence and growth of the whaling industry. Whaling vessels constituted the first regular transpacific traffic, and captains dropped anchor in Pacific harbors to load provisions and to recruit crew members. In these ports they found willing hands in the many natives who agreed to ship for lower pay and shorter spans of duty. These *kannakas* (from *Te Enata*, the Polynesian term for "the men" that Westerners adopted as an ethnic marker) had reputations for their bravery and nautical skills.[8]

Through his fictional portrayal of kannakas in the whaling industry, Melville dramatized the exploitation, alienation, and disillusionment that left natives adrift in the wake of the growing
engine of global capitalism. The variety of types that Melville
represented in his fiction offers an insightful survey of the varied
responses of Asian and Pacific islanders to this intercultural encounter and an open window into Melville's dual modalities of
understanding ethnic difference.

Melville most graphically illustrates the degrading effects of
Western contact in his second book, *Omoo*, by juxtaposing two
vignettes of the Polynesian tradition of the *tayo*—the customary
friendship extended to visitors, which Melville translates as
"bosom friend." At the end of part 1, the narrator tells of a visit
to an isolated island and describes his tayo there—a handsome
youth named Poky who gives the narrator supplies and souvenirs
without demanding any exchange in return. Poky's selfless devotion nostalgically evokes the warmly welcoming original response of Polynesians to the European explorers (152–53). Even in
his diminutive name, Poky embodies the image of innocence
that French writers such as De Bougainville, Diderot, and Rousseau had invented out of their encounters in Polynesia. Melville
acceded to the myth of the noble savage when he argued that
"the virtues of humanity . . . flourish in greater abundance
and attain greater strength among many barbarous peoples"
(*Typee* 202).

In his first two books, he portrayed the infiltration of Euro-
American missionaries and traders as a "fatal embrace" that rav-
ished the innocent peoples and pristine landscapes of the Pacific
by commercializing its cultures (*Typee* 26). At the beginning of
part 2 of *Omoo*, Melville draws a contrasting depiction of a mercenary tayo named Kooloo that demonstrates how Western materialism tempted South Sea islanders to forgo their "authentic
Edens" (*Poems* 295). Although converted by missionaries, Kooloo
employs hospitality only as a strategic extension of his own
greed. After "sponging" the sailors of their possessions, Kooloo
then breaks off his friendships with them, leading Melville to call
him a "man of the world" (157–58). Melville uses these opposing
stories to divide the two parts of his book and to represent the

fall of Tahitian culture, which is the major theme of *Omoo*. As Melville would note in his next book, *Mardi*, "nothing can exceed the cupidity of the Polynesian, when, through partial commerce with the whites, his eyes are opened to his nakedness, and he perceives that *in some things* they are richer than himself" (74; emphasis added).

Melville looks through these opened eyes to register a tragic sense of the personal loss experienced by those Polynesians who perilously agree to be conscripted into the whaling industry. Wymontoo in *Omoo* naively volunteers to join the ship in exchange for a change of clothes and a pipe of tobacco (while a friend of his signs up for ten biscuits and twenty nails, two of which he immediately uses as ear ornaments [28]). Wymontoo's contract is presented as a Faustian bargain through which he sells his soul for the illusory promise of Western materialism—what Melville sardonically called "gewgaw refinement" (*Typee* 189n). After a night of sea-sickness, Wymontoo is baptized with a bucket of salt water and renamed "Luff," a reference to a flapping sail in a losing wind (34). He lapses into melancholy nostalgia, dreaming of the bamboo hut he has left behind. When he spies the clouded peaks of Tahiti in the distance, he believes he is returning to his home beneath the Marquesan mountain of Hivarhoo, only to sink into more dismal depression after discovering his delusion (65). This degradation is also displayed by the "Tahitan" sailor in *Moby-Dick*, who dreams of the same peaks that fooled Wymontoo. His nostalgic vision is so strong that he sees dancing girls in the commotion of the waves and sees his only home as the mat on which he sits. Woven from the green foliage from the island he left behind, this mat is now symbolically "worn and wilted," causing the sailor to ruefully reflect on their common fate, "Ah me!—not thou nor I can bear the change!" (176).

Ishmael in *Moby-Dick* identifies with this loss and translates such dislocation and nostalgia into a universal spiritual condition when he counsels his readers not to abandon the "one insular Tahiti" that lies "in the soul of man . . . full of peace and joy, but encompassed by all the horrors of the half known life" (274). Melville positions his own narrator as a Tahitian Adam exiled from his island Eden, the reader's purity as that possessed by a pagan Polynesian, and the whole colonial enterprise as figuratively fallen and literally lost at sea. All of these alienated vagabonds have pushed off from their isles and can never return to the pristine paradise they left behind.

Some, however, muster up enough courage to return for the patriotic protection of their endangered homelands. *Omoo's* Marbonna, who left his home in the Marquesas on a French whaler, scorns the degeneracy of the colonized Tahitians as he labors to purchase twenty muskets to bring home with him to arm his countrymen against a similar fate. But he is too late. The importation of weapons would itself taint Nukahiva with Western corruption. A more remarkable and successful man is Marnoo, a tabooed Marquesan whose beauty and eloquence lead Melville to call him "the Polynesian Apollo" (*Typee* 135). As Melville's earliest model of cosmopolitan power, Marnoo is empowered by his social affiliations in Nukahiva and the experiential capital he has gained shipping as a seaman to Sydney to function as a transcultural broker. He embodies the local knowledge that Melville is unable to access and is instrumental in orchestrating, with the help of another taboo kannaka named Karakoee, the release of Tommo in exchange for cloth, a musket, and powder. The fact that Tommo bequeaths this musket to his loyal valet, Kory-Kory, symbolizes the fact that this exchange has empowered both the native resolve for resistance and the expansion of Euro-American corruption.

Melville's emergence as an author is premised on his abilities to embody through his narration this native capacity to negotiate cultural taboos. Melville found Polynesia, literally "place of many islands," representative of the fecundity of human creativity. In his third novel, *Mardi*, he literally compressed the whole world into cosmic archipelagoes generated by this oceanic imagination (in which the United States is portrayed as the islands of Vivenza). Melville's depiction of Samoa the Upoluan in *Mardi* in particular dramatizes the symbolic use of the tattooed savage as an emblem of exoticism. With a knife lodged in the lobe of his drooping left ear and a well-polished nail perforating the cartilage of his nose, the Upoluan is "a very devil to behold" (98). But

Melville looks beyond his savage difference, celebrating the "soul in his eye; looking out upon you there, like somebody in him" (99). Indeed Samoa's most spectacular role in *Mardi* is to conduct Melville into his flights of creative imagination. Once arrived in the allegorical islands of Mardi, Samoa becomes "the expounder of all things heathenish and obscure" (172), and it is through his voice that Melville launches into the philosophical disquisitions that characterize the rest of the book (296–97). After this catalyzing role, Samoa becomes a liability, and Melville crudely sacrifices him in favor of his allegorical Mardians—Yoomi, Mohi, and Babbalanja—who are free to philosophize with more orientalized openness because they are less ethnically embodied. When Melville evokes in *Moby-Dick* the mythical lands of Queequeg's Kokovoko (55) and the island of Tranque in the Arsacides (449)—and notes the extravagantly spelled ethnicities of "the Feegeeans, Tongatobooarrs, Erromanggoans, Panannghians and Brighggians" (31) (the latter perhaps an inventive punning on the word *brigands*)—he exemplifies how the ethnic generativity of Polynesia continued to stimulate his creativity.

On a more critical register, however, Melville also used the presence of Polynesians in American ships and cities to parody the foolish habit of universalizing cultural pretensions. In *White-Jacket*, the book that immediately preceded *Moby-Dick*, the commodore of the naval fleet hires the services of a Society islander named Wooloo whom Melville describes as having a "sedate, earnest, and philosophic temperament" (117). Wooloo has never been away from his tropic home and thinks that snow is powdered flour, that hailstones are gems, and that the raisins in his biscuits are bugs. Melville comments:

> [I]n our man-of-war, this semi-savage, wandering about the gun-deck in his barbaric robe seemed a being from some other sphere. His tastes were our abominations: ours his. Our creed he rejected: his we. We thought him a loon; he fancied us fools. Had the case been reversed; had we been Polynesians and he an American, our mutual opinion of each other would still have remained the same. A fact proving that neither was wrong, but both right. (118)

By depicting that all humans are held captive within the "spheres" of their own cultural provincialism, Melville reveals that this puzzling man-of-war world is often a ship of fools in which the hope for a more human perspective emerges from understanding cultural pretensions.

The appearance of Queequeg in the early chapters of *Moby-Dick* enables Melville to synthesize many of his Polynesian observations into one character. New discoveries in Melville's reading reveal that one aspect of Queequeg was based on the account of a Maori chief named Tupai Cupa, who boarded a ship and refused to depart even after being threatened.[9] It is clear that Queequeg is also a composite recreation of Melville's own prior characterizations of Pacific islanders. Queequeg embodies Poky's precolonial institution of the tayo (one of Poky's gifts had even been "a little pocket-idol, black as jet" [*Omoo* 153], which prefigures Queequeg's god Yojo); Wymontoo's alienation from his homeland; and Samoa's heroism of unconscious action and eye of primal wisdom. Queequeg, like Wooloo, becomes the vehicle for humorous relativism when he contrasts his ignorance about how to use a wheelbarrow (he hoists it upon his shoulders) with a sea captain's uncouth washing of his hands in the punchbowl at the wedding of Queequeg's sister (59).

Queequeg's deeper role is to place such reciprocal relativism in the service of cultural criticism. By landing the hideous islander in New Bedford, Melville brings savage difference to bear as a test of the spiritual mettle of sanctimonious New Englanders. By creating Queequeg, Melville realizes his flippant suggestion in *Typee* that "four of five Marquesan Islanders sent to the United States as Missionaries might be quite as useful as an equal number of Americans despatched to the Islands in a similar capacity" (125–26). Melville subverts the evangelical Captain Bildad's construction of Queequeg as a "son of darkness" in need of salvation (87). In fact, it is Queequeg who succeeds in converting Ishmael, and his symbolic body (in the form of the coffin) is the ironic agent of Ishmael's redemption and rebirth as a writer.

Queequeg stands as counterpoint to the famous Hawaiian Henry Opukahaia (Ripped Belly) who was brought from the

Sandwich islands to New Haven in 1809. The legend of "Oboo-kiah" figured him as a tawny alien who was discovered weeping on the classroom steps of Yale College. Taken up by a professor, Obookiah became the inspiration for the establishment of a mission school in Cornwall, Connecticut, in 1816, which in the following decade matriculated students from China, Greece, Tahiti, and the Marquesas as well as Native Americans, Malays, and Portuguese. After his death in 1818, Obookiah became a martyred "matinee idol" of the missionary movement who inspired the founding of a mission to the Sandwich islands (Hawaii) the following year—the first American attempt to evangelize Pacific islanders in their midst.[10] Melville's most vehement critique of Pacific colonization was directed toward this mission where Christians not only failed to inspire the hearts of the natives but instead had them "civilized into draught horses, and evangelized into beasts of burden" (*Typee* 196). Melville deconstructs the myth of Obookiah in his characterization of Queequeg, who is similarly possessed of a "wild desire to visit Christendom" (56). Instead of converting to Christianity, however, the Kokovokan becomes corrupted by Christians, who unfit him for his pagan throne unless he is ironically "baptized" anew into primitivism. Ishmael's ironic advocacy of Queequeg as a member of "the ancient Catholic Church" and as a deacon in the "First Congregational Church of this whole worshiping world," coupled with his own Presbyterian rationalization of worshipping with a pagan, confounds conventional categories of Christian inclusion (87–88). A Rhode Island newspaper account in 1819 ended its announcement of the arrival in Providence of three tattooed Marquesan men from "Madison's Island" with a cosmopolitan plea: "as they are American citizens, having been adopted into the great American family, we trust they will be treated with kindness and hospitality."[11] Through his symbolic naturalization of Queequeg, a Polynesian whose cultural location remains a mystery, Melville challenged the sincerity of American religious and republican inclusiveness. Melville's "wicked" criticism is revealed most forcefully through his annunciation of Ishmael's own apostasy: "Long exile from Christendom and civilization inevitably restores a man to that condition in which God placed him, i.e. what is called savagery. . . . I myself am a savage, owning no allegiance but to the King of the Cannibals; and ready at any moment to rebel against him" (270).

Despite Melville's celebration of the comparative leisure he found in the South Seas, the presence of intertribal violence and cannibalism indicates that Polynesian cultural practices were neither pacific nor immune from the penalties of the Fall. For Melville, the persistence of the aboriginal also revived and represented the postlapsarian antagonisms that sundered the human race. The Pacific contained in its midst not only primeval beauty but also the primal savagery that was the dark source of human destruction. Melville capitalized upon sensational images of Asian and Pacific islanders as embodiments of predatory human cannibalism. Whalers tried to avoid landings in the Fiji islands, known in the mid-nineteenth century as the "Cannibal Isles," because they represented the hell of human barbarism.[12] South Pacific cannibals were featured as exotic spectacles in American museums of the 1830s and 1840s, including an exhibition in Barnum's American Museum in 1842 of one Vendovi, a Fijian chief staged as a living cannibal.[13] Melville's view of the degeneracy of the Fiji islands drew in part from the success of P. T. Barnum's 1842 hoax of the "Feejee Mermaid" in New York, from where it toured the country. While such "mermaids" may have been a type of South Sea fetish sold to sea captains as souvenirs, much in the way that Queequeg—himself a deceptive curiosity—found a market for his New Zealand heads, some viewers foolishly believed that they were evolutionary abortions, literally confirming that "the racism of popular prejudice was artificially joined to a scientific base."[14]

Melville's Pacific savages also embodied a bitter rejection of the fate of earthly exile and through their violence recounted the tragic confirmation of a divided humanity. Melville's prototype for the monomaniacal avenger is Bembo, the Maori ("Mowree") harpooner in *Omoo*. Melville describes the New Zealander as a "dark, moody savage" (71) and introduces him at midnight as he "dances some cannibal fandango all by himself on the forecastle" (13). Maddened by the taunts and insults of the crew members, Bembo bites the neck of a Sydney convict and tries to wreck the ship on a coral reef. Melville's narrator finds Bembo possessed of "a heart irreclaimably savage, and at no time fraternally disposed toward the crew" (92–93). Yet, Bembo's revolt also registers a deep and bitter protest against the deracinating injustices of colonization in which indigenous peoples were stigmatized for cultural behaviors they had been forced to leave behind. Melville revives a more horrific historical scene of Pacific revenge in his dramatization of Babo, the alienated Senegalese slave who devises a mutinous plot in his "hive of subtlety," which confounds Captain Delano and becomes the story of "Benito Cereno" (*Piazza Tales* 116).

Aligned with the representation of the Fijian and Maori as reprehensible figures in Melville's ethnic pageantry are East Asian ethnics, the most prominent of whom were the Malays. For Melville, these sly and shady Asians represent what Ahab called the "dark Hindoo half of nature" (*Moby-Dick* 497). In 1795, the German anatomist Johann Friedrich Blumenbach added the Malayan race to Linnaeus's four original races of mankind—the American Indian, Caucasian, Ethiopian, and Mongolian. At that time, the prototype for the Malay was Omai, the Tahitian boy who had been brought back to London in 1774 between Captain Cook's second and final expeditions (prompting Melville to speak of "Omai's olive race" in *Clarel* [4.18.43]).[15] By the time of Melville's journeys, encounters with actual Malays had distinguished them from Polynesians and invested them with the reputation of being shadowy pirates of terror. Melville derived these images from reading about the Malay specter in Thomas de Quincey's *Confessions of an Opium-Eater* and printed accounts of the frigate *Potomac*, the finest frigate in the navy, sent by President Andrew Jackson to wreak vengeance on the Sumatran settlement of Kuala Batu for their capture of the American merchant ship *Friendship* in 1831.[16] The dangerous reputation of the East Asian is testified to in "Benito Cereno" and *Mardi*, where captains are wary of boarding listless ships because they fear Malay pirates may be lurking below deck.[17] When Malays waylay the *Pequod* after it sails through the straits of Sunda between Java and Sumatra, Ahab applauds the "inhuman atheistical devils" for encouraging him to quicken his own pursuit of the white whale. Melville links the piracy of these "rascally Asiatics" with the savagery of Ahab's own monomaniacal revenge (383–84).

The fuller representation of Ahab's interiority is of course the nefarious Parsee Fedallah with his crew of "tiger-yellow aboriginal natives of the Manillas" (whom Melville calls "a race notorious for a certain diabolism of subtilty" [217]). In his melodramatic characterization of this shady genie, Melville runs the gamut of orientalist types east of Turkey and Arabia: Fedallah bears the hybrid markers of Parsee, Muslim, and Chinese ethnicity and is compared with those who "now and then glide among the unchanging Asiatic communities, especially the Oriental isles to the east of the continent" (439). A figure of evil fate who remains "a muffled mystery to the last" (231), Fedallah is connected with Ahab as "a shadow is to its substance." In contrast to the mutuality of the monkey rope, Melville finds them both "yoked together, and an unseen tyrant driving them," and they remain in that condition in death, united by whale lines to Moby Dick (538). Representations of Persians as personifications of enervating tyranny also appear in the poems "The Rose Farmer" and "The New Zealot to the Sun," where in the latter a collective "Persian" embodies the obsolete and intractable delusions that hold mankind under an "Arch type of sway" (*Poems* 317). This dark, orientalized despotism is also represented in the evil priest Aleema in *Mardi*, who intends to sacrifice the angelic maiden Yillah but is instead killed by Melville's narrator. Melville links the "dusky" Aleema (142) to the evil Aaron, the Moor of Shakespeare's *Titus Andronicus* (130), and his name evokes the *ulema*, the Persian Shiite clergy. Melville employs his varied cast of enigmatic orientals to embody the mystery of how humans lost their divine connection and, deceived by delusions, perpetuate violence against their own kind. Driven by a spirit of vengeance, these humans are terrorists who prey on each other with little sympathy for the lives they destroy.

Melville also uses the aboriginal as an avatar of savagery as part of the complex anti-Semitism that he shared with many gentile Americans of his age. For example, comparing Aleema to Aaron also evoked the high priest of the Old Testament and the harsh inflexibility of Jewish ritual. His literature portrayed a broad array of Jewish characters, including the misanthropic types of the betraying Judas, the miserly Shylock, and the irreverent materialist represented by the geologist Margoth in *Clarel*. In *Redburn*, Melville capitalized on a popular stereotype of the greedy pawnbrokers of Chatham Street, which George Foster had portrayed a year earlier in *New York in Slices* as "the gathering place of gullibility."[18] Although he depicts the "hooked-nosed" operator as an unprincipled opportunist, he does so to expose the naïveté of his own narrator (*Redburn* 19–22). In contrast to his hopes for the United States, Melville excoriated the narrowness of "a bigoted Hebrew nationality—whose blood has been debased in the attempt to ennoble it" (169).

Yet Melville went well beyond the mere affirmation of conventional anti-Semitism. He also celebrated both the power of dissent of the "bold freethinking Jew" (*Clarel* 2.22.55) and the sensuous vitality of the prodigal Lyonese, who challenges Clarel with the words: "Priests make a goblin of the Jew: / Shares he not flesh with me—and you?" (4.17.247–48). Moreover, Melville found in the story of the Wandering Jew—a doubting man whom Christ had cursed to tarry until the Second Advent—a powerful cosmopolitan myth of alienation with which to supplement the biblical story of Ishmael in explaining the unresolved salvation of humanity. Melville frequently pondered the "deeper mystery" of Jewish persistence: "How Judah, Benjamin, live on— / Unmixed into time's swamping sea / So far can urge their Amazon" (1.2.48–51).

Ultimately Melville viewed Judaism as a global system of primitive orientalism that trapped humanity in regressive patterns of intractable division. Melville's most original characterizations of the Jew—the characters of Abdon and Nathan in *Clarel*—dramatize his appraisal of the atavistic devotion of Judaism to the dried husk of dogma. Abdon is a black Jew who has migrated from Cochin on the southwest coast of India to Jerusalem to live out his last days. As the innkeeper of the establishment in which Clarel resides, Abdon's abiding presence in the first part of Melville's poem symbolizes the desiccated fate of "Jehovah's town" (1.44.39). Melville portrays Abdon as the racialized remnant of "Man's earliest breed" whose survival perversely symbolizes the lasting heritage of human tribalism (1.17.219). Abdon is contrasted with Nathan, an American Adam whose fertile potential for redemptive originality becomes mired in sterile Old World antagonisms with his conversion to Judaism. After migrating to the Holy Land as a Zionist settler, he is murdered by Arabs in reaction to the racism of his "inveterate zeal" (1.17.328). The death of this Illinois farmer in the Holy Land registers Melville's doubt about the capacity of the new nation to manifest its millennial potential. These contrasting characterizations of Jews in the Holy Land embody his ruthless assessment in the journal of his 1857 visit: "in the emptiness of the lifeless antiquity of Jerusalem the emigrant Jews are like flies that have taken up their abode in a skull" (*Journals* 91).

American Savagery and the Expansion of Sympathy

Although Melville often dislocated his criticism of the moral direction of the United States onto other geographies, it was through his fictional treatment of Native Americans that he most fully domesticated his understanding of human savagery. Melville's lifetime spanned the period during which the Native American population was deprived of most of its ancestral lands. The natives' fate in the midst of the American republic caused him to meditate deeply on the ethical shortcomings of the nation, which he symbolized through the dramatic destruction of the *Pequod*, named after a New England native culture decimated by the Puritans. Native American characters in Melville's fiction, despite the "grave and decorous" heritage (*Omoo* 260) embodied by the *Pequod*'s harpooner Tashtego, are hapless peoples "all but exterminated" in a war waged "for their native soil and natural rights" ("John Marr," *Poems* 265). When Melville journeyed up the Erie Canal on his way west to Galena, Illinois, in 1840, he traversed the territory in which his maternal grandfather, General Peter Gansevoort, had slaughtered Mohawks during the Revolutionary War and witnessed remnants of populations suffering the indignities of dispossession. Melville chastised American historian Francis Parkman for his hypocritical attitudes toward Native

Americans in a review of his 1849 book *The California and Oregon Trail*:

> When we affect to contemn savages, we should remember that by so doing we asperse our own progenitors; for they were savages also. . . . Why, among the very Thugs of India, or the bloody Dyaks of Borneo, exists the germ of all that is intellectually elevated and grand. We are all of us— Anglo-Saxons, Dyaks, and Indians—sprung from one head and made in one image. And if we reject this brotherhood now, we shall be forced to join hands hereafter. ("Mr. Parkman's Tour," *Piazza Tales* 231)

Melville criticized Parkman for a lack of charity because he expressed contempt for the natives themselves instead of commiseration for their treatment at the hands of the white settlers. Melville condemned Western violence against the natives as the very embodiment of the savagery projected upon the Indian. Melville berated the barbaric actions of the military in the Second Seminole War (1835–1842), especially through the boastings of a sailor—appropriately named Gun-deck—who shoots a Seminole leader by drawing a bead on a pewter ornament that he wears on his chest (*Redburn* 101). The narrator of *White-Jacket* relates a scene he witnessed on the banks of the Mississippi where a regal Sioux named Red-Hot Coal celebrated scalping a foe by parading a newly painted red hand on the back of his blanket. Melville viewed such pride in the destruction of other creatures as pathetic proof of a persistent paganism. "Poor savage!" wrote Melville, "And you account it so glorious, do you, to mutilate and destroy what God himself was more than a quarter of a century in building?" (266–67).

Melville's use of "you" here conflated any reader who believed that the only good Indian was a dead one with the barbarous exploits of this arrogant Sioux warrior. Such fluidity of ascription is one small example of how Melville, while apparently confirming pejorative stereotypes, resisted confining savagery to any ethnic essentialism. In fact Melville designed the vignette about Red-Hot Coal primarily to censure the naval

custom of making trophies out of captured enemy ships. For
Melville, any act of war—including internecine struggles between Western powers—was an expression of heathen despotism. Warfare between civilized nations was a form of cannibalism that reduced people to the "Feegee standard of humanity"
(*White-Jacket* 320). Melville registered the heartlessness of naval
violence in *White-Jacket* by renaming American warships the *Mo-
hawk*, the *Malay*, the *Algerine*, and the *Buccaneer* (253–54) and in
Mardi by barbarizing British cruisers as the "corsairs of Domi-
nora" (469). Melville was so disgusted by the tyrannical infidelity
of such naval practices as flogging, and Christian worship,
aboard warships that he labeled the Articles of War a "Turkish
Code" and compared the bounty paid to chaplains to the treason
of Judas (*White-Jacket* 297, 157). Violence against one's own kin
and neglect for the welfare of others affirmed the universality of
human barbarism. Melville expressed this common legacy forcefully when he claimed that the French Revolution "levelled the
exquisite refinement of Paris with the blood-thirsty ferocity of
Borneo; showing that broaches and finger-rings, not less than
nose-rings and tattooing, are tokens of the primeval savageness
which ever slumbers in human kind, civilised or uncivilized"
(*Israel Potter* 63). Melville remained fascinated by this slumbering
source of "primeval savageness" and puzzled with the phenomenon of the "mystery of iniquity" right up until his final work,
Billy Budd, in which Claggart, the master-at-arms, is a character
whose depravity is so inborn that his predatory savagery seems
insinuated into the very fabric of human nature.[19]

To Melville, the most savage of Americans was not the Indian
but the citizen of the United States who, though thriving in a
land of republicanism, chose to perpetrate violence and injustice
toward others and brag about his exploits. Melville frequently
presented Americans as hybrid ethnics who remained racialized
primitives in spite of their aspirations to civilization. The wicked
sailor Jackson in *Redburn* is a relative of the Indian fighter Andrew Jackson who sailed through the Middle Passage on slavers.
He is an early example of this misanthropic type, and Melville as-
sociates him with a "Malay pirate," "a wild Indian," and "a Cain
afloat" (*Redburn* 104). Ishmael's description of the "Erie-Canaller"

in *Moby-Dick* again exalts such a type, not as the harbinger of democratic enterprise as the rafters in the paintings of George Caleb Bingham, but as a New World manifestation of "Venetianly" corruption (249) he describes as "your true Ashantee" (249). Melville explores such corruption in *The Confidence-Man* of 1857, his only novel to take place in the interior waters of the United States, most notably in his account of "The Metaphysics of Indian-Hating." In contrast to Frederick Jackson Turner's nostalgic evocation of the frontiersman (two years after Melville's death) as the rugged emblem of democratic equality, Melville's Indian hater is a "backwoodsman" who remains "unsophisticated . . . impulsive . . . [and] unprincipled" (145). He is so utterly convinced that Indians are an inveterately depraved "gang of Cains" (153) that this "instinct of antipathy" (146) becomes his reason for living and reduces him to the same status of savage avenger as those he reviles. Melville similarly deconstructs in *Israel Potter* the legends of the revolutionary naval heroes Ethan Allen and John Paul Jones. For example, he portrays Jones's 1779 naval victory over the HMS *Serapis* not as an inaugural moment of national honor but rather as an emblem of the savagery upon which Americans ironically based their "fancied superiority." The war-mongering commander behaves like a renegade pirate by issuing "sultanical orders" and "concealing the intent of a Turk" (*Israel Potter* 96–97) and possesses the same qualities as the Indian hater par excellence: "intrepid, unprincipled, reckless, predatory, with boundless ambition, civilized in externals but a savage at heart" (120). To Melville, the memorialization of Jones's marauding symbolized a corrupt national enterprise, and he prophesied: "America is, or may yet be, the Paul Jones of nations" (120). By satirizing the custom of making American heroes out of rude barbarians, even as he created an example of the "illustrious damned" in Ahab, who is "alien" to Christendom, Melville dramatized the genetic fluidity of human experience (*Redburn* 276; *Moby-Dick* 153).

When the Civil War brought the barbarism of battle to the valleys of his homeland, Melville salvoed with his 1865 book of poems *Battle-Pieces*. Expanding his examination of the Revolutionary veteran as refugee in Europe in *Israel Potter*, Melville also

explored the Civil War through his invention of the scarred soldier Ungar of *Clarel*. An ex-Confederate of both Cherokee and
Catholic heritage, Ungar internalizes in his own bitter experience
the successive historical campaigns of American persecution. He
serves as an embittered mercenary exiled in the Holy Land, "a
wandering Ishmael from the West" (4.11.189) whose duty it is to
"drill the tawny infantry" of Ottoman armies. A man with an
"Anglo brain, but Indian heart" (4.6.141), Ungar exemplifies in his
unrelenting warfare Melville's angry attack on the perverse
providence of human estrangement—the "abiding malevolence
/ In man toward man" (4.13.228–30). Ungar's unquenched feud
extinguishes any hope for a redemptive project for America.
"The world cannot save the world," Ungar despairs. "And Christ
renounces it" (4.20.35–36). He predicts instead that materialism
and proliferating social division will cause the destruction of the
New World nation—that the post–Civil War society has devolved
into a "civic barbarism" that will "yield to one and all / New confirmation of the fall / Of Adam" (4.21.131–33).[20]

The fact that Melville chose to affirm an affiliation with the
vanquished white southerner who, as he claimed in his prose
supplement to *Battle-Pieces*, was "nearer to us in nature" (*Poems*
184), demonstrates that he shared the limitations of his age in
imagining how to integrate freed African American slaves into
the national body-politic. Melville clearly abhorred slavery, calling it "a blot, foul as the crater-pool of hell [that] puts out the sun
at noon" in *Mardi* (534) and an "atheistic iniquity" in *Battle-Pieces*;
even Ungar was "outspoken" among his friends about the "grief"
of racial bondage (4.5.47–48). Despite this stance, Melville pan-
dered to stereotypes in his early works by humorously playing
the minstrel in his representations of African American cooks,
servants, and entertainers. The fact that Melville's advocacy of
African Americans remained more of a paternal sympathy than a
political engagement has opened him to criticism from contemporary scholars. Melville's poem "Formerly a Slave," a meditation on Elihu Vedder's sketch of the African American mother
Jane Jackson, depicts her in a spiritual reverie through which the
"sybilline, yet benign" light of Emancipation reveals only a mystified and gradual hope of racial advancement (*Poems* 129).

Nevertheless, Melville often used stereotypes as resources for more complex and more critical cultural work. To cite but two brief examples, Melville's satire of *Redburn*'s black cook, Dr. Thompson, is countered by the fact that he earns more profits on this journey than any other member of the crew, and Babo's role as valet in "Benito Cereno" is merely a cover for the cunning of his deceptive authority. Melville's final evocation of the African occurred when he returned to fiction once more in the late 1880s to write *Billy Budd, Sailor*. In a late addition at the beginning of this work, Melville reminisces about the disruptive encounter with racial difference that he experienced during his first journey to Liverpool in 1839. Melville transfigures the barbaric majesty of "unadulterated" African manhood, which he had employed in Daggoo of *Moby-Dick* and Atufal from "Benito Cereno," into an embodiment of the Handsome Sailor as an African Adam—a celebrant of Melville's vision of multicultural fraternity (*Billy Budd* 43–44). The persistence of Melville's dual vision of humanity is clear in his representation of the Handsome Sailor as fraternal in the form of the African sailor and as fratricidal in the fate of the flawed Billy Budd. Melville's racially doubled construction of the Handsome Sailor personifies his persisting belief that humans are a divinely unified race both in the nobility of their creation and in the suffering they endured at the tragic hands of their fellow humans.

The strengths of Melville's ethnic cosmopolitanism emerged from his capacity to maintain this faith in human dignity even when his hopes of a fraternal society recessed into nostalgia. His ability to transform his romantic vision of multiethnic reunion into a deep commiseration for the dignity of his compatriots' despair reflected the growth of his own understanding of human dilemmas. Perhaps Melville's most sympathetic account of human suffering is his remarkable sketch of the widow Hunilla in "The Encantadas," which he published halfway through his life in 1856 in *The Piazza Tales* (151–62). Hunilla is a Chola—a mix between an indigenous native and a person of Spanish descent—from the Peruvian port of Payta who suffers a life of the grimmest desolation imaginable. After being abandoned by a French whaler captain on isolated Norfolk isle in the Galapagos, she witnesses the drowning of her husband and brother, her only human companions. When two ships finally land, they not only fail to rescue her but rather abuse her with further calamities that the narrator has the charity not to mention. A crew that includes Melville's narrator finally recovers her and carries her in their ship back to the Continent. Melville canonizes this forsaken woman, consigned to struggle and suffer in solitude on an empty island, as a saint who embodies the earthly trials of the "lone shipwrecked soul" (157) at the hands of a "feline Fate" (156). The fortitude of her silent pride in the face of torturous experiences inspires Melville's faith in the resilience of dignity. "Humanity, thou strong thing, I worship thee," Melville confesses, "not in the laurelled victor, but in this vanquished one" (157). Here Melville's ethnic cosmopolitanism expands the reach of American literature both by enfranchising indigenous Latin Americans and by widening the community of his fraternity to include the redemptive suffering of women (as he did with other female characters such as Delly and Isabel in *Pierre* and Marianna in "The Piazza"). The forlorn widow allows Melville to meditate further on the struggle of the human spirit in an evolving world whose reigning systems made it expedient to ignore the charity of virtuous action. Such a sketch also charts Melville's fictional fall from his early celebration of a Polynesian paradise to the human agony experienced in the barren cinders of the Galapagos— Pacific islands whose only charm rested in the irony of their name, "The Encantadas."

In 1890, the year before he died, Melville was asked by Havelock Ellis to supply his racial genealogy for a study on literary genius (*Correspondence* 764–65). He dutifully replied by parsing out his northern European ancestry (528–29). Yet Melville's real genius and American originality stemmed not from his own ethnic makeup but from his creative capacity to open the floodgates of the world and feed his own vision with the cosmopolitan tide of humanity. Sharing Ishmael's "everlasting itch for things remote" (*Moby-Dick* 7), Melville rendered such a diverse congregation of multicultural characters in the try-pots of his literature that he was able to generate the very fraternity of which he dreamed in his vision of an interethnic afterworld. Melville's true patriots included a ragged bunch of survivors and hapless rebels who testified to the dignity of human experience despite the struggles the species was destined to suffer. Melville celebrated a hybrid society that did not rope itself off in pallid and incestuous conventions from the fertile contamination of diversity.

The dedication of the Statue of Liberty in 1883, two years before Melville retired from his career in the New York Customs House, welcomed more than twenty years of mass immigration that would swell the city into a space whose diversity Melville could only imagine in his lifetime. New Yorkers read the words from Emma Lazarus's poem "The New Colossus" engraved on Liberty's pedestal: "Give me your tired, your poor, / Your huddled masses yearning to breathe free, / The wretched refuse of your teeming shore." By gathering the "bristling clans of Adam" within the society of his literature, Melville had already delivered them to the nation's shores—and from even more exotic points of origin. "If they can get here, they have God's right to come," wrote Melville about his attitude toward immigration in the 1840s, "[f]or the whole world is the patrimony of the whole world" (*Redburn* 292–93). Melville taught us to see others as integral to the constitution of what we consider "our own." He naturalized the alien and outcast as a potent means of honoring the potential of democracy. Yet he traveled even further, beyond the pale of such imperial inclusion.

Melville challenges us to cast off from our own shores and our "cool, civil deference to the dominant belief" (*Mardi* 370) if we wish to civilize ourselves through the "gentler relief" of human sympathy (*Moby-Dick* 424). By courageously federating a crew of castaways in his literature, Melville created a vibrant representation of cosmopolitan culture. By inaugurating the process of authoring the declaration of interdependence, Herman Melville launched a journey that is still under way.

NOTES

The author would like to express his thanks to Giles Gunn, Wyn Kelley, Philip Gura, and Jane Thrailkill.

Except where noted, all quotations are taken from the Northwestern-Newberry editions of *The Works of Herman Melville* (1968–1993).

1. For a fine analysis of Melville's dissection of antebellum discourse of the racialized body, see Samuel Otter, *Melville's Anatomies* (Berkeley: University of California Press, 1999).

2. *Salem Advertiser* (March 25, 1846), reprinted in *Critical Essays on Melville's "Typee,"* ed. by Milton R. Stern (Boston: Hall, 1982), 34.

3. *The Poems of Herman Melville*, ed. Douglas Robillard (Kent, Ohio, and London: Kent State University Press, 2000), 325 (hereafter *Poems*).

4. For Melville, both the "eternal" ocean and the western wilderness of America preserved a flavor of "those primeval times when Adam walked majestic as a god, bluff-browed and fearless" (*Pierre* 139; *Moby-Dick* 191).

5. Wai-chee Dimock, *Empire for Liberty: Melville and the Poetics of Individualism* (Princeton, N.J.: Princeton University Press, 1989), 8.

6. Robin Grey and Douglas Robillard, "Melville's Milton: A Transcription of Melville's Marginalia in His Copy of *The Poetical Works of John Milton*," *Leviathan: A Journal of Melville Studies* 4:1 and 2 (March and October 2002): 162.

7. Melville examines other evidence of racially based violence in *White-Jacket* when two African American members of the crew are forced to engage in head-butting contests. See W. Jeffrey Bolster, *Black Jacks: African-American Seamen in the Age of Sail* (Cambridge, Mass.: Harvard University Press, 1997), esp. 179–80.

8. Margaret S. Creighton, *Rites and Passages: The Experience of American Whaling, 1830–1870* (New York: Cambridge University Press, 1995), 143.

9. Geoffrey Sanborn, "Whence Come You, Queequeg?" reported in *Moby-Dick*, 2nd critical ed. (New York: Norton, 2002), 59.

10. William R. Hutchinson, *Errand to the World: American Protestant Thought and Foreign Missions* (Chicago: University of Chicago Press, 1987), 67; Rufus Anderson, *History of the Sandwich Islands Mission* (Boston: Congregational Publishing, 1870), 10–12; Samuel Colcord Bartlett, *Historical Sketch of the Hawaiian Mission* (Boston: American Board of Commissioners for Foreign Missions, 1871), 3–4.

11. *Providence Patriot* (April 17, 1819), reprinted in *American Activities in the Central Pacific, 1790–1870*, ed. R. Gerard Wood (Ridgewood, N.J.: Gregg, 1967), 5:244.

12. Richard Ellis, *Man and Whales* (New York: Knopf, 1991), 192.

13. Geoffrey Sanborn, *The Sign of the Cannibal: Melville and the Making of a Postcolonial Reader* (Durham, N.C.: Duke University Press, 1988), 130. See also James W. Cook, "The Feejee Mermaid and the Market Revolution," in his *The Arts of Deception: Playing with Fraud in the Age of Barnum* (Cambridge, Mass.: Harvard University Press, 2001), 73–118.

14. Ter Ellingson, *The Myth of the Noble Savage* (Berkeley: University of California Press, 2001), 151.

15. John C. Greene, *The Death of Adam: Evolution and Its Impact on Western Thought* (Ames: Iowa State University Press, 1959), 225.

16. Francis Warriner, *Cruise of the United States Frigate Potomac Round the World, during the Years 1831–1834* (New York: Leavitt, Lord, 1835); J. N. Reynolds, *Voyage of the United States Frigate Potomac* (New York: Harper, 1835).

17. "Benito Cereno," *Piazza Tales* 68; *Mardi* 58. Even in his poem on the Holy Land, *Clarel*, Melville compares the monks of St. Saba surveying the desert for invading Arabs with a ship's foretopmen looking out over the sea for the "slim Malay," whom he calls a "perilous imp" (*Clarel* 3.21.7–8).

18. Frederic Cople Jaher, *A Scapegoat in the Wilderness: The Origins and Rise of Anti-Semitism in America* (Cambridge, Mass.: Harvard University Press, 1994), 222–23.

19. *Billy Budd, Sailor*, ed. Harrison Hayford and Merton M. Sealts, Jr. (Chicago: University of Chicago Press, 1962), 76. The phrase "mystery of iniquity" is from 2 Thessalonians 2:7.

20. Hilton Obenzinger analyzes Ungar and Nathan in *American Palestine: Melville, Twain, and the Holy Land Mania* (Princeton, N.J.: Princeton University Press, 1999), 138–58 and 84–113.

"Wandering To-and-Fro"

Melville and Religion

Emory Elliott

As the title of Lawrence Thomson's classic study, *Melville's Quarrel with God*, asserts, religious and philosophical ideas were central to Melville's thought throughout his life, and questions involving God, the soul, death and the afterlife, heaven and hell, good and evil are integral to most of his creative works. An abundance of scholarship on Melville and religion testifies to the powerful and persistent presence of religious and philosophical issues in his writings and to the difficulty of drawing any clear, satisfying conclusions about his personal faith, the nature of his beliefs, whether he thought religions were valuable or foolish, or whether he believed in "God."[1]

Nathaniel Hawthorne's succinct observation in 1856 remains perhaps the most accurate description of Melville's relation to religion and to metaphysical questions. From his lengthy conversations with Melville, Hawthorne recognized the depth of Melville's spiritual struggles, and he reflected upon his friend's yearnings, his skepticism, and his spiritual ambiguities:

> Melville, as he always does, began to reason of Providence and futurity, and of everything that lies beyond human ken, and informed me that he has "pretty much made up his mind to be annihilated"; but still he does not seem to rest in that an-

ticipation; and, I think, never will rest until he gets hold of a definite belief. It is strange how he persists—and has persisted ever since I knew him, and probably long before—in wandering to-and-fro over these deserts, as dismal and monotonous as the sand hills amid which we were sitting. He can neither believe, nor be comfortable in his unbelief; and he is too honest and courageous not to try to do one or the other. If he were a religious man, he would be one of the most truly religious and reverential; he has a very high and noble nature, and better worth immortality than most of us.[2]

The evidence in Melville's creative works bears out Hawthorne's conviction that Melville never ceased searching for the answers to the big questions yet always believed that there must be reasonable explanations for the seeming absurdities of life, waiting to be discovered or revealed.

From his early *Typee* (1846), to his long narrative poem *Clarel* (1876), to the manuscript of his last work, *Billy Budd* (w. 1886–1891), Melville used his creative work as opportunities to explore many of the great questions of the nineteenth century when science, philosophy, and religion were engaged in heated contestations over pressing issues that included the validity of miracles; the divinity of Christ; natural evolution and the origin of mankind; the deterministic powers of history, class, genetics, race, and the human psyche; the nature and causes of evil; and the existence of God. As an artist examining his world and as an individual looking for answers to life's mysteries and longing for spiritual peace, Melville wavered all his life between hope and despair. Personal tragedies such as the early death of his father, the family's economic difficulties that followed, and the likely suicide of his first son, Malcolm, challenged the optimism of his youth, deepened his gravity and skepticism, and confirmed his suspicions that the great epics and tragedies of antiquity and of Shakespeare portray the nature of the universal predicament: humans are hardly more than pawns at the mercy of Fate, Nature, Divine Providence, or the gods who sport with us for their pleasure.

In spite of Melville's ceaseless, internal metaphysical conflicts, however, he also recognized the vital role that religions still play in the world and that theologies, dogmas, moral teachings, ethical principles, and religiously endorsed cultural value systems have profound effects upon the lives of millions. While he never resolved the larger questions for himself, he was passionately committed to what he as a writer and intellectual might achieve by furthering human possibilities through the enactment of democratic principles in the social, economic, and political realms. He was greatly disturbed by the hypocrisy and duplicity of the leaders of churches and governments who articulated the ideals of freedom, opportunity, and equality even while they used religion systematically to justify withholding human rights, justice, and humane services from slaves, laborers, sailors, poor mothers and children, and the sick and impoverished. When critiques of religion appear in Melville's texts, they usually take the form of an ironic narrator's satirical observations of the egotism, indifference, or malice of those with power who choose self-interest over the common good. Melville sought to urge readers to consider sharing his passionate commitment to certain moral and ethical values that religions, to his mind, were supposed to teach and support.[3]

For gaining insights into the life of Herman Melville, we are fortunate now to have Hershel Parker's comprehensive, two-volume, definitive biography. Although it is surprising that Parker does not have more to say on the subject of Melville's religious and philosophical ideas, this rich biography is a valuable starting point. In the first volume, there are nine references to Melville's "religious practice," and in the second volume, eighteen pages are indexed under "philosophical and religious views." The most substantial remark on the subject of religion is that "Herman was hopelessly ironical about sentimental racist religiosity."[4] While there is no indication of how often Herman and his wife, Elizabeth, attended church, Parker reports that they "rented a pew at Henry Bellows' All Souls Unitarian Church in Manhattan in 1849" (Parker I:625). Parker also observes that Melville was interested in the religious life of the poet John Milton (Parker I:618); that reviewers attacked him for his anti-religious views in *Typee* and *Mardi* (I:634); and that he sometimes used religious rhetoric satirically (I:655). Melville's mother, Maria, often urged him to attend church (I,:795–96), and in her later years, she became adamant that his refusal to do so created public embarrassment for her. Melville was "perversely relativistic" in regard to religion; he believed that "cultural chauvinism and religious chauvinism were inseparable" (II:39); and he swore a lot (II:48). Parker observes that beginning around 1859, Melville began to identify with Milton as a "rebellious thinker" and shared his "wanderings in religious belief." Like Milton, he "avoided churches, especially those in any way connected to the state" and "rejected settled articles of belief" (II:405).

Of Hawthorne's statement on Melville's religious quest, Parker says:

> This is the only testimony that Melville was obsessed with the problem of his own immortality, although ample evidence suggests that he was obsessed with the cluster of philosophical and theological concepts conveyed by the "Fixed Fate, Free-will, foreknowledge absolute," as he spelled the Miltonic words in his 13 October 1849 journal entry. (II:300)

Given Parker's exhaustive study, it is unlikely that any additional explicit statements will soon be found in which Melville directly declared his personal positions on religion. In his review of Parker's biography, Richard Brodhead says that readers interested in Melville's religious and philosophical ideas "will have to turn to other sources to find these missing dimensions," and he observes that, as much as Melville was obsessed with ideas of religion, theology, and philosophy, he seldom wrote or spoke openly about these subjects in his daily life.[5]

Thus, Melville's readers and critics must continue to rely to a large extent upon the words of the characters and narrators of his creative texts for insights regarding the specifics of his religious thinking. Through these many voices, Melville articulated a wide range of opinions on good and evil, human nature, ethics and morality, determinism and free will, Christianity's positive and negative consequences, the possible existence and nature of God, and the religious diversity in the world. His fictional texts strongly indicate that he knew that his wandering to-and-fro among religious doctrines and philosophical theories would never yield satisfying answers for him, but he appears never to have abandoned the search and was still pursuing it even as he was writing *Billy Budd* at the time of his death. More important, although frustrated in regard to the large metaphysical questions, he channeled his passion for answers not into shaking his fist at the heavens like Ahab, but into challenging the leaders of the churches and governments and his readers to take responsibility for the suffering, ignorance, and neglect of the workers, the poor, and the powerless. His complex allegories operate on several levels with the metaphysical questions always present, but his sharpest criticisms pertain on the social, political, legal, moral and ethical levels of his works.

Before turning to his individual creative works to explore these subjects in greater detail, I want to provide a brief overview of what we do know about Melville's spiritual life, the philosophical issues of his time with which he struggled, and about the immediate social and moral issues that persist throughout his writings.

Religious Background and Contemporary Contexts

Throughout his life, family members and friends who were absorbed by religious ideas surrounded Melville, and many of the writers and intellectuals whom he knew in England and the United States were engaged in the intense theological and philosophical debates of the nineteenth century. In 1819, when Melville was born, the United States was entering a period of tremendous religious and philosophical turmoil that affected every aspect of society. As the nation was just completing three decades of its experiment in constitutional democracy, many political and religious leaders believed that the American people were deplorably lacking in social graces, moral values, and ideas of communal responsibility. European travelers in America, such as Frances Milton Trollope, the mother of the novelist Anthony Trollope, and Alexis de Tocqueville, found the people to be overbearing in their expressions of pride over their independence and democratic government and parochial in their scorn for what they considered to be elitist and corrupt aristocratic societies in Europe. At the same time, such observers also testified that in the city centers and everywhere beyond the eastern seaboard they found a shocking level of alcohol consumption and loutish behavior in public places that included fighting, tobacco chewing, profanity, spitting, and a general lack of manners and morals. Mrs. Trollope's observations were especially excoriating.[6]

Partly in response to such behavior and to what Ralph Waldo Emerson declared to be the general malaise and aimlessness that characterized many young people in the decades following the American Revolution, many clergy and secular idealists began as early as the 1790s to generate religious revivals and self-improvement programs that might kindle in the new immigrants and in the young something of the older Puritan moral consciousness and work ethic.[7] While there was considerable competition for conversions among the various denominations, especially the Baptists, Methodists, and Presbyterians, many clergy of these churches eventually formed the Evangelical United Front. There were also hundreds of untrained itinerant preachers who led camp meetings in the West and the South where they too converted thousands. Within this context of such sweeping religious transformations of the nation, subgroups of Christians and some secular groups formed utopian communities. One of these, Brook Farm, which tried to blend manual labor with intellectual work, was closely connected to Emerson and to members of the transcendentalist movement, the subject of Hawthorne's novel *The Blithedale Romance*.[8]

Parallel to this religious upheaval, there also developed, especially in Boston, New York, and other cities of the Northeast, dozens of secular voluntary associations devoted to the eradication of a range of social and moral problems. Moral crusades arose aimed at abolishing drinking, profanity, prostitution, gambling, infidelity, and family abandonment and encouraging literacy, responsible parenting, and the education of the young in both religious and secular subjects. Missionary societies were founded to convert the indigenous people and the new immigrant settlers, many of whom practiced no religion. They also developed missions in other countries, which were to play a major role in the colonization of the Pacific islands and East Asia. The growing opposition of northerners to slavery led to the formation of antislavery societies, resulting in the religiously inspired abolition movement. In addition to transcendentalism, these decades also gave rise to other religious and spiritual movements such as mysticism, millennialism, illuminism, perfectionism, and pantheism. All of these activities proliferated during the first forty years of Melville's life, and his works reveal that he was highly conscious of the idealism and lofty goals of these efforts as well as the hypocrisy of many, especially clergy and political leaders, who merely gave lip service to such causes.[9]

While there may not have been many written expressions of religion within the Melville household, there is considerable evidence that religion was an important family matter. Herman was born into a family that was steeped in Calvinist religious traditions on both sides. His great-great-grandfather was a Congregationalist clergyman in Scotland for fifty years, and his grandfather Thomas Melvill studied divinity at Princeton with the intention of entering the ministry. By the time that Herman's father, Allan Melvill, was an adult, the liberal influences of Harvard University and of Boston society led him to join the Unitarian Brattle Square Church whose pastor was the young minister, intellectual, and writer Joseph Stevens Buckminster. When Allan became a merchant and married Maria Gansevoort of the rich and powerful Gansevoort clan of Albany, however, he decided to join her Dutch Reformed church both because Maria was very devout and because Allan recognized that many people considered members of the conservative Dutch Reformed church to be more reliable and trustworthy in business than the liberal Unitarians. While the minister of the congregation that Allan and Maria joined, the Reverend Jacob Brodhead, was fairly moderate in his preaching, young Herman would have learned the Calvinistic doctrines of predestination, inherent human depravity, God's sovereignty, and man's helplessness and total dependence on grace. Allan may not have agreed fully with some of these doctrines, but he did have religious convictions and believed in rearing and educating his children within a religious home.[10]

Melville's writings demonstrate that he possessed a remarkably inquiring mind with a strong propensity for engaging philosophical and religious questions. Melville was surrounded by volatile public debates among the Calvinists, Unitarians, free thinkers, pantheists, and advocates of various utopian schemes, and such discussions would have impressed upon him the importance of religious and moral issues for Americans of his generation. In 1830, when Herman was only eleven, the Melvill family moved to central New York state near Albany, the "burned-over district" where huge revivals frequently swept the area like firestorms. Thus, young Herman was steeped in Protestantism at home and in his community, and in spite of his rational rejection of Calvinist doctrines later in his life, he seems never to have escaped the shadow of gloom, guilt, pessimism, and even rage that the deterministic interpretations of Calvin's theology generated. Melville's narrators often express their scorn for the self-righteousness and hypocrisy of those clergy and church members who speak platitudes about Christian charity and love but then fail to help those in distress, as had been the situation for Herman's mother, siblings, and himself when Allan Melvill's business failed in 1830 and when he died in 1832 (Parker I:62–83).

On August 4, 1847, Herman married Elizabeth, daughter of Massachusetts chief justice Lemuel Shaw. In 1849, Lizzie signed up for the rental of a pew at the All Souls Unitarian Church near their first home, and after moves of their home in between, Mrs. Melville rented a modest pew for herself and her daughters again at All Souls in 1863. There is no evidence that Herman attended services with the family in either of these periods. However, in 1884, Herman approached the pastor of All Souls, Dr. Theodore Chickering, and asked to have his name entered as a member of the church. His motives for taking membership at that time remain unclear. He may have felt a personal change of heart about religion, he may have been acting out of loyalty to Lizzie, or there may have been some other reason. Those who use his works to make the case that he became mellow and accepting of divine authority late in his life point to this act as evidence. But ambiguity remains regarding Melville's religious and spiritual life as it does with the meanings of many of his writings. All questions are ours to decide.

Religion and the Writings

Layered, multivocal, indeterminate—such contemporary critical terms seem to have been invented to describe the narrative techniques of Herman Melville. Most of his works are allegories and are highly symbolic so that representations and even single words encompass multiple meanings with readers responding on different registers. Such components of Melville's style and narrative structures make his works both challenging and tremendously rich. An examination of the nature and role of religion in Melville's works must begin with an acknowledgment: to focus on religion is to illuminate particular threads in the narratives that can never be fully unraveled from others—the philosophical, anthropological, political, psychological, economic, sexual, and aesthetic—that constitute the astonishing multiple perspectives of Melville's works. My general approach in this chapter is a blend of literary history, biography, and close reading, which is designed to highlight the role of religion and philosophy in Melville's major works.

Because of his family background, young Herman was expected to embrace one of the Christian denominations, and yet, given Melville's independent, questioning mind, making such a choice would never be easy for him. The fact that he had to leave his formal education at the age of thirteen to earn a living for himself and his family meant that he was not trained to read the works of John Locke, Edmund Burke, Samuel Taylor Coleridge, Immanuel Kant, and others. Thus, he had both the advantage of not having his ideas partially formulated for him by the clergymen professors, and he had the disadvantage of having to discover his own way, rather unsystematically, to the ideas he would need to help him to find his own answers to the many great questions of his times.

Typee: A Peep at Polynesian Life

On January 3, 1841, at the age of twenty-one, Melville departed for the South Pacific on the whaling ship the *Acushnet*, for his second ocean voyage. This adventure seems to have constituted a turning point in Melville's intellectual development, for when he returned in 1844, he began an extraordinary self-education that involved voracious reading in philosophy, religion, and literature. Clearly, his experience of the world, and especially his month of living with the Typee people, was like a graduate education in cultural anthropology that challenged many of his youthful assumptions. When he wrote his fictionalization of his voyage, he was not only recounting his recent adventures, where he had been the naive outsider and provincial American learning of radically different cultures and lifestyles. He was also forced to contrast this so-called primitive world with his own society, and he began to see his "civilization" as highly limited in its range of ideas and possibilities regarding every aspect of life and culture, including religion.

Thus, in this text, Melville created an ambiguous double narrative. The primary story is clearly aimed at a broad audience of American and English readers and is designed to be enchanting, humorous, exotic, and erotic. It is the tale of a young American's first experiences aboard ship and his exposure to the mores and customs of peoples whose lives are different from all he had known previously. He learns that the islanders, and especially the Typees, do not fit the accepted stereotypes of "savages" and "cannibals," and he discovers that he shares a common humanity with them even though their forms of labor, leisure, and religion and their social, moral, familial, and sexual behaviors are remarkably different from those of his society. Melville's narrator, Tommo, describes the islanders' physical habits, such as their going naked much of the time, their open partnership arrangements, and their frank sexuality. At the same time, Melville laces the narrative with critical commentary on a wide range of social, political, moral, and religious issues aimed at stimulating reflection and reassessment of the current policies of imperialistic expansion being conducted by the governments of the United States and Europe.

After the "abandoned voluptuousness" of the island women who greet the ship in chapter 2 gets the reader's attention, the plot that holds the reader follows the development of the narrator, Tommo, and his companion, Toby, during their days among the Typee after they have deserted their ship and escaped into the jungle. After overcoming their fear that the notorious Typee cannibals would eat them, they recognize the people to be kind and loving to each other and to be generous hosts. Fayaway, a beautiful Typee woman, takes Tommo as her lover, and a strong young native named Kory-Kory plays the role of Tommo's personal servant. Tommo observes and participates in the life of the islanders for a month, but as time passes, he and Toby become wary of the motives of the islanders, and Toby leaves to seek help. Later, he returns with a ship, and both sailors escape from what appears to be an effort by the natives to hold them hostage. Fayaway weeps at Tommo's departure, but there is a moment of violence when one of the Typee men tries to prevent them from leaving, and Tommo strikes him below the throat with a boat hook, making Tommo yet another Western aggressor who is altering the lives of the islanders for the worse.[11]

The second story that Melville tells through Tommo depicts the strategies of European and American colonialism and imperialism in action. Long before the military invasion, Christian missionaries were sent to convert the people of the island to Christianity. While the motives of most of the missionaries may have been benevolent, their work did facilitate the invasion, defeat, and destruction of the people whose lives they believed they had come to improve. Weaving passages of ironic critique among the romantic descriptions and humor, Tommo explains that in his first days on the island, he realized that the French military was in the process of systematic conquest. Its fiercest opponents were the Typees, and in one effort to defeat them, the French had forced the Happar and the Nukahiva people, whom the French had already conquered and who were bitter enemies of the Typee, to join them in an assault. Tommo reports that the Typees were still able to drive them out of their valley: "valiantly, although with much loss, the Typees disputed every inch of ground, and after some hard fighting obliged their assailants to retreat and abandon their design of conquest" (41). In contrast to the courage and justified defiance of the Typees, the Christian-led forces commit atrocities in their retreat.

In an ironic tone, Tommo describes the kind of initial colonial encounters that are being repeated across the Pacific and around the globe. When the first "big canoe" arrives in a new harbor bringing the first invaders, the "savages" (his quotation marks)

> rush down to the beach in crowds, and with open arms stand ready to embrace the strangers. Fatal embrace! They fold to their bosoms the vipers whose sting is destined to poison all their joys: and the instinctive feeling of love within their breasts is soon converted into bitterest hate. (41)

These passages and many others, such as those criticizing the American trial and prison systems (*Typee* 172, 272), underscore Melville's early disillusionment with the Christian, capitalist, imperialist project and in particular the use of religious rhetoric and proselytizing as a weapon of such destruction. Several reviews of the popular *Typee* and some of Melville's own family relations expressed displeasure with his antireligious and unpatriotic commentary. When his editors recognized Melville's offenses against religion and the missionaries, they expurgated many passages from subsequent printings.

Such offending passages were only the most conspicuous attacks on Christianity in *Typee*, however. Melville's narrator also questions many fundamental religious, social, and philosophical assumptions shared by wealthy and educated Americans and Europeans. He questions the theory of progress that sprang from the Enlightenment and the new science which held that life in the modern society would continue to improve from the state of barbarism to the high pinnacle of polite society then existing in New York and London. In contrast, Tommo's observations of life in the Typee valley support a countertheory that the happiness, order, peace, and lack of physical needs and hardships of daily life there indicate that "civilization" may be "the worst human state":

I was well-disposed to think that I was in the "Happy Valley" and that beyond those heights there was naught but a world of care and anxiety. . . .

In a primitive society, the enjoyments of life, though few and simple, are spread over a great extent; and are unalloyed; but Civilization, for every advantage she imparts, holds a hundred evils in reserve. . . . the thousand self-inflicted discomforts of refined life, which make up in units the swelling, aggregate of human misery, are unknown among these unsophisticated people. (170–77)

Repeatedly, he blames the missionaries for destroying peace and contentment; creating guilt, anxiety, and self-hatred; and thereby establishing jealousy, conflict, and destructive forces among the peoples of the island cultures. He recognizes that one of the most powerful tools in the arsenal of the missionaries is the idea of millennial expectation, which urges people to labor hard and deny themselves now for a future paradise, a message that enables political and corporate leaders of the West to justify taking the islanders' labor and their natural resources.

While living with the Typees, Tommo attempts to learn as much as he can about the nature of their religion. While he remains mystified about many particular doctrines and the apparent absence of theological disputes, he is struck by the reverence and calm that the people display when involved in their religious activities and the faith displayed in their prayers and ceremonies. He is surprised that they may look forward to a life after death that "afford[s] another evidence of the fact, that however ignorant man may be, he still feels within him his immortal spirit yearning after the unknown future" (237). While Tommo fears the ritual of tattooing and the rumors of cannibalistic feasts and he disapproves of some of the taboos, he admires their separation of church and state and the freedom that the people have to pick their own idols to worship. Tommo notes that in the United States there is supposed to be separation of church and state, but the rule is being violated when the churches and the state work so closely to evangelize and colonize people.

Melville ends the section in which Tommo examines Typee religion with a comic episode in which Kory-Kory attempts to show off one of the large wooden gods only to have the god fall on him, leading him to curse and strike the god repeatedly. Melville uses this event to mock the New England Puritan rhetoric of communal chastisement by putting into Tommo's mouth a jeremiad calling for a spiritual revival:

> When one of the inferior order of natives could show such contempt for a venerable and decrepit God of the Groves, what the state of religion among the people in general is easily to be imagined. In truth, I regard the Typees as a back-slidden generation. They are sunk in religious sloth; and require a spiritual revival. A long prosperity of breadfruit and coco-nuts has rendered them remiss in the performance of their higher obligations. The wood-rot malady is spreading among the idols—the fruit upon their alters is becoming offensive—the temples themselves need re-thatching—the tattooed clergy are altogether too light-hearted and lazy—and their flocks are going astray. (245)

Ultimately, Tommo becomes terrified of losing his Western/American identity by having his face tattooed or by becoming a permanent captive of the Typees, but there are points throughout the narrative at which he expresses a personal epiphany that the experience of living in such a different world has given him. After a short time with the Typees, Tommo says: "I began to experience an elasticity of mind which placed me beyond the reach of those dismal forebodings in which I had so lately been prey" (169). Soon thereafter, he echoes the conversion experiences of Saint Paul and Jonathan Edwards when he says: "In the altered frame of mind to which I have referred, every object that presented itself to my notice in the valley struck me in a new light. . . . There seemed to me no cares, grief's, or troubles or vexations in all Typee" (173).

While Tommo ceases to romanticize the Typee religion and culture, the text still suggests that Tommo's exposure to alternate systems of belief and their different moral consequences awakens him to question his own unexamined Christian assumptions about God, country, and the individual self as those concepts are understood within his own culture. It is also evident that Melville distanced himself from Tommo's timidity by demonstrating the limits of Tommo's engagement with difference. Melville himself would carry these lessons into all of his other voyages and into his writings, which would become more challenging and ambiguous in the years ahead.

The financial success of *Typee* and Melville's sequel, *Omoo*, enabled Melville to marry Elizabeth Shaw in 1847 and to purchase a large house in Manhattan where Herman and Elizabeth lived with seven other family members. Feeling pressure to produce another successful book, Melville entered a highly productive period of writing. *Mardi* and *Redburn* appeared in 1849, *White-Jacket* in 1850, *Moby-Dick* in 1851, and *Pierre* in 1852.

Redburn: His First Voyage

On June 4, 1839, nineteen-year-old Melville signed on as a cabin boy with the merchant ship *St. Lawrence* and headed for Liverpool, where he stayed for three months before returning to New York. This voyage constituted his first encounter with cultural difference and clearly sparked in him a desire to see more of the world and to compare the value systems and beliefs of the people of England and America with those elsewhere. He was not moved initially to write a travel narrative or a novel about this journey, and it was only after his long voyage to the South Seas that began in 1841 was he inspired to record his experience and transform it into a publishable narrative. So the reason to examine *Redburn* after *Typee* is that when he wrote *Redburn*, he drew upon all he had learned in the second voyage of 1841 and in the study he pursued between 1844 and 1849.

Redburn and *White-Jacket* have much in common in regard to Melville's treatment of philosophy and religion. For *Redburn*, Melville created a narrator whose views about religion, morality, social injustice, slavery, racism, and the competition among various religious groups and philosophical positions are very similar to those expressed by Tommo in *Typee* and to Melville's own views, to the degree that we can know them. In *Redburn* and *White-Jacket* the gap between the social and moral ideals expressed in the New Testament and in contemporary Christian rhetoric and the actual conditions of life for the great mass of people is the major target of the shock, anger, and frustration expressed by Melville's narrators.

In *Redburn*, two scenes that strike the young sailor with great force may stand as representative of the outrage Redburn feels in the face of the indifference of society toward human suffering and the unnecessary early deaths of millions. With compassion and delicacy, Redburn describes a starving young mother and her two children whom he discovers in the city beneath a grating under a public street but in plain view of passersby like himself. He tries to get the police or citizens to do something for the family, but they tell him that it is none of his business and that nothing can be done. After checking on them for a few days, he discovers one morning that the three of them have died, and some lime has been spread where the bodies had been. Taking this episode as emblematic of larger historical and economic forces of exploitation, inhumanity, and the crass indifference toward human life that he has discovered in England, Redburn elaborates on numerous examples of poverty and suffering he sees throughout the city.[12]

The other major scene that Redburn describes and interprets in detail is a large statue of Lord Nelson dying in the arms of Victory at the moment of his greatest naval success. At his feet are four black slaves in chains in "various attitudes of humiliation and despair" (149), and Redburn reflects that enabling the slave trade to flourish was one of Nelson's achievements because the African slave trade was once the primary commerce of Liverpool. Redburn reflects upon how most of the Christian churches had supported and benefited from slavery and that even his own father had played an indirect role in supporting it by doing business with Liverpool merchants.

Throughout *Redburn*, there is considerable debate among the crew members on a wide range of issues involving the moral values of democracy versus aristocracy. Redburn is disturbed that so many hierarchical power structures still persist within the United States and England, as in the military and the shipping industry, where the owners and captains of sailing ships and military units have unchecked control. He is convinced that, for Americans at least, the totalizing power of the ship captain must be a violation of constitutional rights. Especially appalling to Redburn is the practice of flogging sailors for even minor offenses and often on one person's word. He also learns that corrupt captains commonly prey upon poor Europeans who seek a new life in the United States by charging them a high passage price and promising them clean and healthful accommodations, only to wait until the ship departs to place them in vile conditions and rob them of their property. Redburn is also shocked by the ways that the ship captains promise a sailor a certain wage only to deduct many hidden charges at the end of the journey, leaving the sailor with nothing. In general, he finds the high degree of poverty and public begging in Liverpool to be shocking, but he wonders if he will not see the same conditions in the United States soon.

There is also a great deal in *Redburn* about books and reading and, in particular, about the Bible and the guidebook that Redburn inherited from his father, which he takes with him to England. At first, he is excited to think that he can follow the paths his father had taken and be with his father vicariously, but then he learns that so much has changed in the twenty years that the guidebook is of no practical use. Besides being a lesson to Redburn in self-reliance and not depending upon the books of the past, as Emerson had argued, the irony of the outmoded guidebook raises questions about the Bible upon which young Redburn relies too heavily. While the innocent and naive Redburn never doubts the relevance of the Bible to serve as a guide for life, Melville, as author, puts the question to the reader.[13] Because so many details are taken from Melville's own life, it is easy to think of Melville and Redburn as one voice. But Redburn is naive, and he is unconsciously complicit with much of the apparatus of control and discipline that he sees operating in the society. For example, for all his protests about the dying mother and children, he seems paralyzed by the spectacle of their condition and is powerless himself to help them. Similarly, at the end of the story, he has become the best friend of the fragile figure Harry Bolton who has come to rely upon Redburn and whose future looks quite bleak. When they reach New York, it is clear that Redburn might invite Harry to meet his family and stay a few days with them, but Redburn offers no such assistance, turning his back on Harry, only to wonder years later what might have become of him.

After Melville raised the issue of the flogging of sailors in *Redburn*, the matter began to receive public attention. So, in *White-Jacket*, he devoted an entire chapter to his argument that flogging is unlawful because "the Captain is made a legislature, as well as a judge and an executive." He also cites military laws that state that a captain cannot order more than twelve lashes unless there is a court-martial. Finally, he asserts that "flogging in the navy is against the essential dignity of man, which no legislature has the right to violate."[14] After *White-Jacket*'s publication, the public outcry against flogging increased, and in 1850 President James Polk appointed George Bancroft to be secretary of the navy, who then abolished the practice.

The other moral, religious, and legal issue that troubled Melville was the contradiction between the constitutional provision for the separation of church and state and the fact that in the military the soldiers and sailors had to attend religious services even if the chaplain of the unit was of a different religion or denomination. Melville also objected to the appointment of clergy to the military as officers who hold a military rank. Just as he complained in *Redburn* of preachers in the churches near the docks who did not know how to communicate with the seamen, in *White-Jacket* he railed against those chaplains who preach on abstruse subjects that have no meaning for the average seaman. Just as he wrote with scorn about the missionaries abroad who tried to preach to Pacific islanders on fine points of theology, so too he abhorred the chaplains who saw around them drunkenness, licentiousness, and vices of all manner and "never said aught" (155).

Mardi: and a Voyage Thither

Between his first journey in 1839 from New York to Liverpool and the remarkable outburst of major fiction that he began to produce in 1849, Melville underwent a self-education of extraordinary dimensions. Then, he departed for London and the Continent in October 1849, and it was during this voyage that he spent many days in intense discussion with the German philologist George Adler, who raised many key issues for Melville, guided him to contemporary philosophical works, and became a lifelong friend. Building upon the new learning that he gained on this journey, Melville took his religious and philosophical questioning to new depths in *Mardi*, *Moby-Dick*, and *Pierre*. Melville recognized that he had reached a spiritual and philosophical maturity, and the profound content and challenging aesthetics of his later works emerged between 1849 and 1852.

While there are passages in *Redburn* and *White-Jacket* that do engage philosophical and theological issues, for the most part, Melville confined his critique of religion in these novels to more practical problems that he saw in the practice of religion and in the failure of American clergy to meet the needs of people and to challenge persistent hypocrisy and corruption. In the three other novels he wrote between 1849 and 1852, Melville may have set out to write books that would be appreciated by the readers of *Typee*, *Redburn*, and *White-Jacket*, but the content, style, and structure of *Mardi*, *Moby-Dick*, and *Pierre* reveal that his mind was actively engaged with the most theoretically complex issues of his time. The result is that in *Mardi* Melville seems to have been thinking through many ideas that he would clarify and bring into coherence in *Moby-Dick*, where he formulated his deepest and most eloquent expressions of the large metaphysical questions that he could never stop asking. In *Pierre*, there is a deconstructive collapse or implosion of thought and action as the philosophical, psychological, aesthetic, and domestic crash into a heap, like the bodies of his characters, on the floor of a prison house of failed reason and incoherent expression.

For any Melville reader interested in the place of philosophy and religion in his works, *Mardi* is essential reading. While contemporary reviewers generally faulted the book as "foggy" or a "rubbishing rhapsody," Melville scholars have praised it as "clearly one of the most profound, witty, and charming" of his works."[15] F. O. Mattheissen gave it high praise: "*Mardi* could serve as a source book for reconstructing the conflicting faiths and doubts that were sweeping this country at the end of the eighteen forties."[16] Tyrus Hillway called *Mardi* "the key to Melville's philosophical, religious, political, and social ideas during the most significant and productive period of his career,"[17] and Raymond Weaver said that "the riddle of *Mardi* goes near the heart of the riddle of Melville's life." "There is infinite laughter in the book," Weaver observed, "but the laughter is at bottom the laughter of despair."[18]

Melville was deeply disappointed that *Mardi* was a critical and financial failure, and he seems not to have fully grasped how different it was from *Typee*. When he began the book, it appears that he intended it to be another travel narrative, and critics believe that had he brought it to a conclusion after the first thirty-eight chapters, he might have had a third successful novel. It appears that he was so preoccupied with his own personal religious and philosophical search that he abandoned his original design and let the writing become an intellectual dialogue of the mind for which he was the primary reader. His move from travel narrative in the first third of the text to satiric allegory in the final third mystified his readers, but that final third is a rich resource for those who seek to grasp the state of Melville's religious and philosophical ideas just before he wrote *Moby-Dick*. Indeed, most Melville scholars see *Mardi* as a text in which Melville was working through many concepts that would give *Moby-Dick* its dazzling intellectual power.

In those final chapters of *Mardi*, the characters of Babbalanja and Azzageddi represent opposing ways of dealing with the great philosophical and religious questions that Melville was now asking. He had come to a vision of the world in which he recognized the folly, hypocrisy, corruption, villainy, violence, and evil which lie beneath the surfaces of society where religion, ideology, patriotic rhetoric, pragmatism, economic necessities, and proper behavior served to disguise or erase the ugly truths that most people want to ignore. Babbalanja is the survivor, for he participates gladly in the masquerade that enables the rich to exploit the poor, the strong to use the weak, and the corrupt to destroy the innocent. On the other hand, Azzageddi is the skeptic who insists on raising the unasked questions and challenging those who pretend that all is well. Melville certainly identifies with Azzageddi as is evident in comments in "Hawthorne and His Mosses," where he proclaims that it is the calling of the artist to expose the suppressed lies and to reveal the truths that most are unable to see and then to insinuate those truths into texts so that capable readers may discover them.[19]

When the characters arrive at the utopian land of Serenia, they encounter a society with democratic social and religious structures that appears to be ideal. In this society based on love and reason, the people of Serenia believe in one spiritual God, and they also attend to the teachings of a human prophet with no pretension to being divine. The political and ethical systems are based on the principles elaborated by Christ in his Sermon on the Mount, Melville's favorite biblical text. Social democracy is practiced so those who are able-bodied support those who are incapable of earning a living. Those who are uncooperative with the community or who seek to harm others are not punished but are placed apart until they reform. There is no poverty or oppression and no fixed theology but a general openness to new truths. Walter Kring has observed that the religion represented on Serenia appears to be very close to the liberal Unitarianism that Melville would eventually claim as his religious affiliation in his last years.[20]

Moby-Dick; or, The Whale

During the summer of 1850, Melville wrote his admiring review of Hawthorne's work, "Hawthorne and His Mosses," and soon thereafter he met Hawthorne, beginning their long friendship. In September, he purchased a farm in Pittsfield, Massachusetts, and at a high point of enthusiasm and intellectual excitement, he began writing Moby-Dick, which he inscribed to the "Genius" of Nathaniel Hawthorne.

In his *Moby-Dick and Calvinism* (1977), Walter Herbert explored the important connections between the Calvinist doctrines central to the seventeenth-century Congregational churches of New England and the theological positions that inform much of the religious thought and language of Melville's novel.[21] New England Puritanism and Ahab's romantic transcendentalism both derive from Plato's idealism, and Herbert demonstrates the close connection between the two. Ahab's assertions about God's relationship to mankind and the rhetoric that he employs to dazzle and control the crew of the *Pequod* resonate with Calvinism. Some scholars have remarked that the sermon preached by Father Maple before Ishmael sets sail demonstrates how well Melville knew that rhetorical form and recognized the continuing power of such rhetoric to motivate and galvanize nineteenth-century congregations or whaling crews. Ahab draws upon the psychic force of Puritan rhetoric when he seeks in the "Quarter-Deck" chapter to inspire and unify the crew to join in covenant with him against the white whale, the living symbol of evil.

By the time he was writing *Moby-Dick*, Melville had become skeptical of the value of those Calvinist doctrines, as had many intellectual figures in New England, like Ralph Waldo Emerson. Emerson and many Christian clergy who were more aligned with Unitarianism believed that the doctrines of Original Sin, the divinity of Christ, mankind's natural depravity, predestination, and limited salvation for a small number of God's elect were discouraging and demoralizing and seemed inconsistent with a loving God who created all humans to share eternity with him. While the rhetorical style of Father Maple's sermon may draw upon the form and imagery of the old Puritan jeremiad, the content of the sermon represents the moderate, more encouraging theology that had evolved in some denominations by the mid-nineteenth century. While useful, recognition of the ties between Calvinism and *Moby-Dick* account for only one of the multiple ways that religious forms and ideas circulate in *Moby-Dick*.

When we move from *Mardi* to *Moby-Dick* in an attempt to assess Melville's religious thinking in the early 1850s, we move from the murky swirl of allegorical forms in the former to a far more sharply defined set of oppositions in the latter. Ahab is a nineteenth-century Puritan who suffers from the American Manichaean dualism constructed by the seventeenth-century New England Puritans. Trapped within the either-or logic of Calvin, he sees the world in terms of stark opposites: saint-sinner, heaven-hell, God-Satan, black-white. Ahab thinks in dualistic terms, and his monomania is similar to a form of mental illness common in Puritan New England in which the believer loses his confidence of salvation and becomes so wracked with fear and self-hatred at his spiritual failure that suicide or the murder of family members may result. For Ahab, there will be no peace or purpose for living unless he can destroy Moby-Dick, the real and symbolic source of his shame and rage. Ahab is a type of American Christian evangelical fervor gone mad and directed toward a single purpose, even if accomplishing that purpose will cost his own life and the lives of many others.

Melville follows the dualistic pattern of polar opposites himself by creating two protagonists, Ahab and Ishmael, who are engaged in an agonistic relationship, vying for center stage of the drama. Within the grander allegory of Melville's design, they also represent major philosophical positions and world views. Ahab encompasses forms of transcendental idealism, whether that be German Romanticism, Calvinist Puritanism, or Platonic idealism. He is not so interested in objects in this world, such as the actual whale, but rather in ideal forms that lie beyond the pasteboard mask where only the eye of God may read the signs. Like Milton's delusional Satan, Ahab is convinced that he knows all he needs to know, that he has nothing to learn from others, and that the world awaits his commands. Ahab's quest takes on the stature of a mythic hero in a larger-than-life battle of wills, human versus the unknowable monster. He is a type of paranoid, fanatical, evil tyrant. The more modest Ishmael is a pluralist, who draws eclectically from different intellectual systems; he is partly a mystic, humanist, hedonist, Romantic, and empiricist who appreciates and takes account of the richness of the physical world and stoically accepts his place in it. He has gone to sea for his own desperate reasons and now accepts his calling as the observer and recorder of the history of Ahab's quest. At the same time, he is attempting to "capture the whale in words" and to reflect upon the development of his own life in the process. While Ishmael's quest may appear less ambitious than Ahab's, it is no less significant for the future of a democratic society. Ishmael seeks to understand the real world of the senses rather than to strike through the real to pursue abstract forms and images.[22]

All of the concerns that had been expressed in Melville's works in fragments before *Moby-Dick* come together in this work, which engages issues involving religion, ethics, morality, and metaphysics. Ahab represents the destructive tendencies of hierarchical religions and political systems in which power and opinion are lodged in the hands of one or a few. He symbolizes the self-righteous arrogance of power and stands indifferent to the pain and suffering of others, who are expendable for the greater purpose. In contrast, Ishmael is open-minded, brings a variety of perspectives to his task, and refuses to let one epistemological position dominate his search for knowledge or his efforts at representation. One moment, he is the empirical scientist cataloging and defining in detail each type of whale in the "Cetology" chapter while at another he is squeezing the sperm and the hands of other seamen, appreciating the universal communication and spirit that flows through them. Whereas Ahab appears to be aloof from personal, emotional relationships and seeks to intimidate people and keep them at a distance, Ishmael seeks to learn from others, appreciates the religions and philosophies of different cultures, and joyfully bonds in a loving marriage with Queequeg, whose religion he respects. In naming himself Ishmael, for the Old Testament figure who is outside the covenant with God or the father, he gains the freedom to form his own types of covenants, as he does with Queequeg. Thus, Ishmael is open to multicultural and democratic perspectives.

While some have argued that Calvinism, as a form of Christianity in America, is Melville's primary religious target in *Moby-Dick*, such a view is really too limiting. Instead, what is faulted are all religions that employ a controlling hierarchy with narrow doctrines that restrain and control people's choices and lives to the extent of limiting democracy and freedom of choice. Because of the capitalistic nature of the ship's ownership, the hierarchy of the officers, and the insignificance of most of the crew as individual workers, there is no democracy or freedom in the community of the *Pequod*. Every sailor is a wage slave, and in slavery there is no freedom or justice for any of the parties.

When examined within the context of the development of Melville's religious thought, *Moby-Dick* does not depict a battle between good and evil with Ahab as the human hero trying to destroy the symbol of evil in the whale. Rather, what we have is a madman who is convinced that he has the right and the power to pursue his personal goal as symbolized in Moby-Dick, a mere creature in nature that has little or no interest in humans. It appears to be Melville's view that what is wrong with most of the world's religions is that they are structured in such ways as to be available to empower an Ahab, who believes that he has the knowledge of good and evil and may act for the rest of his society, nation, or the world. Often, secular governments recognize the political value of dressing themselves in religious trappings and language to generate such fervor for their own purposes. Ahab's quiet enemy is not the whale, but Ishmael, for he possesses the counternarrative that offers hope for evading or escaping the Ahabs of the world. By carefully recording his observations and insights, by producing an engaging narrative that carries the "truths" of what happened, by surviving in order to tell the tale, the artist does not tell people what they should think or do but shows them what is happening now and asks what is to be done.

Pierre; or, The Ambiguities

Shocked by the negative reviews of *Moby-Dick,* Melville promised his publisher and Hawthorne's wife, Sophia, that the new book he was working on in early 1852 was going to be a "rural bowl of milk"—meaning, we may suppose, that it would be sentimental and uplifting, noncontroversial, devoid of abstruse philosophy, and a financial success. In the opening chapters of *Pierre*, Melville presents an Edenic setting in central New York state where three generations of Glendinnings have established an estate on land taken from the native peoples in the late eighteenth century. The present occupants, Mary Glendinning and her son Pierre, live like American aristocrats. Mary awaits the day when Pierre will marry their beautiful neighbor, Lucy Tartan, as Mary and Lucy's mother have planned. After demonstrating in the first third of the text that he could sustain the florid style and playful narrative elements of the highly popular sentimental domestic fictions of the day, Melville begins to transform the romantic middle-class dream into a psychological nightmare and thereby to awaken the reader to recognize that all that she has read thus far has been a mocking parody of such fiction and a bitter critique of the false values underlying them.

Melville's scorn for such books and for the hypocritical life-style they foster becomes evident when Mrs. Glendinning and her clergyman, Reverend Falsgrave, enter into a moral confrontation with Pierre. The minister has come to inform Mary that Delly Ulver, the daughter of one of the farmers who lives on her land, has become pregnant by a married tenant. Pierre's mother decrees that Delly must be banished from the parish. Pierre, who has until now been a model of docility, challenges the decision by invoking the example of Jesus, who forgave the adulteress. With great condescension, Falsgrave support's Mary's decision by saying that one cannot always apply the Bible literarily to life. Disgusted by such an evasion, Pierre becomes determined to become Delly's champion.[23]

Had Melville followed the narrative strategies established in *Typee* and *Redburn*, the reader could expect many more examples of such ironic debunking of self-serving clergy who use such obfuscation to protect and flatter the rich. The elements for another satiric assault on the hollow platitudes of Christianity and the arrogance of power are all in place. For many reasons, however, including Melville's disappointment over the failure of *Moby-Dick,* the lack of support he felt from his friend Hawthorne and from his family members, the growing intensity of his philosophical skepticism and pessimism, and his anger toward the religious and political leadership of his country, Melville decided to let Pierre do what no young man in his society is supposed to do: follow his conscience and his instincts to try to repair damage that he believed his father had done to others.

Shortly before his encounter with Falsgrave and Mary, Pierre has seen the fleeting face of a young woman in the forest, and then he sees her more clearly in public. Haunted by her image and sensing that their lives are somehow intertwined, he soon receives a letter from her in which she claims to be his half sister. This assertion, about which he can never be certain, depends entirely upon his long-felt suspicions about his father's secret identity and upon the wild, Gothic, sentimental narrative that Isabel tells of her mysterious life. Deciding that he has a moral responsibility to provide for and protect Isabel, Pierre ends his engagement to Lucy, and leaves the estate with Delly and Isabel, whom he embraces as his sister but who eventually becomes his lover. Soon thereafter, Mary disinherits Pierre and eventually dies of grief. Lucy Tartan decides to move in with Pierre, Isabel, and Delly in the city, and Pierre tries to earn a living for them by his writing, but it is soon apparent to Melville's readers that Pierre lacks the talent and discipline to succeed as an author.

While being the most deeply psychological of Melville's novels, *Pierre* does not engage to any extent in the metaphysical, religious, and philosophical issues with which Melville was struggling in *Mardi* and *Moby-Dick*. With the focus upon moral and ethical responsibility, especially of those with position and wealth, the narrative at first seems designed to illustrate how the apparatuses of family, church, and society function to resist the righteous moral opposition to the status quo that Pierre's defiance and Lucy's unconventional support for him represents. Indeed, Pierre is stunned when his expectation of help and lodging from his prosperous loving cousin Glen Stanly is denied. Except for Pierre's harsh criticisms of voracious publishers who delude, defraud, and exploit authors and pay only minimal royalties, the text lacks the biting social satire and critique of *Typee* and *Redburn*.

What remains then as the only focal point for serious consideration is the nature of Pierre's Christ-like decision to sacrifice himself for the needs of others. The evidence against Pierre's father would be inadequate for a court to hold his son responsible for Isabel at such a late date. So all depends upon Pierre's choice, but his decision is motivated by passion rather than reason. As an angry young man who lost his father when he was entering puberty and was indulged but tightly controlled by his imperious mother, he has come to feel guilty about and resentful of the contrast between the privileged, but unhappy, life he has lived and the obvious poverty and hardship endured by the vast populace. Thus, in his anger and egotism, he grabs the opportunity to be an enthusiast in the cause of the injured Isabel and refuses to turn from that course in spite of all manner of difficulties.

Nothing in Pierre's life before he met Isabel, however, has provided him with the social skills, knowledge of human nature, and marketable profession needed to be able to find employment that would support himself and three women and enable him to negotiate the complex social obstacles that a person in his situation should expect. While Pierre rants a great deal about his persecution and his potential to reform the evils of society through his writing, he lacks the talent, preparation, and connections to have such an impact. By making no effort when he first decides upon his action to try to console his mother and acquire her partial support, he dooms his mission of mercy from the moment of its conception. While many critics have tended to collapse Melville into Pierre and read the text as veiled autobiography, the narrative actually calls this possible Melville-Pierre fusion into question through the use of humor. There is much that is very funny in the narrator's reports on Pierre's state of mind to such a degree that it appears that the narrator thinks that Pierre is a persistent fool and a terrible writer.

Given Melville's long interest in philosophical questions, the fact that Pierre never does think in philosophical or spiritual terms about his cause or situation would support such a reading. The one engagement with ideas that Pierre does have—his connections to Plotinus Plinlimmon and his pamphlet "Horologicals and Chronometricals"—is a comic scenario. When Pierre takes lodging in a residence hall named the Church of the Apostles, he meets a young enthusiast of transcendentalism, Charlie Millthorpe, who is a follower of an Emerson type of idealist philosopher whom he calls "The Grand Master, Plotinus Plinlimmon." Charlie tells Pierre that he should become a worker in the campaign for the philosophy of Kant: "Pierre, a thought, my boy—a thought for you. You do not say it, but you hint of a low purse. Now I shall help you to fill it—Stump the State on the Kantian Philosophy! A dollar a head, my boy!" (280).

While Pierre fails to see the humor in the absurdity that philosophical ideas have now become a commodity of popular distribution, a product like soap to be hawked on the streets, the narrator sets the stage for Pierre to encounter Plinlimmon in the next chapter. When he sees the grand master, Pierre remembers having once skimmed his pamphlet, and now he feels compelled to go back and read it more carefully. He feels that the knowledge therein might be a key to his search for Truth. He searches his clothing but never finds the pamphlet because it has fallen through a pocket and into the lining of his overcoat only to be discovered after his death. The message of the pamphlet is a pragmatic warning that there is no direct connection between God's time (horologicals) and man's time (chronometricals), so it is foolish and self-destructive to try to aspire to lofty aims that belong to the realm of God.

Having failed to recognize the importance of this anti-idealist lesson when he had the pamphlet and then being unable to find it when he senses the need for such advice, Pierre continues on his course toward a melodramatic ending that takes the reader full circle back to the novel of sentiment of the opening chapters. Shutting himself off from everyone, Pierre remains at his writing desk for days trying to write the great book that will reveal all about Truth and lies and about life and death to the world. Melville's self-mocking in this passage is evident as Pierre struggles to express what he recognizes, but he fails to do so with any coherence. So painful are the truths that he pens that he averts his eyes from the pages because he cannot bear to read what he has written. As he sinks into despair and isolation, Glen Stanly arrives to remove Lucy from his dwelling, and in a rage Pierre shoots and kills Stanly. Lucy and Isabel visit him in his jail cell; he tells Lucy that Isabel is his sister, and she dies of a broken heart. With that, Pierre takes a vial of poison that Isabel has brought with her, and he dies. Isabel takes the last of the poison and falls on the body of Pierre. This scene references the ending of Shake-speare's tragedy *Romeo and Juliet* and parodies the endings of many American sentimental novels so popular at the time.

In regard to Melville's own personal journey toward religious faith or philosophical consolation, *Pierre* marks the low point at which Melville seemed closest to madness. In fact, his family had him examined for his mental health soon after he finished the novel, an experience which he conveys in the story "I and My Chimney." The books that followed *Pierre* were darkly ironic: *The Piazza Tales* (1856), which includes "Bartleby, the Scrivener" and "Benito Cereno," and *The Confidence-Man* (1857), which conveys a deeply cynical view of corrupt human nature. On September 11, 1867, Melville's eldest son, Malcolm, was found dead in his bed of a gunshot to the head. This was a terrible blow to Melville at a time when he was already deeply troubled. Although the family denied that it was suicide and insisted that it was an accident, the coroner's jury first officially listed it as suicide. After Malcolm's younger brother, Stanwix, reported that Malcolm had taken to sleeping with a loaded gun under his pillow, a family friend per-suaded the coroner to modify the verdict to an unpremeditated accident "to clear the reputation of the deceased young man."[24] Melville gave up writing novels after *The Confidence-Man*, which was another failure, and he did not return to writing long fiction until he began to write *Billy Budd* a few years before he died.

Clarel

In 1866, Melville published *Battle-Pieces*, a collection of poems on the Civil War, and then he began to work on his long poem *Clarel*. From October 1856 until May 1857, Melville traveled in Eu-rope and the Holy Land, where he began to conceive of the ideas and to collect material for this poem. Working on it occasionally until after the publication of *The Confidence-Man*, he returned to it more often between 1867 and its publication in 1876. For Melville, working on the poem was a way of working through his many questions about God, religion, faith, and his own soul, which no authorities in the churches or the universities were answering to his satisfaction. One scholar has said that he was documenting a "major crisis in Western civilization—the apparent smash–up of revealed religion in the age of Darwin."[25] Although the poem is highly autobiographical and addresses his own skepticism and search for answers, it also examines some of the ways that other thinkers of his era, such as Tennyson, Arnold, Lowell, and Longfellow, responded to the crisis of faith.

Clarel is a fictional narrative whose hero, Clarel, is a student of theology who is on a journey of ten days through the Holy Land in the hope of finding the answers to many questions he has about revelation, the Scriptures, and religious authority. During his travels, he meets many people whom he interrogates on these issues, and he receives many different responses, but he will not settle for answers from others until he has worked through the problems himself. Soon after arriving in Jerusalem, he falls in love with a young Jewish woman named Ruth, and they become engaged. Her father, an immigrant to Palestine from the United States, is killed in a raid by hostile Arabs. Since Ruth is forbidden from seeing Clarel during the long mourning period because he is not Jewish, he leaves with a group to visit the Dead Sea, Jericho, and Bethlehem. The pilgrimage serves to organize Clarel's conversations with a series of characters, many of whom are presented as types: the Banker, the Syrian Monk, the Apostate, and others. The questions Clarel puts to them are ones that Melville himself had been asking for years. In many cases, the answers are also Melville's, but in certain ones, the replies are based in Melville's reading of the works of others, such as Wordsworth or Coleridge. At the end of the pilgrimage, Clarel returns to Ruth's home to find that she has died of grief. Devastated and furious that he had been forced to stay away from her during the mourning period because he is not Jewish, he curses the elders and returns to Jerusalem to participate in Passion Week. As he prepares to return to America, Clarel feels that he has lost his one chance for true love.

While Clarel, like Melville, has not found a faith nor abandoned skepticism by the end of the poem, Clarel does express some important changes in his views. For one, he decides that science may make people think about nature differently, but it has not changed the need for faith in something beyond the natural world. Thus, the need for religion will continue for the great mass of people. Also, while he agrees that, at the time of Martin Luther, Catholicism was in great need of reform, he believes that now it does provide the believer with important religious elements affecting the emotions, which Protestantism lacks, and for that reason Catholicism will outlast the Protestant churches. For the most part, however, *Clarel* has far more criticism than praise for any organized religion, and like the protagonists in many of Melville's novels, Clarel unleashes some bitter and highly offensive comments about the missionaries, pompous clergy, and poor sermons, with particularly vitriolic remarks aimed at Grace Church in New York. In spite of the fact that Melville, like Clarel, did not find the foundation for faith in the Holy Land, the tone of Clarel's criticisms is less sarcastic and darkly pessimistic than those in *Pierre* and *The Confidence-Man*. In the epilogue, the author addresses *Clarel* with some parting words of hope:

Then keep thy heart, though yet but ill-resigned—
Clarel, thy heart, the issues there but mind;
That like the crocus budding through the snow—
· ·
Emerge thou mayest from the last whelming sea,
And prove that death but routs life into victory.

As Melville expected, however, Clarel sold poorly, and he was again forced to accept gifts from relatives to pay for the printing costs.

Billy Budd

In the mid-1880s, Melville began to collect material that would eventually come together as his unfinished novella, *Billy Budd*. When he died in 1891, his wife put the various versions of the manuscript away and when she died in 1906, it was passed on with the rest of Melville's papers to the estate, where it remained until 1924 when a version of it was published. Because there were various versions of the manuscript, different scholars edited and published different versions between 1924 and 1962, leading to directly opposed readings of the work especially in regard to Melville's personal religious and philosophical positions near the end of his life.

In brief, the story tells of a Handsome Sailor whose striking appearance, personal warmth, and boyish innocence have made him a favorite among seamen on the British merchant ship the *Rights-of-Man*. It is a time of war, however, when seamen can be impressed into military service at the whim of the captain of a naval vessel, and Billy is forced to join the crew of the warship the HMS *Bellipotent*. He immediately becomes popular among the crew, but he becomes the object of jealousy and antipathy for the master-at-arms, John Claggart. Billy is quite innocent, and he does not believe it when a friend tries to warn him that Claggart is out to get him. It happens that there is unrest on the ship because of the policies of Captain Edward Fairfax Vere, scornfully named "Starry Vere" by fellow captains because he is bookish and aloof. Claggart is aware of the possible plot in motion, and he notices that one of the rebels approaches Billy, who rejects his invitation. Still, Claggart uses the fact of this conversation as evidence and tells Captain Vere that Billy is brewing mutiny. Billy is brought before the captain to confront his accuser, and when Claggart makes his charge, Billy, who suffers with a stutter, is unable to speak and in anger and frustration strikes Claggart on the temple, killing him. Captain Vere reacts by saying, "Fated boy what have you done? Struck dead by an angel of God! Yet the angel must hang!"[26]

Because he fears a possible mutiny, and because he is generally insecure as a leader who does not have respect among his peers, Vere is convinced that he must take decisive action immediately. So he appoints a drumhead court of officers and serves as Billy's prosecutor. Although the other officers want to consider the mitigating circumstances and find a path to leniency, Vere insists on death for Billy, and he gets his verdict: Billy is to be hung at dawn. During the night, Vere pays a visit to Billy, but the nature of the conversation is not reported. In the morning, as the crew looks on, Billy says as he is about to die: "God Bless Captain Vere!" In the rest of the narrative, various other accounts of the events are presented, among them, newspaper reports on the mutiny, historical accounts, and legal records from the hearing held back in port. In time, Billy becomes a mythic, Christ-like figure to the sailors, who keep relics of his clothing and pass them along to others. It becomes evident that there will be many versions of the events in the world and that the "true" story will never be known.

For scholars who are interested in Melville's final personal positions about religion, the text of *Billy Budd* has been a battlefield because for decades there was no authoritative version of the story. One version seems to support the authority of Captain Vere as the appointed representative of the king and God who must act as he did for the greater good of society, and in this version Billy's final words acknowledge the wisdom of humbly accepting Vere's decision. Those who embraced this reading saw in it Melville's reconciliation with God and with organized religion and authority. Others used different versions of the final work to show that Vere is a villain and that Melville is being consistent to a lifetime of rebellion against arrogant authority figures by exposing Vere's self-interest and hypocrisy.

In 1962, after years of painstaking research, Harrison Hayford and Merton M. Sealts, Jr., produced a "genetic text" in which they reproduced and dated all of the variations of the manuscript that Melville produced. From this work, they fashioned their best guess about what would be a legitimate text for readers today, but they acknowledged that Melville left a work in progress and that there is no way to know exactly what he would have produced as his final version.

Thus, Melville's final work does not provide conclusive evidence of his religious or philosophical state of mind at the time of his death, but as always he offers complex, tantalizing intricacies for those who wish to continue to join him, in Hawthorne's words, "to wander to-and-fro over these deserts, as dismal and monotonous as the sand amid which we were sitting."

Conclusion

In her remarkable 1998 essay, "Melville's Traveling God," the late Jenny Franchot asserted that Melville's journey at the age of twenty-two to the South Seas deeply affected his evolving religious views and his literary aesthetic. While many scholars before Franchot have held that Melville was a radical critic of organized religion, with the possible, much-debated exception of a late return to religious authority which some perceive in *Billy Budd*, Franchot held that from very early on Melville's narratives reinvigorated Christianity and breathed new life into the yearning for a personal God. For other writers and intellectuals in the nineteenth century, God was already dead and religion was irrelevant, but in Franchot's view Melville refused to accept this finality and made an aesthetic move to absorb the creeds, dogmas, Scriptures, and daily acts of faith and belief into "the absorbing domain of ambiguous literary narrative."[27] Yet, she says, at the same time Melville's works so fully absorb religion as the opposing Other that they drain religion of its last vestige of authority as a real force and presence in the world, making it into a character or puppet of Melville's more powerful art. Franchot's argument explains the complex ways that Melville's aesthetic forms and allegorical style reveal the hybridity of all world religions. Each great religion, including Christianity, has borrowed concepts, stories, characters, images, and even theological doctrines from prior religions, altered those components, formed new ones, and woven new narratives and sacred texts for new times and places.

For understanding these dimensions of Melville's treatment of religion as a component of Melville's aesthetics and metaphysical speculations, Franchot's essay is provocative and insightful. For her, Melville persists in seeking his own personal God and individual truth while repeatedly demonstrating and resuscitating Christianity in the admittedly futile hope that it may live up to its promises.

Yet, this reading seems to deny or avoid what so many readers find compelling in Melville's treatment of religion: the persistent, often bitter and angry, critique of the hypocrisy and corrupt complicity of too many of its leaders with the inhumanity, injustice, and immorality that were rampant in his own country and around the globe. Melville gave a new and different meaning to religion in his texts because he recognized that—whether or not he was a believer in a particular faith—religion, at its worst, inspired millions of believers to condone slavery, colonization, ruthless forms of political and economic imperialism, racism, class warfare, and global wars; and it served to allow people to avert their eyes from the poverty, injustice, suffering, and violence endured by millions even in the richest countries. At the same time, the powerful anger expressed in Melville's texts over these contradictions as embodied by religious leaders and their followers demonstrates that Melville did, in his own way, resurrect religion because, though lacking intellectual viability, it remained alive in the hearts and minds of millions and possessed great potential as a force in the world, a force that could bring terrible destruction or the human benefits of understanding and peace.

NOTES

1 Lawrence R. Thompson, *Melville's Quarrel with God* (Princeton, N.J.: Princeton University Press, 1952).

2 Randall Stewart, ed., *The English Notebooks by Nathaniel Hawthorne* (New York: Russell and Russell, 1941), pp. 432–33.

3 Nancy Fredricks, *Melville's Art of Democracy* (Athens: University of Georgia Press, 1995), pp. 3–13.

4 Hershel Parker, *Herman Melville: A Biography*, 2 vols. (Baltimore, Md.: Johns Hopkins University Press, 1996, 2002), I:618; hereafter in text as Parker.

5 Richard H. Brodhead, "All in the Family," *New York Times Book Review* (June 23, 2002), pp. 13–14.

6 Frances Milton Trollope, *Domestic Manners of the Americans* (London: Whittaker, Treacher, 1832); and Alexis de Tocqueville, *Democracy in America* (London: Saunders and Otley, 1835).

7 Emory Elliott, *Revolutionary Writers: Literature and Authority in*

the New Republic, 1725–1810 (New York: Oxford University Press, 1982), pp. 1–25.

8 Nathaniel Hawthorne, *The Blithedale Romance and Fanshaw* (Columbus: University of Ohio Press, 1964).

9 Sydney Ahlstrom, *A Religious History of the American People* (New Haven, Conn.: Yale University Press, 1972), pp. 385–510.

10 Walter Donald Kring, *Herman Melville's Religious Journey* (Raleigh, N.C.: Pentland, 1997), pp. 1–19; and William Braswell, *Melville's Religious Thought* (New York: Octagon, 1973), pp. 1–18.

11 Herman Melville, *Typee: A Peep at Polynesian Life*, ed. Jay Leyda, in *The Portable Melville* (New York: Viking, 1972), p. 27.

12 Herman Melville, *Redburn: His First Voyage*, ed. Harrison Hayford, Hershel Parker, and G. Thomas Tanselle (Evanston, Ill.: Northwestern University Press, 1969), pp. 180–84.

13 Emerson, "An American Scholar," in *The Selected Writings of Ralph Waldo Emerson*, ed. Brook Atkinson (New York: Random House, 1950), p. 49. Emerson says: "Instantly the book becomes noxious; the guide is a tyrant."

14 Herman Melville, *White-Jacket* (Evanston, Ill.: Northwestern University Press, 1979), pp. 143–44.

15 Quoted in Laurie Robertson-Lorant, *Melville: A Biography* (Amherst: University of Massachusetts Press, 1996), p. 192.

16 F. O. Mattheissen, *American Renaissance: Art and Expression in the Age of Emerson and Whitman* (New York: Oxford University Press, 1941), p. 122.

17 Tyrus Hillway, *Herman Melville* (New York: Twayne, 1963), quoted in Kring, *Herman Melville's Religious Journey*, p. 60.

18 Raymond Weaver, *Herman Melville: Mariner and Mystic* (New York: Doran, 1921), p. 274.

19 Herman Melville, "Hawthorne and His Mosses, in *The Portable Melville*, ed. Jay Leda (New York: Viking, 1972), pp. 407–9.

20 Kring, *Religious Journey*, p. 67.

21 T. Walter Herbert, *Moby-Dick and Calvinism: A World Dismantled* (New Brunswick, N.J.: Rutgers University Press, 1977).

22 Fredricks, *Art of Democracy*, pp. 28–33.

23 Herman Melville, *Pierre; or, The Ambiguities* (Evanston, Ill.: Northwestern University Press, 1971), pp. 98–101.

24 Robertson-Lorant, *Melville*, p. 515.

25 Walter E. Bezanson, "Introduction," *Clarel* (New York: Hendricks House, 1960), p. x.

26 Herman Melville, *Billy Budd, Sailor (An Inside Narrative)*, ed. Harrison Hayford and Merton M. Sealts, Jr. (Chicago: University of Chicago Press, 1962), pp. 99–101.

27 Jenny Franchot, "Melville's Traveling God," in *The Cambridge Companion to Herman Melville*, ed. Robert S. Levine (Cambridge: Cambridge University Press, 1998), pp. 157–85.

ILLUSTRATED
CHRONOLOGY

Historical Events	Melville's Life
1819: Florida purchased; University of Virginia founded.	**1819:** Herman Melville born August 1, the third child of Allan Melvill (1782–1832), importer and merchant, and Maria Gansevoort (1791–1872), daughter of General Peter Gansevoort, a member of an important Albany family and American Revolution hero. Brothers and sisters include Gansevoort (1815–1846), Helen Maria (1817–1888), Augusta (1821–1876), Allan (1823–1872), Catherine (1825–1905), Frances Priscilla (1827–1885), and Thomas (1830–1884).
1820: Missouri Compromise outlaws slavery in lands of Louisiana Purchase.	
1821: Santa Fe Trail mapped between Independence, Missouri, and Santa Fe, New Mexico.	
1823: Monroe Doctrine enunciated.	
1825: John Quincy Adams elected sixth president of the United States; Erie Canal completed.	**1825–1829:** Enters New York Male High School with Gansevoort; named best speaker in high school's Introductory Department; enters grammar school of Columbia College.
1826: First lyceum to provide educational opportunities for adults.	

Allan Melvill, 1820. Courtesy of Berkshire Athenaeum.

Maria Gansevoort Melvill, c. 1814. Courtesy of Berkshire Athenaeum.

1827: Slavery is abolished in the state of New York.

1828: Andrew Jackson is elected president for two terms in a victory for the new Democratic party.

1830: Joseph Smith founds Church of Jesus Christ of Latter-Day Saints (Mormons); congressional passage of the Indian Removal Act forces Native Americans to move west of the Mississippi.

1831: Nat Turner mounts a slave insurrection that kills more than 57 whites.

1832: South Carolina precipitates the nullification crisis, threatening to secede from the Union, by finding two national tariffs illegal.

1833: American Anti-Slavery Society founded.

1834: Whig party replaces the New Republicans as the anti-Jackson party.

1836: In the Battle of the Alamo with Mexico, 183 Americans die, including the trapper Kit Carson.

1837: Martin van Buren's election as eighth president of the United States is accompanied by five years of economic difficulties.

1830: Father's business fails and family moves to Albany; attends Albany Academy with Gansevoort; Lemuel Shaw, Herman's future father-in-law, named chief justice of the Supreme Judicial Court of Massachusetts.

1832: Father dies, probably as a result of pneumonia contracted while crossing the frozen Hudson River on foot; due to family's debts, Melville is taken out of school and works as clerk at New York State Bank; mother adds the "e" to Melvill sometime during the next two years.

1833: Melville vacations at his uncle Thomas Melville's farm (later "Broadhall") in Pittsfield, Massachusetts.

1834: Melville works at uncle Thomas's farm; brother Gansevoort's business is destroyed by fire.

1835: Melville clerks in fur store, joins Albany Young Men's Association, enters Albany Classical School.

1836: Melville joins the Ciceronian Debating Society; as family debts increase, mother mortgages inherited property.

1837: Gansevoort's business fails in financial panic; Melville teaches at Sikes District School, Pittsfield.

1838:   Underground Railroad founded to assist slaves in escaping to the North.

1839:   Economic depression spreads, causing bankruptcies and defaults on loans by several states.

1840:   Election of William Henry Harrison puts the Whigs in power; Cyrus McCormick invents the mechanical reaper.

1841:   Harrison dies after only one month in office and is succeeded by John Tyler; Brook Farm established in West Roxbury, Massachusetts, as a utopian experiment; Emerson's *Essays: First Series* is published.

1838:   Melville becomes president of Albany's Philo Logos Debating Society, moves with family to Lansingburgh, takes course in surveying and engineering at Lansingburgh Academy.

1839:   In May, *Democratic Press & Lansingburgh Advertiser* publishes Melville's "Fragments from a Writing Desk"; in June, Melville sails for Liverpool and *St. Lawrence*, a trader; in the fall, Melville teaches school in Greenbush and, briefly, in Brunswick, New York.

1840:   Melville visits his uncle Thomas in Galena, Illinois, and takes a voyage on a Mississippi River steamer; in December, after failing to find work on his return to New York, Melville signs on the whaling ship *Acushnet*.

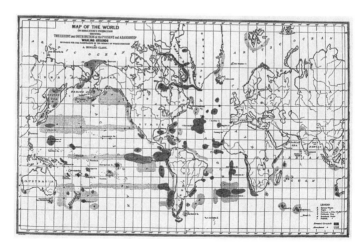

Whaling grounds map. © Mystic Seaport, Mystic, Conn.

Charles W. Morgan *under sail.* © *Mystic Seaport, Mystic, Conn.*

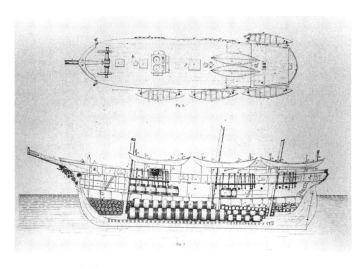

Cutaway view of whaler. © Mystic Seaport, Mystic, Conn.

Whale and whaleboat. © Mystic Seaport, Mystic, Conn.

Lithograph, "Sperm Waling No. 2: The Conflict." © Mystic Seaport, Mystic, Conn.

Cutting into whale with tryworks. © Mystic Seaport, Mystic, Conn.

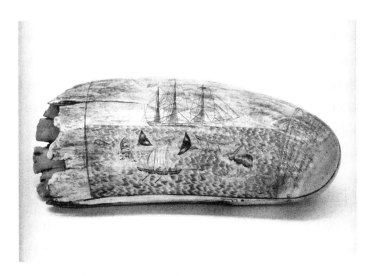

Scrimshaw tooth. © Mystic Seaport, Mystic, Conn.

Two men at masthead. © *Mystic Seaport, Mystic, Conn.*

1843:   The Oregon Trail is opened.

1844:   Texas is annexed from Mexico; Samuel F. B. Morse invents the telegraph.

1845:   James Polk becomes president; the term "manifest destiny" is used for the first time by James L. O'Sullivan to justify national expansion; the first clipper ship is launched.

1846:   War with Mexico begins (1846–1848); the Wilmot Proviso banning slavery in the lands acquired from Mexico fails to pass; many members of the Donner party expire in the Sierra Nevadas on their way to California.

1841:   The *Acushnet* leaves Fairhaven on its maiden voyage for the Pacific Ocean on January 3, stops at Rio de Janeiro, rounds Cape Horn, and visits Santa, Peru, before cruising through Galapagos islands.

1842:   The *Acushnet* arrives at Marquesan islands in June; on July 9, Melville and Tobias Greene desert the ship and escape to interior of Nukahiva; after a month in the valley of the Typees, Melville signs on the Australian whaler *Lucy Ann* on August 9 and is imprisoned in Tahiti on September 24 by the British consul for refusing duty; in October, Melville escapes to Eimeo with John B. Troy and works on a potato farm before signing on as boat steerer on the Nantucket whaler *Charles & Henry* bound for Hawaii.

1843:   The *Charles & Henry* reaches Lahaina in Hawaiian islands in April; in May, Melville is discharged and sent to Honolulu, where he works at odd jobs, including store clerk and setter of pins in a bowling alley; in August, Melville signs on as ordinary seaman of frigate *United States*, where he meets his friend John J. Chase.

1847: Free Soil party established (1847–1854).

1848: Seneca Falls Convention on women's rights; antislavery Free Soil party receives 10 percent of the vote in the presidential election that brings Zachary Taylor to the White House; Treaty of Guadalupe Hidalgo ends Mexican War and gives the United States the lands of California, New Mexico and parts of Arizona and Nevada for $15 million; political revolutions sweep Europe.

1849: The California gold rush commences; U.S. Department of the Interior is established.

1850: Millard Fillmore inaugurated thirteenth president after Zachary Taylor dies sixteen months into his first term; in the Compromise of 1850, California is admitted as a free state and New Mexico and Utah are organized as territories; Fugitive Slave Act is passed; Emerson's *Representative Men* and Hawthorne's *The Scarlet Letter* are published.

1851: Sojourner Truth speaks at women's right convention in Ohio.

1852: Franklin Pierce is elected president, *Uncle Tom's Cabin* published by Harriet Beecher Stowe.

1844: On its return home, the *United States* visits the Marquesas, Tahiti, Valparaiso, Callao, Lima, and Rio Harbor before arriving in Boston in October; Melville is discharged on October 14 and returns to Lansingburgh, where he soon begins writing his adventures in the book to be entitled *Typee*.

1845: *Typee* is rejected by Harper Brothers in New York but is then accepted by British publisher John Murray through the efforts of Melville's brother Gansevoort, secretary of the American legation in England.

1846: Gansevoort's political career blossoms; published in London on February 26 under the title *Narrative of a Four Months' Residence among the Natives of a Valley of the Marquesas Islands, Typee* is published by the American firm Wiley & Putnam toward the end of March; on May 12, Gansevoort dies in London; in July, Tobias Greene verifies the experiences recorded in *Typee*, and Melville composes a sequel for a revised edition; *Omoo* is accepted by Murray and Harper's.

Elizabeth Shaw Melville, c. 1847.
Courtesy of Berkshire Athenaeum.

1847:   Melville seeks a government position in Washington, D.C.; *Omoo* is published in London on March 30, in the United States a month later; Melville begins publishing anonymous reviews and political satires for the *Literary World*, edited by his friend Evert A. Duyckinck, and for *Yankee Doodle*, edited by Cornelius Mathews, a member of Duyckinck's circle; on August 4, Melville marries Elizabeth Shaw (June 13, 1822–July 31, 1906), daughter of Massachusetts chief justice Lemuel Shaw (1781–1861), and moves to Manhattan where they set up housekeeping at 103 Fourth Avenue, New York City, along with brother Allan and his wife, Melville's mother, and unmarried sisters.

1849:   His first son, Malcolm, is born on February 16 (dies September 11, 1867); *Mardi* is rejected by the London publisher of *Omoo*, John Murray, but is then published in England by Richard Bentley in March and in the United States by Harper's in April; Melville writes *Redburn* and *White-Jacket* in an astonishingly creative period of four months; *Redburn: His First Voyage* is published by Bentley in London on September 29 and by Harper's in New York on November 14; on October 11, Melville sails for England with proofs of *White-Jacket*, visits Paris, Brussels, Cologne, and the Rhineland, then departs for New York on Christmas morning.

1853:   Rise of Know-Nothings and political nativism.

1854:   Whig party collapses and is replaced by new Republican party; Kansas-Nebraska Act repeals Missouri Compromise and opens western territory to slavery.

1856:   James Buchanan elected president; Senator Charles Sumner of Massachusetts is assaulted in Congress by Preston Brooks of South Carolina and nearly killed when he speaks on "The Crime against Kansas"

1857: The *Dred Scott* decision by the Supreme Court denies citizenship to blacks and declares the Missouri Compromise to be unconstitutional; financial panic spreads.

1858: Abraham Lincoln debates Senator Stephen Douglas; Lincoln delivers his "House Divided" speech.

1859: Radical abolitionist John Brown raids the federal arsenal at Harpers Ferry, Virginia, to incite a slave revolt; his capture, trial and execution are subjects of national discussion.

1850: *White-Jacket* is published by Bentley in February and Harper's in March; Melville and his family spend the summer in Pittsfield, Massachusetts; Duyckinck visits him there and attends the excursion to Monument Mountain and Icy Glen, where Melville meets Nathaniel Hawthorne, then living in Lenox; *Literary World* publishes "Hawthorne and His Mosses"; in September, Melville receives a loan from his father-in-law and buys a farm in the Pittsfield area near Hawthorne's, which he names "Arrowhead"; the family is moved in by October; Melville begins writing "The Whale."

Arrowhead. Courtesy of Berkshire Athenaeum.

Interior of Arrowhead, Chimney Room. Courtesy of Berkshire Athenaeum.

A Burnham Shute, "Aye, the Piquod [sic]—that ship here." American Publisher's Corporation, 1896, facing p. 90.

1851:   A second son, Stanwix, is born on October 22 (dies February 23, 1886); in October, Bentley published *The Whale*; in November, Harper's publishes it as *Moby-Dick*.

1852:   In the spring, Bentley refuses publication of *Pierre* unless it is expurgated, but Harper's publishes it in August; Melville visits New Bedford, Nantucket, and the islands and seeks a consular post abroad.

1853:   Concerned about Melville's health (he is plagued by recurrent bouts of depression that are exacerbated by increasing financial insecurity), his family tries to obtain a consulship for him abroad; first daughter, Elizabeth, is born on May 11 (dies May 26, 1908); Melville contributes to *Putnam's* and *Harper's* monthly magazines.

I. W. Taber, Queequeg and his harpoon. *Charles Scribner's Sons, 1899; facing p. 78.*

A Burnham Shute, Next instant, the luckless mate was smitten bodily into the air. *American Publisher's Corporation, 1896, p. 299.*

I. W. Taber, Moby Dick swam swiftly round and round the wrecked crew. *Frontispiece. Charles Scribner's Sons, 1899.*

1854: *Putnam's* begins serial publication of *Israel Potter* (at first subtitled "or, Fifty Years of Exile. A Forth of July Story").

1855: Second daughter, Frances, is born on March 2 (dies January 15, 1938); *Israel Potter* is published in March by Putnam in New York after serialization in *Putnam's Monthly Magazine* from July 1854 to March 1855; a pirated edition (a fate experienced by earlier works) is produced in England by George Routledge in May: at his family's request, Melville is examined by Dr. Oliver Wendell Holmes.

1860: Abraham Lincoln is elected president and at Cooper Union delivers a speech on the problem that slavery creates for the U.S. Constitution; the Pony Express is established.

1861: Ten southern states secede from the Union, and Jefferson Davis is elected president of the new Confederate States of America; Fort Sumter is attacked and war is declared; Richmond becomes the capital of the Confederacy; the First Battle of Bull Run is fought; Matthew Brady begins to photograph the Civil War.

1856: *The Piazza Tales* (including five of the *Putnam* stories and a new introduction) is published in March by Dix and Edwards in New York and distributed later in England by Sampson and Low; "The Bell-Tower" is rejected for publication; on October 11, with financial assistance from his father-in-law, Melville sails for Europe and the East, visiting Hawthorne in Liverpool before traveling to Malta, Syria, Salonica, Constantinople, Alexandria, Cairo, and the Holy Land, where he gathers material that will wind up in *Clarel*.

Melville children, c. 1860. Courtesy of Berkshire Athenaeum.

Herman and Thomas Melville, 1860. Courtesy of Berkshire Athenaeum.

Herman Melville, 1861. Corutesy of Berkshire Athenaeum.

1857: On his way home, Melville visits Greece, Sicily, Naples, Rome, Florence, Pisa, Padua, Venice, Milan, Turin, Genoa, Switzerland, Germany, the Netherlands, and England; *The Confidence-Man* is published in April both by Longman Brown, Green, Longmans & Roberts in England and by Dix, Edwards in the United States.

1858: Melville begins an ill-starred career on the lecture circuit that lasts three years, his subjects each of the three seasons being, respectively, "Statues in Rome," "The South Seas," and "Traveling"; these lectures carry him as far as Tennessee and Ohio.

1859: Melville's lectures continue as far as Milwaukee; he writes poetry and offers it for publication.

1860: Melville's brother Thomas, captain of the clipper ship *Meteor*, invites him to sail for San Francisco on May 28; he returns to New York on the *North Star* on November 12.

1861: Melville travels to Washington, D.C., seeks a consular appointment; Lemuel Shaw, his father-in-law, dies.

1862: Melville, ill with rheumatism, is seriously injured in a road accident.

North Field, Arrowhead, during the 1890s. Courtesy of Berkshire Athenaeum.

1862:   The Battles of Shiloh, Antietam, Fredericksburg, and Second Bull Run are waged along with the siege of Vicksburg; the Homestead Act is signed, offering 160 acres of free land in the western territories to anyone willing to work it for five years.

1863:   The Emancipation Proclamation is signed, freeing the slaves; further battles occur at Chancellorsville, Cemetery Ridge, Chattanooga, and Gettysburg, where Lincoln delivers his famous address; the National Banking Act is signed.

1863:   Melville trades Arrowhead for his brother Allan's home at 104 East 26th Street, New York.

1864:   Melville visits the Virginia front to see his cousin Colonel Henry Gansevoort in April.

1865:   Melville protests the reissue of *Israel Potter* under the title *The Refugee*.

1864: Ulysses Grant takes over the Union armies, and General William T. Sherman makes his march to the sea; Nathaniel Hawthorne dies.

1865: General Robert E. Lee surrenders at Appomattox; President Lincoln is assassinated; the Thirteenth Amendment to the Constitution is ratified, abolishing slavery; the Freedman's Bureau is created (1865–1869) to provide education, food, and jobs for former slaves; The Ku Klux Klan is organized; Andrew Johnson becomes president.

1866: The Civil Rights Bill signed into law.

1867: The Reconstruction Act is passed over Johnson's veto.

1868: The Fourteenth Amendment to the Constitution is ratified, granting citizenship to all persons born in the United States; Andrew Johnson is impeached and acquitted.

1869: Ulysses Grant becomes president; the transcontinental railroad is complete; the Knights of Labor is founded.

1870: The Fifteenth Amendment, forbidding states from denying African-American men the right to vote, is ratified; the Standard Oil Company is founded.

U.S. Customs House. Library of Congress, Prints and Photographs Division, Detroit Publishing Company.

1866: *Harper's Monthly* publishes four of Melville's poems from the forthcoming *Battle-Pieces and Aspects of the War*, which appears from Harper's on August 23; on December 5, Melville is sworn in as deputy inspector of customs at the port of New York.

1867: Elizabeth Melville consults with her family and her minister about the possibility of legally separating from Melville, whose bouts of depression and rage have become intolerable to her; their son Malcolm is found dead of a self-inflicted pistol shot on September 11.

1869: Stanwix goes to sea.

1870: Stanwix returns; Melville begins his long poem *Clarel*; his portrait is painted by Joseph Oriel Eaton; in the 1870s, Stanwix regularly appears and disappears, and many of Melville's close relatives and friends die.

1871:   The Tweed ring in New York is overthrown; Chicago is ravaged by fire.

1873:   Financial panic spreads; silver is discovered in Nevada.

1874:   The Woman's Christian Temperance Union is founded; Massachusetts legalizes a ten-hour workday for women.

1875:   Bell Telephone is established; Centennial Exposition is held.

1876:   The Battle of Little Big Horn is fought.

1877:   Reconstruction ends; Chief Joseph of the Nez Perce leads his people on a doomed march; Thomas Edison invents the phonograph.

1879:   Edison announces his invention of the incandescent lamp.

1880:   The literary magazine the *Dial* is founded (1880–1929).

1881:   James Garfield's brief administration is succeeded by Chester Arthur's; the American Federation of Labor is established.

1882:   Chinese immigration is suspended; the outlaw Jesse James is killed.

1872:   Melville's brother Allan and his mother die; Elizabeth Melville's property is destroyed in a Boston fire.

1873:   The New York Customs House threatens to dismiss Melville.

1875:   Melville projects a volume of prose and poetry, "Parthenope"; his uncle Peter Gansevoort offers to pay for the publication of *Clarel*.

1876:   *Clarel* is published; uncle Peter and sister Augusta die.

1877:   The New York Customs House again threatens to dismiss Melville.

1878:   Elizabeth Melville inherits a substantial sum of money.

1879:   Daughter Elizabeth is stricken with severe arthritis; son Stanwix is stricken with tuberculosis in California.

1880:   Daughter Frances marries Henry B. Thomas.

1882:   First grandchild, Eleanor Thomas, is born.

1884:   Melville's brother Thomas dies.

1883: The Civil Service Reform Act is established; the Brooklyn Bridge is completed; the Metropolitan Opera is founded in New York City.

1885: Grover Cleveland begins his first administration; the Washington Monument is dedicated.

1886: The Haymarket Riot in Chicago spreads fears of social anarchy when a bomb is thrown at police, many of whom are injured or killed, and the police open fire on the crowd; the Statue of Liberty is dedicated.

1887: The Interstate Commerce Act is signed; the first electric streetcars appear.

1889: Benjamin Harrison becomes president; the first Pan-American Conference is held; Jane Addams founds Hull House in Chicago.

1890: The Sherman Anti-Trust Act is established; The U.S. Census announces that the frontier is closed; the Battle of Wounded Knee in South Dakota marks the end of the wars with Native Americans.

Wooden box used for papers by Herman Melville. Ends are initialed HM. Courtesy of Berkshire Athenaeum.

1885: Melville's sister Frances Priscilla dies; Melville's poem "The Admiral of the White" is published in New York and Boston newspapers; Melville resigns as customs inspector on December 31.

1886: Stanwix dies in San Francisco.

1888: Melville voyages to Bermuda, returning via Florida; *John Marr and Other Sailors* is privately printed at the De Vinne Press in an edition of 25 copies; Melville begins writing *Billy Budd, Sailor*.

Herman and Elizabeth Melville's graves. Courtesy of Berkshire Athenaeum.

1891:   The Populist party is founded; the Forest Reserve Act is signed.

1890:   Melville suffers an attack of erysipelas.

1891:   *Timoleon* is published privately at the Caxton Press in May in an edition of 25 copies; on September 28, Melville dies. leaving a number of unpublished poems and *Billy Budd, Sailor* in manuscript.

Bibliographical Essay

Giles Gunn

When Melville died in 1891, only two of his books, *Pierre* and *Battle-Pieces*, remained in print in the United States. Copies of *Omoo*, *White-Jacket*, and *Moby-Dick* were no longer available from Harper Brothers, his main American publisher, by 1887, and in the firm's 1892 catalog, *Typee*, *Mardi*, and *Redburn* were no longer listed. John Murray, one of Melville's English publishers, kept *Typee* and *Omoo* available until after 1891, but Melville's other English publisher, Richard Bentley, let the next four titles go out of print as soon as their initial stock was depleted. Melville's other texts fared no better, whether in England or America, even in unauthorized editions. The reprinting of Melville's works, which began almost immediately after his death, played an important role in the reestablishment and development of Melville's reputation, but the scholarly attempt to produce authoritative editions of all of his writings, which continues to the present day, constitutes a story of its own of nearly epic, and certainly heroic, proportions.

It is important to understand that the complications of this latter story were originally introduced by the publishing history of each of Melville's books during his lifetime. It would have been complex enough if that history were merely restricted to the differences between subsequent editions of the same text, which often increased because of Melville's penchant for corrections and revisions. But add to this the fact that seven of Melville's books (the first six plus *The Confidence-Man*) were originally published separately in America and England and most of the contents of another (*The Piazza Tales*) were published in *Putnam's Monthly Magazine* and *Harper's Magazine*. Furthermore, the English editions of Melville's works, with the exception of *The Confidence-Man*, were published several weeks earlier than the American editions. This permitted English publishers to get the jump on their American counterparts for establishing copyright, such that only the first of Melville's texts, *Typee*, was set from a manuscript provided by Melville, the other texts using proof sheets from the American editions. As Sheila Post makes clear in her contribution to this volume, this practice allowed American publishers to assess the response of British readers before deciding to produce an American edition.[1] This cross-patching and confusion of the publishing record means that scholars have faced a monumental task in establishing among the variations in punctuation, wording, and printing reliable texts of the books that Melville actually intended to write.

The attempts to produce more accurate individual texts of Melville's main body of writing, together with efforts to bring previously unpublished or uncollected writings into print, are too copious to record here. Even though much energy has been devoted to making more of Melville's writing available in trustworthy form, the more exciting and eventually significant efforts have been focused on developing editions of the whole, or what was assumed to be the whole, body of Melville's texts. The first of such efforts was the creation, between 1922 and 1924, of the Constable Edition under the supervision of Michael Sadleir, which collected all of Melville's known writings in sixteen volumes. Published in 750 sets, the Constable was considered for more than two decades to be the standard edition, but by the late 1940s that title shifted to the Hendricks House Edition. This new edition, produced under the general editorship of Howard P. Vincent, was originally projected to include fourteen volumes available either with or without textual notes, but in the end no more than seven volumes appeared, some with as many inaccuracies as the Constable version they were designed to replace. Raymond Weaver also organized a Pequod Edition of Herman Melville, published by Albert and Charles Boni, but it only managed to yield four volumes of Melville's work before it was permanently suspended.

In the meantime, some of the important textual work of the immediate postwar period found its way into important collections of Melville's writings, such as Willard Thorp's *Herman Melville: Representative Selections* (1938) and Jay Leyda's *The Portable Melville* (1952). Melville's lectures were published in 1957 by Merton M. Sealts, Jr., and his letters in 1960 by Merrell R. Davis and William H. Gilman, along with classroom editions of particular texts like *Moby-Dick*. The most famous examples of these latter projects were the collaboration between Harrison Hayford and Morton Sealts to produce a truly dependable text (actually two versions of it) of *Billy Budd* (1962) and the mutually fruitful collaboration between Harrison Hayford and Hershel Parker to produce an almost "definitive" edition of *Moby-Dick* (1967).

The success of these two projects also helped to nourish plans, long under discussion, to develop as fully accurate as possible an edition of all the writings of Herman Melville. Those plans brought together the resources of the Newberry Library of Chicago and Northwestern University Press and were formalized in 1965, but they had been laid several years before when the American Literature Group of the Modern Language Association established, in 1963, a Center for Editions of American Authors, which would eventually oversee the development of accurate editions of the writings of many canonical American writers, principally but not exclusively from the nineteenth century. Adapting editorial principles accepted by the center, the editorial board of the Melville edition agreed that, in the words of one of its members:

> The aim of the edition was to establish texts that reflected Melville's final intentions, as faithfully as the editors' judgment of all surviving evidence would allow. That evidence includes in addition to such documents as letters, manuscript drafts, and publishers' records, the result of collations of mul-

tiple copies of all authorized editions of Melville's writings during his lifetime.[2]

The Northwestern-Newberry Edition, or NN, as it is called, issued its first volume in 1968. Based on the most scrupulous examination ever made of the record of the editing, printing, and publishing of Melville's writings, the NN is without question a monumental textual achievement. Yet even now, scholars are continuing to discover new material that calls some of the judgments of the NN into question. Along with a group of letters by various members of the Melville family, an early draft of *Typee* has recently turned up that will alter at least some of the judgments that informed the NN edition of Melville's first book, and there is every reason to think that additional textual discoveries may be made in the future. Nonetheless, if the goal of such investigations is to determine as exactly as possible what Melville's actual intentions were for his texts, this is perhaps as it should be. The evidence of those intentions, after all, is left behind in words, and even if we were to get the words exactly as Melville meant them to be, we would still be left with the challenge of deciding exactly what they mean.

We can be thankful, however, that the scholarly editions of many of Melville's writings produced by the NN have also been made available to the general public through various reprintings. The most significant of those reprintings are associated with the Library of America, a nonprofit enterprise launched in 1979 by grants from the Ford Foundation and the National Endowment for the Humanities to produce accurate editions of the works of American authors in uniform collections at a reasonable price. So far, three different volumes, each collecting six or more texts and miscellaneous prose, have been issued by the Library of America, and more may be planned.

For many years, the chief authority on Melville's life was Leon Howard's biography *Herman Melville* (1951). Based on Jay Leyda's *The Melville Log* (1951; supplemented 1968), which is an astonishing two-volume collection of facts about Melville and documentary excerpts, Howard's narrative was complemented by the still-prescient critical biography *Herman Melville* (1950) by

Newton Arvin. In the intervening years, Melville's life has been further explored in a variety of biographical studies, the most detailed, comprehensive, and lively being Laurie Robertson-Lorant's energetic *Melville: A Biography* (1996) and Hershel Parker's magisterial two-volume *Herman Melville: A Biography* (1996, 2002). The long and fascinating history of writings about Melville, including reviews, articles, essays, and books, is slowly being compiled by Brian Higgins in his projected three-volume *Herman Melville: An Annotated Bibliography* (1979–). Foreign-language editions as well as some reviews and articles of Melville's writings can be found in Leland Phelps's *Herman Melville's Foreign Reputation* (1983). Various checklists of Melville criticism have been published over the years, but the most accurate, annotated compilations of recent criticism of Melville are to be found in the chapters published on him annually since 1965 in the pages of *American Literary Scholarship*.

There are several concordances of separate volumes of Melville's work, including *Moby-Dick*, *Pierre*, and *Clarel*, and a number of other useful biographical and critical resources. Merton M. Sealts, Jr., has compiled virtually all of the biographical material published during Melville's lifetime in *The Early Lives of Melville* (1974), and in 1966 he listed all of the books Melville owned or borrowed in a book entitled *Melville's Reading*. While Sealts updated that list in a book rehearsing the search for those sources, *Pursuing Melville* (1982), his collection has been further superseded by a 1984 dissertation from Northwestern University authored by Mary K. Madison entitled "Melville's Sources."

NOTES

1. Since the royalties for American books published in America were not protected by international copyright law, American authors, as Sheila Post also points out, were obliged to publish their writings first in England rather than the United States or risk having their work pirated by European publishers.

2. G. Thomas Tanselle, "Melville and the World of Books," in *A Companion to Melville Studies*, ed. John Bryant (New York: Greenwood, 1986), 816.

Studies of Melville

ARCHIVAL MATERIAL

Albany Institutes of History and Art
Berkshire Athenaeum
Lansingburgh Historical Society
Jay Leyda Collection, University of California at Los Angeles
Melville Family Papers, Houghton Library, Harvard University
Morewood Collection, Berkshire County Historical Society
Murray Papers, Harvard University Archives
Museum of the City of New York
Newberry Library of Chicago
New-York Historical Society
New York Public Library, Augusta Papers, Gansevoort-Lansing
    Collection
New York Public Library, Gansevoort-Lansing Collection
Osborne Collection of Melville Materials at Southwestern University
Rockwell Papers, Lenox (Mass.) Library
Shaw Papers, Massachusetts Historical Society

SELECTED EDITIONS OF MELVILLE'S WORKS

The Battle-Pieces of Herman Melville, ed. Hennig Cohen. New York:
    Yoseloff, 1964.
Billy Budd, Sailor (An Inside Narrative): Reading Text and Genetic Text,
    ed. Harrison Hayford and Merton M. Sealts, Jr. Chicago:
    University of Chicago Press, 1962.
Clarel: A Poem and Pilgrimage in the Holy Land, ed. Harrison Hayford,
    Hershel Parker, and G. Thomas Tanselle. Evanston and
    Chicago: Northwestern University Press and Newberry
    Library, 1991.
Collected Poems of Herman Melville, ed. Howard P. Vincent. Chicago:
    Packard and Hendricks House, 1947.
The Confidence-Man: His Masquerade, ed. Harrison Hayford, Hershel
    Parker, and G. Thomas Tanselle. Evanston and Chicago:
    Northwestern University Press and Newberry Library, 1984.
Correspondence, ed. Lynn Horth. Evanston and Chicago: Northwest-
    ern University Press and Newberry Library, 1993.
Israel Potter: His Fifty Years of Exile, ed. Harrison Hayford, Hershel

Parker, and G. Thomas Tanselle. Evanston and Chicago: Northwestern University Press and Newberry Library, 1982.

Journals, ed. Howard C. Horsford and Lynn Horth. Evanston and Chicago: Northwestern University Press and Newberry Library, 1989.

The Letters of Herman Melville, ed. Merrell R. Davis and William H. Gilman. New Haven, Conn.: Yale University Press, 1960.

Mardi: and a Voyage Thither, ed. Harrison Hayford, Hershel Parker, and G. Thomas Tanselle. Evanston and Chicago: Northwestern University Press and Newberry Library, 1970.

Moby-Dick; or, The Whale, ed. Harrison Hayford, Hershel Parker, and G. Thomas Tanselle. Evanston and Chicago: Northwestern University Press and Newberry Library, 1988.

Moby-Dick; or, The Whale. Northwestern-Newberry Editions, with introduction by Andrew Delbano, notes and explanatory text by Tom Quirk. New York: Penguin, 1992.

Omoo: A Narrative ofAdventures in the South Seas, ed. Harrison Hayford, Hershel Parker, and G. Thomas Tanselle. Evanston and Chicago: Northwestern University Press and Newberry Library, 1968.

The Piazza Tales and Other Prose Pieces, 1839–1860, ed. Harrison Hayford, et al. Evanston and Chicago: Northwestern University Press and Newberry Library, 1987.

Pierre; or, the Ambiguities, ed. Harrison Hayford, Hershel Parker, and G. Thomas Tanselle. Evanston and Chicago: Northwestern University Press and Newberry Library, 1971.

Redburn: His First Voyage, Being the Sailor-boy Confessions and Reminiscences of the Son-of-a-Gentleman, in the Merchant Service, ed. Harrison Hayford, Hershel Parker, and G. Thomas Tanselle. Evanston and Chicago: Northwestern University Press and Newberry Library, 1969.

Typee: A Peep at Polynesian Life, ed. Harrison Hayford, Hershel Parker, and G. Thomas Tanselle. Evanston and Chicago: Northwestern University Press and Newberry Library, 1968.

Weeds and Wildings Chiefly: With a Rose or Two, by Herman Melville: Reading Text and Genetic Text, ed. Robert Charles Ryan. Evanston, Ill.: Northwestern University Press, 1967.

White-Jacket; or, The World in a Man-of-War, ed. Harrison Hayford, Hershel Parker, and G. Thomas Tanselle. Evanston and

Chicago: Northwestern University Press and Newberry Library, 1970.

BIOGRAPHIES AND BIOGRAPHICAL INFORMATION

Allen, Gay Wilson. *Melville and His World*. New York: Viking, 1971.

Arvin, Newton. *Herman Melville*. New York: Sloane, 1950.

Charvat, William. "Melville's Income." *American Literature* 15 (1943): 251–61.

Davis, Merrell R. "Melville's Midwestern Lecture Tour, 1859." *Philological Quarterly* 20 (1941): 46–57.

Dillingham, William B. *Melville and His Circle: The Last Years*. Athens: University of Georgia Press, 1997.

Freeman, John. *Herman Melville*. New York: Macmillan, 1926.

Gilman, William H. *Melville's Early Life and Redburn*. New York: New York University Press, 1951.

Hardwick, Elizabeth. *Herman Melville*. New York: Viking, 2000.

Hillway, Tyrus. *Herman Melville*. New York: Twayne, 1963.

Howard, Leon. *Herman Melville*. Berkeley: University of California Press, 1951.

Leyda, Jay. "An Albany Journal by Gansevoort Melville." *Boston Public Library Quarterly* 11 (1950): 327–47.

———. *The Melville Log: A Documentary Life of Herman Melville, 1819–1981*. 2 vol. New York: Harcourt, 1951.

Mayoux, Jean-Jacques, *Melville*. Translated by John Ashbery. New York: Grove, 1960.

Metcalf, Eleanor. *Herman Melville: Cycle and Epicycle*. Cambridge, Mass.: Harvard University Press, 1953.

Miller, Edwin Haviland. *Herman Melville: A Biography*. New York: Braziller, 1975.

Mumford, Lewis. *Herman Melville*. New York: Harcourt, Brace, 1929.

Parker, Hershel. *Herman Melville: A Biography*. 2 vols. Baltimore, Md.: Johns Hopkins University Press, 1996, 2000.

Robertson-Lorant, Laurie. *Melville: A Biography*. New York: Clarkson Potter, 1996, 2002.

Rosenberry, Edward H. *Melville*. London: Routledge and Kegan Paul, 1979.

Sealts, Merton M., Jr. *The Early Lives of Melville: Nineteenth-Century*

Biographical Sketches and Their Authors. Madison: University of Wisconsin Press, 1974.

———. *Melville as Lecturer.* Cambridge, Mass.: Harvard University Press, 1957.

Stone, Geoffrey. *Melville.* New York: Sheed and Ward, 1949.

Weaver, Raymond. *Herman Melville: Mariner and Mystic.* New York: Doran, 1921.

Young, Philip. *The Private Melville.* University Park: Pennsylvania State University Press, 1993.

CRITICAL STUDIES

Adler, Joyce. *War in Melville's Imagination.* New York: New York University Press, 1981.

Baird, James. *Ishmael: A Study of the Symbolic Mode in Primitivism.* Baltimore, Md.: Johns Hopkins University Press, 1956.

Bellis, Peter. *No Mysteries Out of Ourselves: Identity and Textual Form in the Novels of Herman Melville.* Philadelphia: University of Pennsylvania Press, 1990.

Berthoff, Warner. *The Example of Melville.* Princeton, N.J.: Princeton University Press, 1962.

Bickley, R. Bruce, Jr. *The Method of Melville's Short Fiction.* Durham, N.C.: Duke University Press, 1975.

Bowen, Merlin. *The Long Encounter: Self and Experience in the Writings of Herman Melville.* Chicago: University of Chicago Press, 1960.

Braswell, William. *Melville's Religious Thought: An Essay in Interpretation.* Durham, N.C.: Duke University Press, 1943.

Brodtkorb, Paul, Jr. *Ishmael's White World: A Phenomenological Reading of Moby-Dick.* New Haven, Conn.: Yale University Press, 1965.

Bryant, John. *Melville and Repose: The Rhetoric of Humor in the American Renaissance.* New York: Oxford University Press, 1993.

Chase, Richard. *Herman Melville: A Critical Study.* New York: Macmillan, 1949.

Cowan, Bainard. *Exiled Waters: Moby-Dick and the Crisis of Allegory.* Baton Rouge: Louisiana State University Press, 1981.

Creech, James. *Closet Writing/Gay Reading: The Case of Melville's Pierre.* Chicago: University of Chicago Press, 1993.

Davis, Merrell R. *Melville's Mardi: A Chartless Voyage.* New Haven, Conn.: Yale University Press, 1952.

Dillingham, William B. *An Artist in the Rigging: The Early Work of Herman Melville.* Athens: University of Georgia Press, 1972.

———. *Melville's Later Novels.* Athens: University of Georgia Press, 1986.

———. *Melville's Short Fiction, 1853–1856.* Athens: University of Georgia Press, 1977.

Dimock, Wai-chee. *Empire for Liberty: Melville and the Poetics of Individualism.* Princeton, N.J.: Princeton University Press, 1989.

Dryden, Edgar A. *Melville's Thematics of Form: The Great Art of Telling the Truth.* Baltimore, Md.: Johns Hopkins University Press, 1968.

Duban, James. *Melville's Major Fiction: Politics, Theology, and Imagination.* DeKalb: University of Illinois Press, 1983.

Finkelstein, Dorothy Metlitsky. *Melville's Orienda.* New Haven, Conn.: Yale University Press, 1961.

Fisher, Marvin. *Going Under: Melville's Short Fiction and the American 1850s.* Baton Rouge: Louisiana State University Press, 1977.

Franklin, H. Bruce. *The Wake of the Gods: Melville's Mythology.* Stanford, Calif.: Stanford University Press, 1963.

Garner, Stanton. *The Civil War World of Herman Melville.* Lawrence: University Press of Kansas, 1993.

Herbert, T. Walter. *Marquesan Encounters: Melville and the Meaning of Civilization.* Cambridge, Mass.: Harvard University Press, 1980.

———. *Moby-Dick and Calvinism: A World Dismantled.* New Brunswick, N.J.: Rutgers University Press, 1977.

James, C. L. R. *Mariners, Renegades, and Castaways: The Story of Herman Melville and the World We Live In.* 1953. Reprints, London: Allison and Busby, 1985.

Karcher, Carolyn. *Shadow over the Promised Land: Slavery, Race, and Violence in Melville's America.* Baton Rouge: Louisiana State University Press, 1980.

Kelley, Wyn. *Melville's City: Urban and Literary Form in Nineteenth-Century New York.* New York: Cambridge University Press, 1996.

Kenny, Vincent. *Herman Melville's Clarel: A Spiritual Autobiography.* Hamden, Conn.: Shoe String, 1973.

Markels, Julian. *Melville and the Politics of Identity: From King Lear to Moby-Dick*. Urbana: University of Illinois Press, 1993.

Martin, Robert K. *Heroes, Captains, and Strangers: Male Friendship, Social Critique, and Literary Form in the Sea Novels of Herman Melville*. Chapel Hill: University of North Carolina Press, 1986.

McCall, Dan. *The Silence of Bartleby*. Ithaca, N.Y.: Cornell University Press, 1989.

Miller, James E., Jr. *A Reader's Guide to Herman Melville*. New York: Farrar, Straus, & Cudahy, 1962.

Olson, Charles. *Call Me Ishmael: A Study of Melville*. San Francisco: City Lights, 1947.

Otter, Samuel. *Melville's Anatomies: Bodies, Discourse, and Ideology in Antebellum America*. Berkeley: University of California Press, 1998.

Parker, Hershel. *Reading Billy Budd*. Evanston, Ill.: Northwestern University Press, 1990.

Post-Lauria, Sheila. *Correspondent Colorings: Melville in the Marketplace*. Amherst: University of Massachusetts Press, 1996.

Quirk, Tom. *Melville's Confidence Man: From Knave to Knight*. Columbia: University of Missouri Press, 1982.

Rampersad, Arnold. *Melville's Israel Potter: A Pilgrimage and a Progress*. Bowling Green, Ohio: Bowling Green University Popular Press, 1969.

Renker, Elizabeth. *Strike through the Mask: Herman Melville and the Scene of Writing*. Baltimore, Md.: Johns Hopkins University Press, 1996.

Rogin, Michael Paul. *Subversive Genealogy: The Politics and Art of Herman Melville*. New York: Knopf, 1983.

Rosenberry, Edward H. *Melville and the Comic Spirit*. Cambridge, Mass.: Harvard University Press, 1955.

Sachs, Viola. *The Game of Creation: The Primeval Unlettered Language of Moby-Dick; or, The Whale*. Paris: Maison des sciences de l'homme, 1982.

Sachs, Viola, ed. *L'Imaginaire-Melville: A French Point of View/Textes Reunis et Presentes*. Saint-Denis, France: University Press of Vincennes.

Samson, John. *White Lies: Melville's Narrative of Facts*. Ithaca, N.Y.: Cornell University Press, 1989.

Schultz, Elizabeth. *Unpainted to the Last: Moby-Dick and Twentieth-Century American Art.* Lawrence: University Press of Kansas, 1995.

Sealts, Merton M., Jr. *Pursuing Melville, 1940–1980.* Madison: University of Wisconsin Press, 1982.

Sedgwick, William Ellery. *Melville and the Tragedy of the Mind.* Cambridge, Mass.: Harvard University Press, 1944.

Seelye, John. *Melville: The Ironic Diagram.* Evanston, Ill.: Northwestern University Press, 1971.

Sherrill, Rowland A. *The Prophetic Melville: Experience, Transcendence, and Tragedy.* Athens: University of Georgia Press, 1979.

Short, Bryan C. *Cast by Means of Figures: Herman Melville's Rhetorical Development.* Amherst: University of Massachusetts Press, 1992.

Shurr, William H. *The Mystery of Iniquity: Melville as Poet, 1857–1891.* Lexington: University Press of Kentucky, 1972.

Spanos, William V. *The Errant Art of Moby-Dick: The Canon, the Cold War, and the Struggle for American Studies.* Durham, N.C.: Duke University Press, 1995.

Stein, William Bysshe. *The Poetry of Melville's Late Years: Time, History, Myth, and Religion.* Albany: State University of New York Press, 1970.

Sten, Christopher. *The Weaver-God, He Weaves: Melville and the Poetics of the Novel.* Kent, Ohio: Kent State University Press, 1996.

Stern, Milton R. *The Fine Hammered Steel of Herman Melville.* Urbana: University of Illinois Press, 1957.

Thompson, Lawrence R. *Melville's Quarrel with God.* Princeton, N.J.: Princeton University Press, 1952.

Tolchin, Neal L. *Mourning, Gender, and Creativity in the Art of Herman Melville.* New Haven, Conn.: Yale University Press, 1988.

Trimpi, Helen P. *Melville's Confidence Men and American Politics in the 1850s.* Hamden, Conn.: Archon, 1987.

Vincent, Howard P. *The Tailoring of White-Jacket.* Evanston, Ill.: Northwestern University Press, 1970.

———. *The Trying Out of Moby-Dick.* Kent, Ohio: Kent State University Press, 1980.

Wallace, Robert K. *Melville and Turner: Spheres of Love and Fright.* Athens: University of Georgia Press, 1992.

Wenke, John. *Melville's Muse: Literary Creation and the Forms of Philo-*

sophical Fiction. Kent, Ohio: Kent State University Press, 1995.

Zoellner, Robert. *The Salt-Sea Mastodon: A Reading of Moby-Dick.* Berkeley: University of California Press, 1973.

LITERARY AND HISTORICAL STUDIES WITH SECTIONS ON MELVILLE

Some of the most influential work on Melville has appeared in historical, cultural, and theoretical studies that include a number of authors. Selected Melville texts under discussion are indicated parenthetically.

Aaron, Daniel. *The Unwritten War: American Writers and the Civil War.* New York: Oxford University Press, 1973.

Bell, Michael Davitt. *The Development of American Romance: The Sacrifice of Relation.* Chicago: University of Chicago Press, 1980.

Bercovitch, Sacvan. *The Rites of Assent: Transformations in the Symbolic Construction of America.* New York: Routledge, 1993. (*Pierre*)

Bercovitch, Sacvan, and Myra Jehlen, eds. *Ideology and Classic American Literature.* New York: Cambridge University Press, 1986.

Brodhead, Richard H. *Hawthorne, Melville, and the Novel.* Chicago: University of Chicago Press, 1976.

Brown, Gillian. *Domestic Individualism: Imagining Self in Nineteenth-Century America.* Berkeley: University of California Press, 1990. (*Pierre*, "Bartleby")

Cameron, Sharon. *The Corporeal Self: Allegories of the Body in Melville and Hawthorne.* Baltimore, Md.: Johns Hopkins University Press, 1981.

Caserio, Robert L. *Plot, Story, and the Novel: From Dickens and Poe to the Modern Period.* Princeton, N.J.: Princeton University Press, 1979. (*White-Jacket, Moby-Dick*)

Castronovo, Russ. *Fathering the Nation: American Genealogies of Slavery and Freedom.* Berkeley: University of California Press, 1995. (*Moby-Dick, Israel Potter*)

Charvat, William. *The Profession of Authorship in America, 1800–1870: The Papers of William Charvat.* Ed. Matthew J. Bruccoli. Columbus: Ohio State University Press, 1978.

Dekker, George. *The American Historical Romance.* New York: Cambridge University Press, 1987.

Douglass, Ann. *The Feminization of American Culture*. New York: Knopf, 1977.

Eigner, Edwin M. *The Metaphysical Novel in England and America: Dickens, Bulwer, Melville, and Hawthorne*. Berkeley: University of California Press, 1978.

Fiedelson, Charles. *Symbolism and American Literature*. Chicago: University of Chicago Press, 1953.

Fiedler, Leslie. *Love and Death in the American Novel*. New York: Criterion, 1960.

Franchot, Jenny. *Roads to Rome: The Antebellum Protestant Encounter with Catholicism*. Berkeley: University of California Press, 1994. ("Benito Cereno")

Franklin, H. Bruce. *Prison Literature in America: The Victim as Criminal and Artist*. New York: Oxford University Press, 1989.

Fussell, Edwin S. *Frontier: American Literature and the American West*. Princeton, N.J.: Princeton University Press, 1965. (*Moby-Dick, The Confidence-Man*)

Gilmore, Michael T. *American Romanticism and the Marketplace*. Chicago: University of Chicago Press, 1985. (*Moby-Dick*, "Bartleby")

Hoffman, Daniel. *Form and Fable in American Fiction*. New York: Oxford University Press, 1961. (*Moby-Dick, The Confidence-Man*)

Irwin, John T. *American Hieroglyphics: The Symbol of the Egyptian Hieroglyphics in the American Renaissance*. Baltimore, Md.: Johns Hopkins University Press, 1980. (*Moby-Dick, The Confidence-Man*)

Jehlen, Myra. *American Incarnation: The Individual, the Nation, and the Continent*. Cambridge, Mass.: Harvard University Press, 1986. (*Pierre*)

Johnson, Barbara. *The Critical Difference: Essays in the Contemporary Rhetoric of Reading*. Baltimore, Md.: Johns Hopkins University Press, 1980. (*Billy Budd*)

Lawrence, D. H. *Studies in Classic American Literature*. 1923. Reprint, New York: Penguin, 1977.

Leverenz, David. *Manhood and the American Renaissance*. Ithaca, N.Y.: Cornell University Press, 1989. (*Moby-Dick*)

Levin, Harry. *The Power of Blackness: Poe, Hawthorne, Melville*. New York: Knopf, 1958.

Levine, Robert S. *Conspiracy and Romance: Studies in Brockden Brown,*

Cooper, Hawthorne, and Melville. New York: Cambridge University Press, 1989. ("Benito Cereno")

Lewis, R. W. B. *The American Adam: Innocence, Tragedy, and Tradition in the Nineteenth Century.* Chicago: University of Chicago Press, 1955. (*Billy Budd*)

Lindberg, Gary. *The Confidence-Man in American Literature.* New York: Oxford University Press, 1982. (*The Confidence Man*)

Marx, Leo. *The Machine in the Garden: Technology and the Pastoral Ideal in America.* New York: Oxford University Press, 1964. (*Moby-Dick*)

Matthiessen, F. O. *American Renaissance: Art and Expression in the Age of Emerson and Whitman.* New York: Oxford University Press, 1941.

Miller, Perry. *The Raven and the Whale: The War of Words and Wits in the Era of Poe and Melville.* New York: Harcourt Brace & World, 1956.

Mizruchi, Susan. *The Science of Sacrifice: American Literature and Modern Social Theory.* Princeton, N.J.: Princeton University Press, 1998.

Nelson, Dana D. *The Word in Black and White: Reading "Race" in American Literature, 1638–1867.* New York: Oxford University Press, 1992. ("Benito Cereno")

Pease, Donald E. *Visionary Compacts: American Renaissance Writings in Cultural Context.* Madison: University of Wisconsin Press, 1987. (*Moby-Dick*)

Railton, Stephen. *Authorship and Audience: Literary Performance in the American Renaissance.* Princeton, N.J.: Princeton University Press, 1991. (*Moby-Dick*)

Reynolds, David S. *Beneath the American Renaissance: The Subversive Imagination in the Age of Emerson and Melville.* New York: Knopf, 1988.

Reynolds, Larry J. *European Revolutions and the American Literary Renaissance.* New Haven, Conn.: Yale University Press, 1988.

Richardson, Robert D., Jr. *Myth and Literature in the American Renaissance.* Bloomington: Indiana University Press, 1978.

Rowe, John Carlos. *At Emerson's Tomb: The Politics of Classic American Literature.* New York: Columbia University Press, 1997. (*Pierre*)

———. *Through the Custom-House: Nineteenth-Century American Fic-

tion and Modern Theory. Baltimore, Md.: Johns Hopkins University Press, 1982. ("Bartleby")

Sedgwick, Eve Kosofsky. *Epistemology of the Closet.* Berkeley: University of California Press, 1990. (*Billy Budd*)

Slotkin, Richard. *Regeneration through Violence: The Mythology of the American Frontier, 1600–1860.* Middletown, Conn.: Wesleyan University Press, 1973. (*Moby-Dick*)

Smith, Henry Nash. *Democracy and the Novel: Popular Resistance to Classic American Writers.* New York: Oxford University Press, 1978. (*Moby-Dick*)

Stuckey, Sterling. *Going through the Storm: The Influence of African-American Art in History.* New York: Oxford University Press, 1994. ("Benito Cereno")

Sundquist, Eric J. *Home as Found: Authority and Genealogy in Nineteenth-Century American Literature.* Baltimore, Md.: Johns Hopkins University Press, 1979. (*Pierre*)

———. *To Wake the Nations: Race in the Making of American Literature.* Cambridge, Mass.: Harvard University Press, 1993. ("Benito Cereno")

Thomas, Brook. *Cross-Examinations of Law and Literature: Cooper, Hawthorne, Stowe, and Melville.* New York: Cambridge University Press, 1987.

Wadlington, Warwick. *The Confidence Game in American Literature.* Princeton, N.J.: Princeton University Press, 1975.

Wald, Priscilla. *Constituting Americans: Cultural Anxiety and Narrative Form.* Durham, N.C.: Duke University Press, 1995. (*Pierre*)

Weinstein, Cindy. *The Literature of Labor and the Labors of Literature: Allegory in Nineteenth-Century American Fiction.* New York: Cambridge University Press, 1995.

Weisbuch, Robert. *Atlantic Double-Cross: American Literature and British Influence in the Age of Emerson.* Chicago: University of Chicago Press, 1986. ("Bartleby")

Weisburg, Richard H. *The Failure of the Word: The Protagonist as Lawyer in Modern Fiction.* New Haven, Conn.: Yale University Press, 1984. (*Billy Budd*)

Williams, Susan S. *Confounding Images: Photography and Portraiture in Antebellum America.* Philadelphia: University of Pennsylvania Press, 1997. (*Pierre*)

Yellin, Jean Fagan. *The Intricate Knot: Black Figures in American Literature, 1776–1863.* New York: New York University Press, 1972. ("Benito Cereno")

Ziff, Larzer. *Literary Democracy: The Declaration of Cultural Independence in America.* New York: Viking, 1981. (*Mardi, Moby-Dick, The Confidence Man*)

Contributors

LEON CHAI is professor of English at the University of Illinois at Urbana. He is the author most recently of *Jonathan Edwards and the Limits of Enlightenment Philosophy*. He has also written *Aestheticism: The Religion of Art in Post-Romantic Literature* and *The Romantic Foundations of the American Renaissance*. A specialist in American literature, British and European Romanticism, critical theory, and later nineteenth-century British and French literature, Chai is currently finishing books on Emily Dickinson and Romantic theory.

EMORY ELLIOTT is university professor in the Department of English at the University of California at Riverside. His monograph *American Puritan Literature* appears in volume 1 of the multivolume Cambridge History of American Literature. He has also written *Power and the Pulpit in Puritan New England* and *Revolutionary Writers: Literature and Authority in the New Republic*. He has also edited a large number of other volumes, including *The Columbia Literary History of the United States*, *American Literature: A Prentice-Hall Anthology,* and the *Columbia History of the American Novel*. He is also series editor of *The American Novel* and *Penn Studies in Contemporary American Fiction*. He is currently working on a book on the social and political implications of the use of cultural memory and history in American fiction in a group of writers from Brockden Brown, Hawthorne, and Stowe to Morrison, Pynchon, and DeLillo, as well as a collection of essays that examine the consequences of Puritanism, fundamentalism, and political ideology in nineteenth- and twentieth-century American literature.

GILES GUNN is professor of English and of global and international studies and director of the American Cultures and Global Contexts Center at the University of California at Santa Barbara. His most recent book is *Beyond Solidarity: Pragmatism and Difference in the Globalized World*. Author of many other volumes, including *F. O. Matthiessen: The Critical Achievement*, *The Interpretation of Otherness: Literature, Religion, and the American Imagination*, *The Culture of Criticism and the Criticism of Culture*, and *Thinking across the American Grain: Ideology, Intellect, and the New Pragmatism*, he has also co-edited, with Stephen Greenblatt, *Redrawing the Boundaries: The Transformation of English and American Literary Studies* and edited *New World Metaphysics, Early American Writing*, *William James' Pragmatism and Other Writings*, and *Global Studies*. He is currently at work on a new book on the human in a world of terror.

MYRA JEHLEN is Board of Governors Professor of Literatures in the Department of English at Rutgers University. She is the author most recently of *Readings at the Edge of Literature*. A specialist in transatlantic cultural relations, literature and history, and literary aesthetics, she has also written *American Incarnation: The Individual, the Nation, and the Continent* and *Class and Character in Faulkner's South*; co-edited, with Michael Warner, *The English Literatures of America, 1500–1800*; co-edited, with Sacvan Bercovitch, *Ideology and Classic American Literature*; and edited *Herman Melville: A Collection of Critical Essays*. She is finishing a book titled *The Face of Hamilcar* about literary form as an instrument of knowledge.

TIMOTHY MARR is assistant professor in the American studies curriculum at the University of North Carolina at Chapel Hill. He has published in *Leviathan: A Journal of Melville Studies* and in

Melville *"Among the Nations."* He is a co-editor of *Ungraspable Phantom,* a volume of essays selected from the sesquicentennial celebration of the publication of *Moby-Dick* in 2001. He is completing a book on imaginations of Islam, which traces the cultural work of orientalism in Melville's writings as well as in early American discourses such as eschatology, despotism, and reform.

ROBERT MILDER is professor of English at Washington University in St. Louis. He is the author most recently of *Reimagining Thoreau* and the editor of *Billy Budd, Sailor, and Selected Tales.* He is the author of "Herman Melville" in *The Columbia Literary History of the United States* and numerous essays on Emerson, Hawthorne, and Melville, including "The Ugly Socrates: Melville, Hawthorne, and Homoeroticism," "Old Man Melville: The Rose and the Cross," "An Arch between Two Lives: Melville in the Mediterranean," and "Hawthorne's Winter Dreams." He is presently working on a book on Melville titled *Exiled Royalties.*

SHEILA POST, formerly a professor of English at the University of Massachusetts, Boston, is the author of *Correspondent Coloring: Melville and the Marketplace.* A specialist in early American writing as well as New England literature and culture, she is now devoting herself fulltime to creative writing and is currently at work on a novel called *Waumbek: Or; The White Bear,* a retelling of *Moby-Dick* from the narrative perspective of Tashtego, the only Native American in Melville's tale.

Index

Page numbers in *italics* indicate illustrations.

abolition, 33, 173. *See also* slavery

Adam, 147–48. *See also* creation story

Adler, George J., 30, 185

"Aeolian Harp, The" (Melville), 51

affect, 71–72

Africans (ethnic group), 160–61. *See also* slavery

"After the Pleasure Party" (Melville), 51

Aids to Reflection (Coleridge), 69–70

Alighieri, Dante, 90

Allan, Ethan, 159

allegory, 75–76, 111, 137

All Souls Unitarian Church, 169, 174

America

European views of, 171–72

Melville's distaste for and desire for cultural revolution in, 33–34, 41, 45

Melville's multicultural aspirations for, 140–41

American Literary Scholarship, 229

American Literature Group (MLA), 227

American Publishers' Circular, 120

American Renaissance (Matthiessen), 10

American Review, 117

"Andrew Crabelly: Attorney at Law" (Curtis), 126

anti-Semitism, 154–56

anti-sentimentalism, 124–30

antislavery societies, 173. *See also* slavery

Arnold, Matthew, 48, 61, 197

Arrowhead (farm), 31, 38, 215, 220

artist, role of the, 139, 187, 194

Arvin, Newton, 20, 228

Athens, 41

Atlantic Monthly, 92

audience

"cultured" or "intellectual," 107–10, 124

diversity of American, 106–8, 116

English vs. American, 9, 24, 35, 39, 105–6, 108

247